LEADERSHIP
AND
SOCIAL CHANGE

LEADERSHIP
AND
SOCIAL CHANGE

Third Edition (Revised and Updated)

Edited by
William R. Lassey and Marshall Sashkin

UNIVERSITY ASSOCIATES, INC.
8517 Production Avenue
P.O. Box 26240
San Diego, California 92126

pd
9-14-84

Preface to the Third Edition

When the first edition of this volume was completed in 1971, no other book provided a broad overview of leadership theory, research, and practice. During the intervening years, much has been written about leadership, but no treatment is more complete than the Second Edition of *Leadership and Social Change*, which appeared in 1976. Consequently, the present authors and the publisher concluded that a Third Edition was in order.

The present version has been thoroughly revised and updated. Conceptual boundaries have been extended to include a focus on social movement and political leadership. There is greater emphasis on research findings as well as on theory and practice from a broad range of disciplines, in order to incorporate the best contemporary scholarship on the subject of leadership.

More than 70 percent of the articles in the Second Edition were published prior to 1970; over 75 percent of the contributions in this new edition were published after 1970, and 50 percent have appeared since 1975, thus increasing the currency and relevance of the selections. We hope that readers will agree that the "classic" materials have been retained and that new works of major significance have been added. The new contributions should substantially increase the book's usefulness to previous audiences as well as to new ones.

This Third Edition also introduces Marshall Sashkin as co-editor. Marshall has wide experience in the development of leadership theory, leadership training, and research. He is responsible for locating and editing much of the new selections. Our joint effort has been thoroughly collaborative; we each attempted to increase the quality of introductory sections as well as the selections in each Part, while co-authoring three articles that we felt were needed to provide a comprehensive treatment of the literature.

We wish to extend our thanks and appreciation to Anne K. Nelsen, who made a major contribution to the initial search of the literature for this revision. Our appreciation is also extended to the publishing staff of University Associates; without its encouragement, patience, assistance, and support, it is unlikely that two otherwise fully occupied academicians would have found the time to produce this work.

William R. Lassey
Pullman, Washington

Marshall Sashkin
College Park, Maryland

March 1983

Contents

Introduction

Effective leadership requires an understanding, at the very least, of two basic characteristics of human nature: the rational tendency and the emotional need. Individuals and social groups require structure and a sense of order for the achievement of goals but, as social animals, also demand to be treated with concern and respect. These two factors are critical to an understanding of why some leaders are effective while others make the effort but fail. A leader must balance attention to personal feelings against the need for achievement of individual and group tasks.

This conclusion is based on the recurring appearance of two primary sets of activities in the reports of theory, research, and practice throughout this volume. "Task" activities focus on accomplishing specific jobs such as achieving the mandate of a governmental body, producing automobiles, or delivering public and private services. Rational and orderly activities are required to effectively achieve these tasks. "Maintenance" activities, on the other hand, focus on sustaining or increasing individual and group feelings of satisfaction in the process of achieving the task. People's emotional needs must be met while the job is being done, or they are likely to lose interest in the goal.

Individuals seem to perform most productively and contentedly when they are treated as integrated human beings, as individuals who want to accomplish specific goals while maintaining social and psychological balance in the process. This is the theme of classic works by McGregor, Blake and Mouton, and Gibb. It reappears in more recent writings about theory, research results, and practical applications.

The readings and original articles in this volume draw from a wide range of disciplines, including psychology, sociology, communication science, political science, public administration, and business management. In order to locate the best available work, we have, of necessity, reviewed the bulk of all publications in the social-behavioral sciences. Although the literature on leadership is multidisciplinary and scattered among the specialized journals and books, we rarely found appropriate material in more than one volume of any journal or more than one chapter of any book.

Although we believe that "nothing is as practical as a good theory," our concern in editing this book has been to select theoretical and research articles that have direct implications for practical application to specific leadership situations, in work groups of all kinds, in organizations of varying complexity, in formal and informal educational settings, in various types of communities, and in diverse social and political movements. We believe that the five parts of this book provide a basis for leadership development in all of these diverse contexts.

MAJOR SECTIONS

Part 1, Basic Concepts, is intended to provide an introductory overview of theory and practice as well as a comprehensive summary of several approaches to research. These themes are refined and applied to specific leadership contexts in later sections.

Part 2, Leadership in Complex Organizations, deals primarily with business management, but the theory has wide application to all forms of public and private organization. The research on business leadership is much more abundant and cumulative than the research for other leadership situations. Fortunately, the authors maintain broad perspectives, which make applications to nonbusiness settings eminently clear. Furthermore, several articles deal with leadership in government, military, voluntary, and other organizations, usually emphasizing "participative" management as the most effective approach (Sashkin, 1982).

Part 3, Leadership in Educational Settings, emphasizes the special circumstances and uniqueness of these contexts. Weick (1976) refers to educational units as "loosely coupled systems." In Part 3, Cohen and March refer to higher education as "organized anarchy," which they view as quite descriptive of the leadership pattern—particularly in large state universities.

Community Leadership is the focus of Part 4. Two types of leaders are examined: indigenous individuals who attempt to provide direction from within and external, professional "consultants" who attempt to assist communities through a range of roles and activities. The emphasis is on what is needed to develop or enhance the community as a social unit.

Social Movement and Political Leadership are the topics discussed in Part 5. Although both are pervasive in society and although these "types" of leadership obviously affect large masses of the population and have great impact on the course of events, there has been very little well-grounded theory or research to increase our knowledge of how leaders function in these situations. Therefore, the articles in this part could serve as the basis for new and productive research.

Although we have somewhat arbitrarily chosen to divide the book in the manner described, there are clear linkages among many of the selections in the five parts. For example, many of the principles generated by investigators of profit-oriented organizations have direct application to communities, most forms of government, and some forms of education. Much of the research on community leadership has implications for social movement and political leadership. This is, in part, because the study of leadership adds to the understanding of basic human characteristics and social processes, which has implications for many forms of social systems.

It is clear to us that the theoretical and practical knowledge of leadership remains incomplete. However, we believe that the richness of the readings in this volume provides a sound basis for understanding and practicing more effective leadership.

References

Weick, K.E., Jr. Educational organizations as loosely coupled systems. *Administrative Science Quarterly*, 1976, *21*, 1-19.

Sashkin, M. *A manager's guide to participative management.* New York: American Management Associations, 1982.

Basic Concepts

Introduction to Part 1:
Basic Concepts

Although leadership is exercised in numerous variations in widely divergent social units, certain basic patterns of leadership appear to have widespread applicability. We refer to these patterns, or characteristics, as "basic concepts" because they help to establish the knowledge base that is necessary to understand the more specific and more complex explanations in later sections.

The first selection, by the co-editors, introduces elementary definitions of leadership concepts, identifies critical activities and skills, discusses the roles of authority and power in leadership practice, and confronts the issue of leadership as both the cause and effect of goal-oriented social organization. This article provides one answer to the question "What is leadership?," although a universally acceptable answer undoubtedly eludes us.

In the second article, Bass offers an overview of leadership in the context of a partially tested analytical model. He identifies the important variables associated with the three-part concept: attempted, successful, and effective leadership. This approach deals as much with the characteristics of followers as it does with those of leaders. Psychological and social factors such as motivation, power, status, esteem, and conflict are variables in a set of predictive relationships that lead to effective or ineffective results. The model recognizes the potential difference between the leader's and followers' perceptions of effectiveness: from the viewpoint of group members, effectiveness may be interpreted as whether they feel personally rewarded, while the leader may perceive goal achievement to be the appropriate measure. The Bass theory does not deal with "effectiveness" from the perspective of the organization or social system. Nonetheless, this theory is a helpful basis for understanding significant relationships among leadership variables. The theory is expanded in Bass (1981), which is too extensive for inclusion here.

The article by Tannenbaum and Schmidt is a classic conception of key issues in leadership; it has had widespread influence on the study of leadership styles. Since publication of their original article in 1958, considerable thought and research in the field of managerial leadership has led the authors to update their analysis of the leadership role and the leader-follower relationship.

In the original article, the degree of authoritarian leadership is contingent on the manager's assessment of personal forces, as well as forces in subordinates and in the situation. To attempt a completely democratic style in a context appropriate to a more authoritarian approach would introduce destructive inconsistency. The manager thus requires a sophisticated understanding of the forces at work, as well as of the alternative leadership styles, in order to choose an effective leadership pattern.

The retrospective commentary by Tannenbaum and Schmidt re-evaluates the original emphasis on hierarchical structure and the unilateral decision-making power of the manager. In addition to evaluating the forces in one's self, one's employees, and the situation, the manager's analysis should include recognition of the interdependency of the various forces. The authors now take a more balanced view of the distribution of power within and among organizations. They incorporate the effects of external social forces as an important basis for understanding the internal dynamics of the organization. Perhaps the most significant change is the pervasive shift toward greater manager-nonmanager participative involvement, reflected in the revision (Exhibit II) of their classic diagram (Exhibit I) describing the continuum of leadership behavior.

The fourth selection, by Kerr and Jermier, is important because it represents the first recognition that leadership has clear limits. Other forces can *substitute* for leadership. For example, when a task is very clearly structured, the leader does not need to engage in "structuring" behaviors. Prior planning of task structure is a "substitute" for leadership.

Unnecessary structuring is a waste of time as well as a source of possible resentment among subordinates. Kerr and Jermier suggest an important distinction between substitutes for leadership and "neutralizers" —factors that do not lead to the desired results. Yukl (1981) illustrates the point: when a leader does not control rewards, it is not possible to promise those rewards to employees as performance incentives. Such leader behavior is neutralized. Similarly, if the leader can provide a reward that the employee does not want, the employee motivation factor neutralizes the reward as an incentive.

There has been, in Kerr and Jermier's view, too much assumption that leadership is always critical (although styles or details may differ in varying circumstances). It is a refreshing viewpoint, suggesting that leaders search for substitutes that could facilitate task achievement while preventing subordinate disenchantment.

Next, Denmark's article is important because it debunks the myth of male-female differences in leadership. After a careful review of the literature, Denmark concludes that no major differences exist; the only minor difference generally agreed on is women's greater concern for relationships among people. This conclusion is strongly supported by an extensive study of male and female leaders reported by Hall and Donnell (1980). They identified over nine hundred male and nine hundred female managers and matched the samples by age and achievement. No differences were found on forty-one of forty-three measures of personality and behavior. Female managers were *more* achievement-oriented than their male counterparts, while males (in contrast to Denmark's report) were somewhat more interpersonally competent as well as more open and candid. Both results can be explained readily; women in the business world probably must have much greater achievement motivation in order to succeed. The men studied by Hall and Donnell were probably more "comfortable" and accepted as managers in their organizations and, thus, may have appeared to be more socially skilled. Denmark's conclusions indicate that opportunity is what women need most to be effective leaders.

The final selection in this section represents the editors' effort to provide a comprehensive summary of leadership theory and research. The objective is to demonstrate how leadership theory has become increasingly sophisticated over time. Approaches that seem at first to be inconsistent are found, on examination, to complement one another. We trace the development of concepts from static "traits" or "personal qualities" to dynamic behavior that interacts with the situation. Finally, the notion emerges of the fully "proactive" leader as a person who designs and directs situations as well as people.

References

Bass, B.M. *Stogdill's handbook of leadership*. New York: Free Press, 1981.

Hall, J., & Donnell, S. Men and women as managers: A significant case of no significant differences. *Organizational Dynamics*, 1980, 8(4), 60-77.

Yukl, G.A. *Leadership in organizations*. Englewood Cliffs, NJ: Prentice-Hall, 1981.

Dimensions of Leadership

William R. Lassey and Marshall Sashkin

The study of leadership has a long and somewhat troubled history. Early definitions of leadership were based largely on "traits" by which leaders or leadership behavior could be identified. However, this process proved frustrating because each student of leadership created different definitions based on selected sets of traits. There were few characteristics that could be universally identified as leadership behavior. Requirements for leadership, characteristics of leaders, and definitions of what constitutes leadership vary widely, depending on circumstances. Therefore, analysis in the most recent decades has concentrated on examination of leadership behavior in various contexts.

In a review of the leadership literature, Stogdill (1974) suggests eleven perspectives. Leadership may be defined as:

1. a function of group process
2. personality or effects of personality
3. the art of inducing compliance
4. the exercise of influence
5. a form of persuasion
6. a set of acts or behaviors
7. a power relationship
8. an instrument of goal achievement
9. an effect of interaction
10. a differentiated role
11. the initiation of structure

Any one or all of the meanings noted by Stogdill might apply to a particular circumstance, but no single definition is universally applicable. However, leadership is clearly a role that leads toward goal achievement, involves interaction and influence, and usually results in some form of changed structure or behavior of groups, organizations, or communities. Strength of personality and ability to induce compliance or to persuade are critical variables in the effectiveness of leaders, but their relative influence depends on time and circumstance.

Other leadership variables are more directly applicable to behaviors in group situations. These might be classified as functional definitions of the leadership role. Anyone who performs these functions is fulfilling a leadership role, regardless of his or her formal status in the group.

FUNCTIONAL DIMENSIONS OF LEADERSHIP

Two sets of functions have been identified by Benne and Sheats (1948) as critical: *task functions* must be executed to rationally select and achieve goals; *maintenance functions* associated with emotional satisfaction are required to develop and maintain group, community, or organizational viability.

Task Functions

Initiating Activity: proposing solutions; suggesting new ideas; providing new definitions of the problem, attacking problems in new ways, or organizing material.

Information Seeking: asking for clarification of suggestions; requesting additional information or facts.

Information Giving: offering facts or generalizations; relating one's experience to group problems as illustration.

Opinion Giving: stating an opinion or belief about a suggestion (or one of several suggestions), particularly concerning its value rather than its factual basis.

Elaborating: clarifying by giving examples or developing meanings; trying to envision how a proposal might work if it were adopted.

Coordinating: showing relationships among various ideas or suggestions; trying to pull ideas and suggestions together; trying to draw together activities of various subgroups or members.

Summarizing: pulling together related ideas or suggestions; restating suggestions after the group has discussed them.

Testing Feasibility: making application of suggestions to real situations; examining practicality and workability of ideas; evaluating possible decisions.

Evaluating: submitting group decisions or accomplishments to comparison with group standards; measuring accomplishments against goals.

Diagnosing: determining sources of difficulties, appropriate steps to take next, and primary blocks to progress.

Maintenance Functions

Encouraging: being friendly, warm, and responsive to others; praising others and their ideas; agreeing with and accepting the contributions of others.

Gatekeeping: trying to make it possible for another member to make a contribution to the group; suggesting a limited talking time for each member so that everyone will have a chance to be heard.

Standard Setting: suggesting standards for the group to use in choosing its content or procedures or in evaluating its decisions; reminding the group to avoid decisions that conflict with group standards.

Following: going along with the decisions of the group; passively accepting the ideas of others; serving as an audience during group discussion and decision making.

Expressing Group Feelings: sensing and summarizing group feelings; describing group reactions to ideas or solutions.

Consensus Taking: tentatively asking for group opinions in order to find out if the group is nearing consensus on a decision; sending up "trial balloons" to test group opinions.

Harmonizing: mediating; conciliating differences in points of view; making compromise solutions.

Tension Reducing: draining off negative feelings by jesting or pouring oil on troubled waters; putting a tense situation into a wider context.

Nonfunctional Behavior

Some participants in groups regularly deter achievement. The more common types of nonfunctional behavior include:

Aggression: working for status by criticizing or blaming others; showing hostility against the group or some individual; deflating others.

Blocking: interfering with the progress of the group by going off on a tangent; citing personal experiences unrelated to the problem; arguing too much about a point; rejecting ideas without consideration.

Self-Confessing: using the group as a personal sounding board; expressing personal feelings or points of view that are not related to the group.

Competing: vying with others to produce the best ideas, talk the most, play the most roles, or gain favor with the leader.

Seeking Sympathy: trying to induce other group members to be sympathetic to one's problems or misfortunes; deploring one's own ideas to gain support.

Special Pleading: introducing or supporting suggestions related to one's own concerns or philosophies; lobbying.

Horsing Around: clowning; joking; mimicking; disrupting the work of the group.

Recognition Seeking: attempting to call attention to one's self by loud or excessive talking, extreme ideas, or unusual behavior.

Withdrawing: being indifferent or passive; resorting to excessive formality; daydreaming; doodling; whispering to others; wandering from the subject.

When functional or nonfunctional behaviors occur in settings in which leadership is under study, they can be recognized quickly. Understanding behaviors that help or hinder achievement helps the individual to appreciate how improved performance on the part of the leader can increase the effectiveness of a group, organization, or community.

LEADERSHIP ACTIVITIES AND SKILLS

The Benne and Sheats (1948) formulation can be used to define two broad categories of productive leader behavior and many specific leadership roles within each category. Additional types or categories of important leadership activities have been suggested to increase our understanding of the leader's role. Mann (1965) defined four basic types of activity.

The first type consists of *technical* work, the performance of specific production-task activities involved in manufacturing or service. The second type involves *interpersonal* activities, work focused on the management of interpersonal relations. This would include most of the maintenance functions defined earlier and would also encompass all of the "human relations" activities that a leader might need to undertake. The third type is *administrative* work—planning, organizing, coordinating, and, in general, attending to the normal responsibilities of a manager. The fourth and final type is what Mann called *institutional* activities, representing the organization to other organizations (e.g., government agencies) and to the public in general. In 1982, Lee Iacocca, president of the Chrysler Corporation, provided one particularly clear example of this latter set of leader activities in television commercials and representation of his organization before the U.S. Congress.

Mann (1965) also suggested that certain skills are needed in order for a leader to perform the four leadership activities effectively (see Exhibit 1). Specific managerial jobs can be described in terms of the *mix* of the four types of leadership activities and skills needed for a particular job. Mann argued that a key factor is the level of the job, whether it is a first-line supervisory position, a mid-level management job, or a high-level executive position. At the lowest levels, a supervisor might need quite a bit of technical and human relations skills, a little skill in administration, and almost no institutional skill. At mid-levels, managers might require little or no technical skill, quite a bit of human relations and administrative skills, and very little institutional skill. Finally, at top levels, executives would need a great deal of institutional skill, some administrative and human relations skills, and almost no technical skill. This argument is illustrated in Figure 1.

Exhibit 1. Categories of Leadership Skills

Technical Skills. The ability to use pertinent knowledge, methods, techniques, and equipment necessary for the performance of specific tasks and activities. Technical skills may be acquired through formal training in professional schools, informal on-the-job training, or combinations of school and apprenticeship programs.

Human Relations (Interpersonal) Skills. The ability to use pertinent knowledge and methods for working with people. This includes an understanding of general principles of human behavior, particularly those that involve interpersonal relations and motivation, and the use of this understanding in day-to-day interactions with others in the work situation.

The supervisor with human relations skills understands how the principles of behavior affect not only others but oneself as well. He or she knows how both his or her own and others' frames of reference color what is perceived and assumed; how attitudes, beliefs, opinions, and values affect behavior and learning; and how needs and aspirations shape an individual's investment of energy. Included in these skills is the ability to represent the needs and goals of members at different levels in the organization so that each can comprehend the problems faced by the others. Central to human relations skills is the ability to integrate the goals of individuals with the objectives of the organization. The supervisor must be able to identify those needs of others that are central to their self-concepts and to relate these to organizational objectives in a manner that is psychologically meaningful and rewarding to the specific individuals. Overall, this area of skill involves managing the emotional and motivational dimensions of interpersonal relations in an organization.

Administrative Skills. The ability of the manager to think and act in terms of the organization within which he or she operates; the functions and tasks that must be fulfilled in order to effectivly perform the job as it relates to the tasks and goals of the organization. Administrative skills include planning, organizing, assigning the right tasks to the right people, giving people the right amount of responsibility and authority, inspecting and following up on the work, and coodinating the efforts and activities of different organizational members, levels, and departments.

Institutional Skills. This set of skills involves representing the entire organization in interaction with the other organizations, groups, and government agencies that form the environment of the organization. People differ in their ability to see, think clearly about, appraise, predict, and understand the demands and opportunities posed to the organization by its environment. If a leader is seriously mistaken about the requirements or needs of the organization or about the demands of the environment, his interpersonal and administrative skills may become liabilities for the organization. It is worse to be wrong AND influential than to merely be wrong; thus, the top-level executive needs institutional skills the most. Part of this category of skills is an "external perspective"—an accurate and comprehensive view of the organization-environment relationship—which includes a sensitivity to environmental demands and opportunities (the possibilities of achieving a more advantageous relationship with the environment) and a sensitivity to trends and changes in the environment.

This exhibit is based partly on a chapter by Floyd C. Mann in R. Dubin, G.C. Homans, F.C. Mann, and D.C. Miller, *Leadership and Productivity* (San Francisco: Chandler, 1965), and partly on discussions with Floyd Mann.

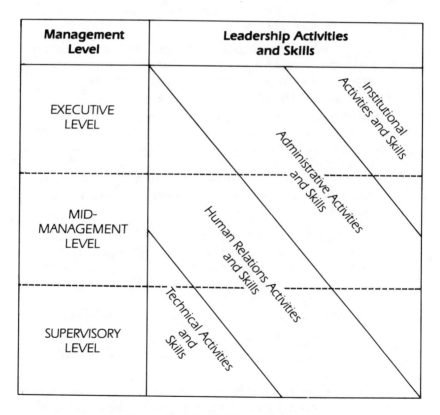

Figure 1. The Skill-Mix Model

AUTHORITY AND POWER

Although identification of specific behaviors is a first step in understanding and performing leadership functions, authority and power are important dimensions in determining the appropriateness of any such behavior. Individuals achieve positions of leadership for a variety of reasons. An individual may (a) be perceived by superiors or colleagues to have leadership potential; (b) inherit a leadership role; (c) assume the role by default because no one else is available or willing to perform the function; or (d) use physical or economic force to achieve the role (Crookston, 1961).

The processes through which a "leader" achieves authority or power vary widely, again depending on the leadership context and the forms of desirable leadership behavior in the group, organization, or community. Obviously, behavior that is perceived as highly desirable in a street gang may be totally unacceptable in a civic club.

A leader vested with authority and power necessarily takes on greater "psychological size" than other members of a group, organization, or community, in part because of:

1. *Individual attitudes toward authority.* These are conditioned by life experiences, beginning with the mother, father, and then other persons who control childhood behavior or set and enforce rewards and punishments. Those who control a child's life are usually physically and psychologically larger. Childhood feelings and attitudes toward authority may be projected onto leaders.

2. *Individual needs for security.* Some individuals prefer a psychologically larger leader. They want protection or are fearful of taking responsibility for themselves. Therefore, the more psychologically important the leader is perceived to be, the greater is his perceived protective role and the higher is his potential status.

The psychologically larger leader encounters several basic types of reactions from the group members (Crookston, 1961):

1. *Dependency.* Members demonstrate submissiveness or willingness to go along with the leader's proposals.

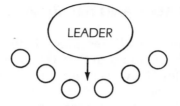

2. *Counterdependency*. Members demonstrate reactive, opposing, resisting behavior of two types: individual opposition or organized opposition, often typified by labor-management or student-faculty relationships.

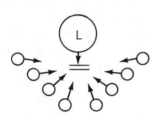
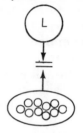

Individual Opposition   Organized Opposition

Dependent reactions are related to desires for security. Counterdependent reactions may be related to perceived leader inadequacies, task difficulties, or individual attitudes toward authority.

Most groups and organizations contain both dependent and counterdependent members, and a group may change from being predominantly dependent to counterdependent. Both reactions may exist in most people—a kind of ambivalence toward powerful leaders. The individual may welcome the leader's direction and protection, yet resent the leader's power.

3. *Interdependence*. If the authority problem is resolved, people are able to perceive the leader in a more realistic psychological dimension. If the difference in psychological size between the individual and the leader is minimal, mutual respect is likely to increase. The individual becomes interdependent in his relationship with the leader and a more collaborative, democratic process can then evolve.

THE LEADER AND THE SITUATION

Identifying the important dimensions of the leader's job is central to most of the readings in Part 1—and is a salient issue in many later articles. However, leadership is not the only factor important to organizational effectiveness and may not even be the most important factor. Some social scientists argue that leadership is more likely to be an *effect* of other organizational variables—such as the nature of the technology used by the organization—rather than a cause, and may even be irrelevant to organizational effectiveness. One expression of this view can be found in traditional bureaucratic theory (Weber, 1947), which essentially holds that leader behavior is (a) a dependent, not a causal, variable and (b) an outcome of organizational structure rather than a cause or predictor of organizational effectiveness. Bureaucratic theory classifies leaders as charismatic, traditional (such as kings), or rational-legal, in terms of their authority base. The aim, explicitly identified by Weber, is to eradicate the first two types of leaders and to create organizations that are based solely on rational-legal authority and which do not require "leaders."

A more recent and possibly more sophisticated view is expressed by Perrow (1970), who argues that certain types of technology both require and cause certain approaches to leadership. The classic studies of Woodward (1965), for example, demonstrated that organizations using continuous-process technology (such as chemical plants or oil refineries) were most profitable when the "span of control"—the average number of workers reporting to a supervisor—was around ten. However, organizations engaged in unit-production technology (such as building locomotives) were most profitable when the supervisory span of control was around four, with each supervisor overseeing a relatively small number of workers and able to exercise closer control. The assorted reasons underlying such findings are quite complex; Perrow (1970) makes a valid point: "leadership does play a role, but not necessarily the most important one; it is better to begin...by examining the situation which the leader confronts" (p. 14).

In summary, there is no clear-cut agreement on the meaning of leadership for all circumstances. Leadership can probably be best understood by submitting specific behaviors and roles to careful study. Fortunately, leadership is subject to refinement and, presumably, can be learned through systematic acquisition of the knowledge and skills appropriate to specific leadership roles.

References

Benne, K.D., & Sheats, P. Functional roles of group members. *Journal of Social Issues*, 1948, 4(2), 41-49.

Crookston, B.B. Leadership. Paper presented at the Intermountain Laboratory for Group Development, Cedar City, Utah, 1961.

Mann, F.C. Towards an understanding of the leadership role. In R. Dubin, G.C. Homans, F.C. Mann, & D.C. Miller, *Leadership and productivity*. San Francisco: Chandler, 1965.

Perrow, C. *Organizational analysis: A sociological view*. Monterey, CA: Brooks/Cole, 1970.

Stogdill, R.M. *Handbook of leadership*. New York: Free Press, 1974.

Weber, M. *The theory of social and economic organization*. (T. Parsons, trans.) New York: Free Press, 1947.

Woodward, J. *Industrial organization: Theory and practice*. London: Oxford University Press, 1965.

Some Observations About a General Theory of Leadership and Interpersonal Behavior

Bernard M. Bass

STUDYING BEHAVIOR IN GROUPS

The productive capacity of modern man and his machines, and the increased complexity of organized activity, have increased our awareness of the significance of understanding, predicting, and controlling interpersonal behavior—although the matter has been of interest to man throughout history. To understand human behavior, we must develop methods and principles for studying behavior in groups, for a large proportion of human activity takes place within groups. The universality of interpersonal phenomena is attributed to the prolonged biological dependence of the mammalian, particularly the human child, on his parents.

The study of interpersonal behavior is complicated by the elusiveness of its effects and the fact that individuals belong to several groups at the same time. Until recently, theory about social behavior was mainly speculative and seldom subjected to experimental test. Now, a variety of rigorous "small" theories are being developed about leadership, compliance, evaluation, and other interpersonal phenomena.

Reprinted from *Leadership, Psychology, and Organizational Behavior* by Bernard M. Bass. (New York: Harper & Row, 1960.) Copyright © 1960 by Bernard M. Bass.

The importance of the group, the situation, and the individual members are relative matters. We can increase or decrease the significance of each at will. We need to develop ways of studying and describing the interacting effects of all three. We think we should begin with concepts rooted in individual behavior.

NATURE AND PURPOSE OF THEORY

The purpose of a theory is to promote understanding. Theory provides the concepts and definitions which abstract the important elements in the observable phenomena we are interested in describing. Operations proceed on two planes: the empirical and the rational. The constructs of the rational plane are connected to the observables of the empirical plane by operational definitions. Propositions are deduced from the postulated relationships among the constructs. They are also induced from examining the empirical relationships among the observables. Validating the propositions by both means increases our confidence that we understand the phenomena. Yet, while the observable relationships are likely to withstand much further change (although they may become more precise), the rationale accounting for the relationship is likely to be modified and replaced by a newer and better model.

GROUP EFFECTIVENESS

A group is defined as a collection of individuals whose existence as a collection is rewarding to the individuals (or enables them to avoid punishment). A group does not necessarily perceive itself as such. The members do not have to share common goals. Nor are interaction, interlocking roles, and shared ways of behavior implied in the definition, although these are common characteristics of many groups.

The extent to which a group actually rewards its members is the group's effectiveness. The extent to which members anticipate such reinforcement is the attractiveness of the group. In natural groups, goals and goal attainment are likely to be multidimensional. The source of reward may be the task or the interaction among members, or both. Rewards may be *relevant* or *irrelevant, immediate* or *delayed, partial* or *total.* Generally, task effectiveness accompanies interaction effectiveness, although situations can be described where only the task or only the interaction is positively reinforcing. It is particularly important to know whether the goal attainment producing effectiveness is relevant to the members. Mere productivity indices may be irrelevant to workers. Group goal attainment will modify subsequent behavior to the extent it is relevant to the members of the group. While goals may be immediate or distant, it is probable that immediate rather than ultimate effectiveness is more significant for understanding interaction among individuals.

GROUP ATTRACTIVENESS

A group is more attractive the greater the rewards which may be earned by membership in the group and the greater the subjective expectancy that these rewards will be obtained through membership. Attraction to a group may be modified, therefore, by changing the amount or intensity of rewards for members and by changing expectations about obtaining the rewards. The clearer are the rewards of the group, the more attractive will the group be. Similarly, the more members share the same goals obtainable through cooperative effort, the more they will be attracted to each other.

Individuals are attracted to groups because groups tend to be more rewarding than isolated activity. The more rewarding or effective are the groups, the more members will be attracted to them. The more attracted to the groups, the more members will attempt to behave in a way to maintain or increase the effectiveness of the groups.

LEADERS AND LEADERSHIP

Interaction occurs when one member's behavior stimulates another whose resultant change (or lack of change) in behavior in turn stimulates the first member. Formal interactions occur between occupants of positions, while informal ones occur between persons regardless of their positions. The formal organization is a consistent pattern of formal interactions. The corresponding pattern of consistent informal interactions, the informal organization, arises in response to changing problems not solved by the more formal rigid organization. For example, it may arise because of failure in formal communications. But, in doing so, it may aid rather than conflict with the formal organization, depending on other factors.

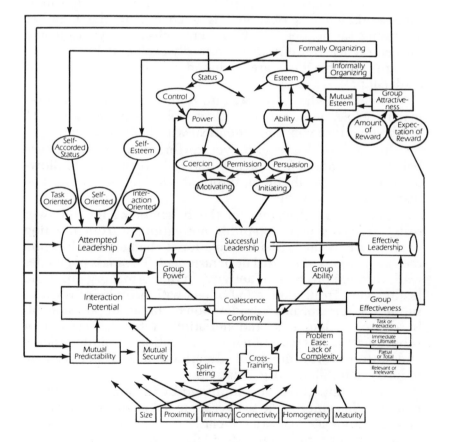

Figure I. Some Assumed and Deduced Relations of the Theory of Leadership and Group Behavior.

The large numbers of types of leaders described by earlier investigators fall into a few categories. Some have equated leadership with status, the importance of position. Others have equated leadership with esteem, the value of the person regardless of their [sic] positions. Still others have singled out certain behaviors and called those behaviors leadership.

The definition used in our theory is similar to those earlier ones defining leadership as influence on others in a group. Leadership is the observed effort of one member to change other members' behavior by altering the motivation of the other members or by changing their habits. If the leadership is successful, what is observed is a change in the member accepting the leadership. Changing behavior by disturbing the central nervous system is arbitrarily excluded, but psychotherapy and teaching are included within the meaning of leadership.

Members who lead may also do other things. The foreman may keep inventory records as well as exhibit leadership. But being a foreman is not identical with being a leader.

Related to leadership, yet different in meaning, are behavioral contagion, influence, and followership. But following is not necessarily the opposite of leading; sometimes one may lead by following.

The observed change in the behavior of the follower results from the alteration of his motivation, or from initiating of structure by the leader. Motivation is changed by changing the expectations of reward or punishment. The mass persuader leads through this type of activity. In the formal organization, leaders vary from motivating others with promise of reward, support, affection, and consideration to threats of punishment, burdensome demands, and deflation of the self-esteem of subordinates. This variation in consideration is unidimensional and accounts for much of described leader behavior in industry and military organizations.

Leadership also is accomplished by initiating structure—making others more able to overcome the obstacles thwarting goal attainment. Activities include instructing, supervising, informing, ordering, and deciding. Again a single factor describes how leaders in formal organizations vary in such initiation.

Conceiving leadership in this way permits an easier integration of theories concerning the perception, learning, and behavior of the individual in a nonsocial (isolated) situation with theory emerging from research on perception, learning, and behavior of individuals in groups.

MEASUREMENT AND EVALUATION OF LEADERSHIP

Our understanding of leadership will depend on how we measure and evaluate it. Earlier investigators using wisdom research, case history analyses, nomination, ratings, and categorization did not attempt to distinguish between attempted, successful, and effective leadership. But a dynamic analysis of the leadership process requires differentiation. Nonobjective assessment methods are not likely to as readily provide the necessary discrimination because of the halo error in ratings and other difficulties of discrimination.

An objective method of assessing attempted leadership is to measure the amount of time a subject participates in an initially leaderless discussion. The reliability of this and related measures of participation is high and accounts for much of the observed and evaluated differences in leadership among discussants.

One possible objective approach to assessing successful leadership is to present a group with a problem whose solution requires ranking the alternative answers to the problem. Each member is asked to report privately his own initial opinion. Then the members interact—usually in discussion. They reach another decision or decisions, as a group or as individuals. Who has influenced whom is gauged from the changes in correlations among the various members' rankings from before to after they interact.

Effective leadership is exhibited by successful leaders of groups which become effective as a consequence of the leadership. Measurement requires assessing the effectiveness of the groups led as well as the success of the leadership.

LEADERSHIP AND GROUP EFFECTIVENESS

Changes occur in the behavior of members of a group in order to increase the rewards for performance. While such changes can be initiated by individual isolated trial and error or other personal means, it is assumed that they more often are the product of interaction, since evidence indicates that (1) more changes occur when interaction is possible; (2) the changes occur faster; (3) interaction brings rewards not possible in isolation; and (4) isolated individuals are likely to reduce the variability of their behavior or withdraw from the environment if it is not a stimulating one.

If group effectiveness depends on the occurrence of interaction, it also depends on the occurrence of attempted and successful leadership, since leadership is interaction. The more difficult are the problems facing the group and blocking goal attainment or the less able the membership to cope with their problems and reach their goals, the more the leadership is necessary and likely to be attempted and successful. But if the difficulties are too great, members' expectations of failure may make the group sufficiently unattractive to cause the members to withdraw from it, rather than attempt to solve the problems or attempt and succeed as leaders.

MOTIVATION TO ATTEMPT LEADERSHIP

Individuals differ in personality and personal goals, and in whether they are task-oriented, self-oriented or interaction-oriented. This results in further individual differences in tendency to attempt leadership. Also, energetic persons, regardless of other conditions, are more likely to attempt more leadership than those less active generally. Similarly, persons with strong needs to achieve are more likely to attempt leadership than those without such needs. Again, members more attracted to the group, expecting more rewards for goal attainment, will be more likely to attempt leadership than those lower in attraction to the group.

Idealized types of task-, interaction-, and self-oriented members can be conceived, although naturally most persons will exhibit some of all three tendencies, depending to some extent on the situation. Task-oriented members are most attracted to the group by expectations of task success and its rewards. They are reinforced primarily by task effectiveness. Others are similarly more concerned with interaction and interaction effectiveness. Still other members are primarily attracted to a group as a source of esteem, status, or direct reward to themselves regardless of task and interaction effectiveness. An analysis of a particular group's goals and those of its members often is required to determine whether the various members are self-, task-, or interaction-oriented. A member high personally in need achievement may exhibit interaction orientation at a social gathering, and task orientation in a work group.

Orientation changes with the aging of a group in existence over long periods of time. Members tend to be attracted to each other initially to complete some tasks they cannot handle alone. Then the groups tend to move from task orientation to a concern with interaction as an end in itself. Finally, self-orientation comes to the fore prior to the disintegration of the groups.

The self-oriented leader is more concerned with his success as a leader than the task or interaction effectiveness of his leadership. Therefore, the self-oriented leader is usually detrimental to group effectiveness. He is less likely to change his behavior to meet changing group needs. He may even try to divert the group from one goal to another. But the self-oriented member is less likely to persist in the face of failure to lead others.

The task-oriented leader will attempt leadership only when the group is attractive because of its tasks and the rewards for task success. He will more readily cease attempting leadership if his successes are ineffective.

The interaction-oriented leader will avoid attempting leadership likely to disrupt current patterns of interaction. He will attempt leadership mainly when interaction difficulties present themselves and he sees himself as able to cope with them.

ABILITY AND PERSUASIVE LEADERSHIP

One member can persuade another if he has demonstrated his ability to solve the other member's problems. In persuasive leadership, the leader serves as a secondary reinforcer of the behavior of the follower.

A variety of generalized aptitudes and more specific proficiencies are associated with observed success as a leader. In a wide variety of situations, the more fluent, intelligent, original, and adaptable member is more likely to succeed as a leader. The member more empathic or sensitive to the needs of his group is more likely to succeed as leader. Proficiency in the activities of the group also characterizes successful leaders.

Again, ability derived from a member's position can also produce successful leadership.

But the would-be leader cannot be too much more able than those he leads to succeed maximally as a leader. Moreover, his ability must be relevant or significant for solving the problems of the groups he expects to lead.

DEVELOPMENT AND TRANSFER OF ABILITY TO LEAD

It is assumed that positive transfer, the facilitation of new performance by earlier behavior, is greater the more similar the new and old performances. But negative transfer will occur if the new situation is seen as similar and is responded to as if it is similar when it is actually different from the old. Both positive and negative transfer are common in social development.

It follows from these assumptions that the leader successful and effective earlier will succeed and be effective to a maximum in a new situation the more it resembles the earlier one and is perceived as similar. The earlier-effective leader will attempt less leadership in the new situation if he sees it as different. He will be least effective in the new situation if it is seen as similar to the earlier one but is not.

The leader successful and ineffective earlier will attempt less leadership in a new situation seen as similar. If others see it as similar, he will be less successful in influencing them.

An unsuccessful leader of an earlier situation will attempt less leadership in a new one if he sees the new one as similar to the earlier situation. If he does attempt leadership and the other members see the situation as similar, he will be less likely to succeed.

One is more likely to attempt leadership in a new situation if he attempted it in an earlier one seen as similar.

Most of these and related deductions have not been tested as yet, but various studies can be arranged to lend empirical support to some of the propositions. For example, consistency of leadership displayed by individuals in early and later leaderless discussions decreases insofar as the later discussions are among differently composed groups, about different problems, and further away in time from the earlier discussions. Similarly, there is a much higher correlation between leadership displayed in junior high school and high school by students than among students in elementary school reexamined in high school.

Considerable additional evidence supports the generality of transfer across changing situations, but the evidence does not indicate how the consistency or generality is affected by the similarity or differences between situations. The observed generality suggests the utility of situational tests, such as the leaderless group discussion, for assessing future leadership potential in "real-life" situations.

But, while illustrations of negative transfer from industry and government can be cited, no experimental evidence has been uncovered.

The transfer phenomena suggest that the interaction experiences of children and adolescents with their parents, siblings, peers, and other adults play an important role in the development of leadership potential. The ability of biographical information blanks to forecast future leadership success and the biographical analyses of "great men" suggest the utility of further exploration of the links between childhood and adult leadership behavior.

From studies of the social development of the child, a number of factors are likely to affect the future success of the adult as a leader, particularly if the conditions persist into and through adolescence. These include the early pattern of interaction with the mother, and later the father and teacher; family factors such as birth order and number; parental attitudes toward children; and adolescent opportunities for social learning.

MANAGEMENT DEVELOPMENT

There have been almost no specific tests contrasting the efficacy of various methods of executive training as now practiced in industry. The leadership training apparently aims to (1) increase the ability to solve the problems of those to be led; (2) reinforce success as a leader by giving opportunities to attempt leadership and to see the effects of the attempts; and (3) increase motivation to attempt leadership.

It is probable that those programs attempting to increase proficiencies rather than to modify aptitudes or personality traits are more likely to succeed. Particularly important is the need for the superiors of the trainees to provide active support and acceptance of what is to be learned.

Training may include coaching by superiors; guided experience; understudy training; management apprenticeships; job rotation; counseling by professional consultants; and project assignments. Use may be made of problem-solving discussions, case history analyses, and role playing, in addition to many formal and informal class and course procedures.

POWER AND COERCIVE LEADERSHIP

While a member with ability can successfully persuade others to follow him, a member with power can coerce others to follow. His power may derive from his person or his position. A powerful person can directly reinforce the behavior of others by granting or denying rewards or punishments to the others, depending on their behavior. A person has power over others if he controls what the others want. If the other members are not motivated to gain these goals, the control does not yield power. The stronger the motivation, the greater the resulting power.

Coercion occurs when members publicly but not privately comply with the suggestions or direction of another member. But the inhibition of their own preferences results in dissatisfaction and frustration, which in turn may lead to a variety of attempts to reduce the frustration. Coercion may produce hostility among the coerced. Or the less powerful members may withdraw from the situation. Or they may overreact, resulting in a loss in task effectiveness. Or they may compensate by forming a new informal organization to counter the frustrating effects of being coerced.

Power provides successful coercive leadership but it is not as likely to be effective as far as the coerced members are concerned.

ABILITY, POWER, AND PERMISSIVE LEADERSHIP

To lead successfully and permissively, a member must have the power to impose restrictions on what other members are permitted to do, and he must have the ability to know when such restrictions are necessary and when he would do better to avoid such impositions. While power used to coerce will produce hostility, withdrawal, apathy, "forced" behavior toward irrelevant goals, the same power, coupled with ability, can be used permissively. Permissiveness is less likely to result in hostility and withdrawal since the goals selected by those led permissively are likely to be relevant to them.

Group decision-making is usually involved in permissive leadership. As such, the permissive leader can avoid using his power to coerce (except when necessary to impose some restrictions on the interacting members). Instead, he can make use of the power of the group and the members' acceptance of the group as more able than themselves as individuals.

Memberships in groups facilitates compliance with suggestions. The tendency to conform to majority opinion, to the norms established by the group, to modal behavior, seems to be a universal phenomenon. Such compliance is found in adolescent cliques, in conformity to cultural values, in military discipline, in the typical work group, in delinquent gangs, and in the laboratory.

The more attractive a group, the more rewards expected from it, the more power it will have over its members, and the more members will conform to group standards. Conformity will be greater the more certain or clear are the standards, and when the group is made more important to its members. Conformity is greater among the less confident members, the more acquiescent members, and those closer initially to the majority position.

A great deal of evidence suggests that permissive leadership, group decision-making, and permission to interact prior to reaching such decisions produce more effective groups and more satisfied members. Exceptions are likely to occur when members are under severe stress or are of low ability.

STATUS AND LEADERSHIP

Status is the worth or value to the organization of the occupant of a position, regardless of who the occupant is personally. Status provides the power to coerce, the ability to persuade as well as the power and ability to be a permissive leader, but status is not leadership.

Status can be gauged from the rank or echelon of an occupant's position in an organization. Also, various methods of job evaluation can be used to determine the worth of the various positions making up the formal organization. Special sociometric analyses also can be employed.

Status is usually accompanied by visible symbols of position and worth. Sometimes, however, the symbols remain after the status has disappeared. While habitual compliance to the symbols may be maintained, the loss of status and of the power and ability accompanying it results in a loss in likelihood of success as a leader.

Considerable experimental evidence and related research support the theorem that the higher one's status, the more likely he is to succeed as a leader among those of lower status. This generalization applies equally well to status and leadership in societies, in formal industrial and military organizations as well as to impromptu initially leaderless group discussions. But the control accompanying status must be of what is potentially rewarding to those of lower status. Otherwise, the status will yield control, but not power, resulting in less leadership success.

ESTEEM AND LEADERSHIP

Esteem is the worth of an individual to his group, regardless of his position. Esteem contributes to subsequent status, and heightened status tends to increase one's esteem. Esteem depends to some extent on what abilities are relevant to goal attainment by the group; to what the group values. Esteem is not popularity, although they tend to be related, particularly when the group is mainly concerned with pleasant interactions.

Esteem is measured by some form of merit rating by superiors, peers, or subordinates in formal organizations, or by one's associates in informal organizations. Or it can be estimated by outside observers. Sociometric ratings by peers tend to be consistent over considerable periods of time, particularly for more mature subjects.

Esteemed members tend to be more able, more likely to conform, better adjusted, seemingly more similar in attitudes and attributes to the average member and more like other esteemed members.

The esteemed member can successfully coerce others by means of his personal power or he can successfully persuade them because of his apparently greater ability. Since continued coercion is likely to produce a loss of esteem, permissive or persuasive leadership must be emphasized by an esteemed member in order for him to maintain his esteem.

Esteem has been found associated with success in leading initially leaderless group discussions, with success in military leadership, and with success in leading other children. The effects can be reproduced in the laboratory.

Mutual esteem is positively associated with the attractiveness of a group. Since attractiveness contributes to effectiveness, mutual esteem likewise is related to group effectiveness. In the same way, conformity in groups is likely to be greater when mutual esteem is high.

Self-esteem presages attempted leadership. Self-esteem increases with success and in turn reduces tendencies to conform or acquiesce. Self-accorded status operates in a similar way.

CONFLICT

Leadership may be rejected despite the ability or power behind it because of a variety of conflicts.

Events preceding the attempted leadership, or taking place concurrently, may result in the failure of what would have been successful leadership. The attempted leadership may require excessive energy expenditure not commensurate with promised rewards for compliance; it may demand unacceptable distribution of rewards; it may threaten loss of esteem or status. In all of these cases, despite the power or ability promoting success, the attemped leadership may be rejected. Or followers may resort to pseudosolutions, such as rationalization for acceptance, withdrawal, and displaced aggression, rather than reject power figures openly.

The would-be leader is often the "man-in-the-middle" caught between the demands of his superiors and the desires of his subordinates. A variety of resolutions of his dilemma have been adopted, some regarded as tactful, others as hypocritical. Many comment on the need of a leader caught in such conditions to wear a mask, to be a good actor.

If one's self-esteem is higher than the esteem he is accorded by other members, he is likely to attempt more leadership and succeed less than a member whose esteem matches his high self-esteem. Status and self-accorded status follow the same proposition, but self-esteem is more likely to be overestimated than is self-accorded status.

Since status or esteem produces success as a leader, if the high-status member is not esteemed or vice versa, conflict is likely. Status-esteem incongruencies lead to a variety of conflicts, if the high-status and the high-esteem members differ in their respective ideas and goals. Ways of mitigating status-esteem incongruence include ensuring the promotion of the esteemed, increasing or maintaining the esteem of those promoted to higher status, and increasing the agreement about aims of the formal and informal organizations.

Ability-esteem or ability-status incongruence not only bring[s] conflict, but also group ineffectiveness. If the powerful member lacks ability, he may succeed as a leader but is less likely to be effective than the powerful member with ability to solve the group's problems. Again, one solution avoiding this difficulty is to ensure promoting the most able members. Another is for lower-status members to mask their abilities, avoiding conflict, but not fostering group effectiveness.

INTERACTION POTENTIAL

Interaction potential is the tendency of any pair of a group to interact. As interaction potential increases between two individuals, we observe an increase in:

1. The probability of their interacting in a given amount of time.
2. Rate or frequency of interaction between the pair.
3. Speed of initiation of an interaction between the pair.
4. Duration of interaction between the pair.
5. The total amount of interaction in a group composed of many small pairs.

A pair of individuals are [sic] more likely to interact if they are:

1. Members of a small rather than a large group.
2. Geographically and socially close.
3. Connected by a communication channel free of "noise" or blockage, free to contact each other rather than lacking in opportunity for contact and meeting.
4. Intimate and familiar and experienced with each other rather than distant and unfamiliar.
5. Mutually esteemed.
6. Attracted to each other.

7. Similar in abilities and attitudes rather than different.
8. More mature than young children.
9. More in contact with reality, energetic and outward-oriented.

Other factors that increase interaction potential may include alcohol, boredom, third parties, interaction primacy, the importance of message, the amount of situational stimulation, the time available to interact, and the amount of coordination required for completion of the task.

INTERACTION POTENTIAL AND GROUP EFFECTIVENESS

If groups tend to move toward greater effectiveness and if most changes in groups are by means of interaction, then it follows that increased effectiveness accompanies increased interaction among members. Large, distant, disconnected, unfamiliar, and heterogeneous groups of members will be less likely to reach a given state of effectiveness compared to small, proximate, connected, intimate, homogeneous groups. We must qualify this generalization as we consider each variable separately. However, the qualifications themselves logically follow from the differences that exist among such diverse variables as size, propinquity, connectedness, and so on and some of their unique effects on behavior in groups, above and beyond considerations of interaction potential. Thus, increased homogeneity in attitudes is accompanied by increased willingness to express hostility openly as well as increased interaction potential.

OVERCOMING INEFFECTIVENESS DUE TO LACK OF INTERACTION POTENTIAL

A variety of techniques and modifications are introduced into group activities in order to counteract the effects of initially lower interaction potential.

Some raise effectiveness by raising interaction potential directly, while others raise interaction potential indirectly or attack effectiveness rather than interaction potential as such. The processes or techniques include establishing formal organization and increasing the differentiation of members in status (which, in turn, may create new difficulties for the group); increasing the training of assigned leaders; increasing the educational level or degree of understanding of the members of the group activities; establishing and reinforcing reliable common sources of information for all members; increasing the rapidity and frequency of transmittal of information; and splintering the group.

More direct methods include increasing propinquity mechanically; restricting size arbitrarily; increasing familiarity; promoting feelings of homogeneity; increasing mutual esteem; and developing new communication procedures.

Historical developments of civilized societies to some extent may be described in terms of changing interaction potential and its effects.

LEADERSHIP DURING EMERGENCIES

When members must cope with danger, sudden threat, any attempts to aid them in removing themselves from the obvious possibilities will be welcomed. Attempts to lead are more likely to be accepted more readily than if no crises were present. Such attempts are also more likely to be immediately effective.

Since speed of interaction is likely to be effective, groups with greater interaction potential are likely to be more immediately effective when faced with emergencies. Small, intimate, proximate, communicative groups are more likely to be effective in crises. Or stratified groups with highly trained leaders and members are more likely to be able to cope with sudden crises.

Since stress increases with increasing motivation, and since attractiveness also increases with motivation, attractive groups are likely to experience more stress when thwarted from obtaining their goals than unattractive groups.

How To Choose a Leadership Pattern

Robert Tannenbaum and Warren H. Schmidt

Should a leader be democratic or autocratic in dealing with his subordinates—or something in between?

"I put most problems into my group's hands and leave it to them to carry the ball from there. I serve merely as a catalyst, mirroring back the people's thoughts and feelings so that they can better understand them."

"It's foolish to make decisions oneself on matters that affect people. I always talk things over with my subordinates, but I make it clear to them that I'm the one who has to have the final say."

"Once I have decided on a course of action, I do my best to sell my ideas to my employees."

"I'm being paid to lead. If I let a lot of other people make the decisions I should be making, then I'm not worth my salt."

"I believe in getting things done. I can't waste time calling meetings. Someone has to call the shots around here, and I think it should be me."

Each of these statements represents a point of view about "good leadership." Considerable experience, factual data, and theoretical principles could be cited to support each statement, even though they seem to be inconsistent when placed together. Such contradictions point up the dilemma in which the modern manager frequently finds himself.

NEW PROBLEM

The problem of how the modern manager can be "democratic" in his relations with subordinates and at the same time maintain the necessary authority and control in the organization for which he is responsible has come into focus increasingly in recent years.

Earlier in the century this problem was not so acutely felt. The successful executive was generally pictured as possessing intelligence, imagination, initiative, and the capacity to make rapid (and generally wise) decisions, and the ability to inspire subordinates. People tended to think of the world as being divided into "leaders" and "followers."

New Focus

Gradually, however, from the social sciences emerged the concept of "group dynamics" with its focus on *members* of the group rather than solely on the leader. Research efforts of social scientists underscored the importance of employee involvement and participation in decision making. Evidence began to challenge the efficiency of highly directive leadership, and increasing attention was paid to problems of motivation and human relations.

Through training laboratories in group development that sprang up across the country, many of the newer notions of leadership began to exert an impact. These training laboratories were carefully designed to give people a firsthand experience in full participation and decision making. The designated "leaders" deliberately attempted to reduce their own power and to make group members as responsible as possible for setting their own goals and methods within the laboratory experience.

It was perhaps inevitable that some of the people who attended the training laboratories regarded this kind of leadership as being truly "democratic" and went home with the determination to build fully participative decision making into their own organizations. Whenever their bosses made a decision without convening a staff meeting, they tended to perceive this as authoritarian behavior. The true symbol of democratic leadership to some was the meeting—and the less directed from the top, the more democratic it was.

Some of the more enthusiastic alumni of these training laboratories began to get the habit of categorizing leader behavior as "democratic" or "authoritarian." The boss who made too many decisions himself was thought of as an authoritarian, and his directive behavior was often attributed solely to his personality.

New Need

The net result of the research findings and of the human relations training based upon them has been to call into question the stereotype of an effective leader. Consequently, the modern manager often finds himself in an uncomfortable state of mind.

Often he is not quite sure how to behave; there are times when he is torn between exerting "strong" leadership and "permissive" leadership. Sometimes new knowledge pushes him in one direction ("I should really get the group to help make this decision"), but at the same time his experience pushes him in another direction ("I really understand the problem better than the group and therefore I should make the decision"). He is not sure when a group decision is really appropriate or when holding a staff meeting serves merely as a device for avoiding his own decision-making responsibility.

The purpose of our article is to suggest a framework which managers may find useful in grappling with this dilemma. First we shall look at the different patterns of leadership behavior that the manager can choose from in relating himself to his subordinates. Then we shall turn to some of the questions suggested by this range of patterns. For instance, how important is it for a manager's subordinates to know what type of leadership he is using in a situation? What factors should he consider in deciding on a leadership pattern? What difference do his long-run objectives make as compared to his immediate objectives?

RANGE OF BEHAVIOR

Exhibit I presents the continuum or range of possible leadership behavior available to a manager. Each type of action is related to the degree of authority used by the boss and to the amount of freedom available to his subordinates in reaching decisions. The actions seen on the extreme left characterize the manager who maintains a high degree of control while those seen on the extreme right characterize the manager who releases a high degree of control. Neither extreme is absolute; authority and freedom are never without their limitations.

Boss- centered leadership	←					Subordinate- centered leadership

Use of authority by the manager						Area of freedom for subordinates
Manager makes decision and announces it.	Manager "sells" decision.	Manager presents ideas and invites questions.	Manager presents tentative decision subject to change.	Manager presents problem, gets sug- gestions, makes decision.	Manager defines limits, asks group to make decision.	Manager permits subordi- nates to function within limits defined by superior.

Exhibit I. Continuum of Leadership Behavior

Now let us look more closely at each of the behavior points occurring along this continuum:

The Manager Makes the Decision and Announces It.

In this case the boss identifies a problem, considers alternative solutions, chooses one of them, and then reports this decision to his subordinates for implementation. He may or may not give consideration to what he believes his subordinates will think or feel about his decision; in any case, he provides no opportunity for them to participate directly in the decision-making process. Coercion may or may not be used or implied.

The Manager "Sells" His Decision.

Here the manager, as before, takes responsibility for identifying the problem and arriving at a decision. However, rather than simply announcing it, he takes the additional step of persuading his subordinates to accept it. In doing so, he recognizes the possibility of some resistance among those who will be faced with the decision, and seeks to reduce this resistance by indicating, for example, what the employees have to gain from his decision.

The Manager Presents His Ideas, Invites Questions.

Here the boss who has arrived at a decision and who seeks acceptance of his ideas provides an opportunity for his subordinates to get a fuller explanation of his thinking and his intentions. After presenting the ideas, he invites questions so that his associates can better understand what he is trying to accomplish. This "give and take" also enables the manager and the subordinates to explore more fully the implications of the decision.

The Manager Presents a Tentative Decision Subject to Change.

This kind of behavior permits the subordinates to exert some influence on the decision. The initiative for identifying and diagnosing the problem remains with the boss. Before meeting with his staff, he has thought the problem through and arrived at a decision—but only a tentative one. Before finalizing it, he presents his proposed solution for the reaction of those who will be affected by it. He says in effect, "I'd like to hear what you have to say about this plan that I have developed. I'll appreciate your frank reactions, but will reserve for myself the final decision."

The Manager Presents the Problem, Gets Suggestions, and Then Makes His Decision.

Up to this point the boss has come before the group with a solution of his own. Not so in this case. The subordinates now get the first chance to suggest solutions. The manager's initial role involves identifying the problem. He might, for example, say something of this sort: "We are faced with a number of complaints from newspapers and the general public on our service policy. What is wrong here? What ideas do you have for coming to grips with this problem?"

The function of the group becomes one of increasing the manager's repertory of possible solutions to the problem. The purpose is to capitalize on the knowledge and experience of those who are on the "firing line." From the expanded list of alternatives developed by the manager and his subordinates, the manager then selects the solution that he regards as most promising.[1]

The Manager Defines the Limits and Requests the Group To Make a Decision.

At this point the manager passes to the group (possibly including himself as a member) the right to make decisions. Before doing so, however, he defines the problem to be solved and the boundaries within which the decision must be made.

An example might be the handling of a parking problem at a plant. The boss decides that this is something that should be worked on by the people involved, so he calls them together and points up the existence of the problem. Then he tells them:

"There is the open field just north of the main plant which has been designated for additional employee parking. We can build underground or surface multilevel facilities as long as the cost does not exceed $100,000.00. Within these limits we are free to work out whatever solution makes sense to us. After we decide on a specific plan, the company will spend the available money in whatever way we indicate."

The Manager Permits the Group To Make Decisions Within Prescribed Limits.

This represents an extreme degree of group freedom only occasionally encountered in formal organizations, as, for instance, in many research groups. Here the team of managers or engineers undertakes the identification and diagnosis of the problem, develops alternative procedures for solving it, and decides on one or more of these alternative solutions. The only limits directly imposed on the group by the organization are those specified by the superior of the team's boss. If the boss participates in the decision-making process, he attempts to do so with no more authority than any other member of the group. He commits himself in advance to assist in implementing whatever decision the group makes.

KEY QUESTIONS

As the continuum in Exhibit I demonstrates, there are a number of alternative ways in which a manager can relate himself to the group or individuals he is supervising. At the extreme left of the range, the emphasis is on the manager—on what *he* is interested in, how *he* sees things, how *he* feels about them. As we move toward the subordinate-centered end of the continuum, however, the focus is increasingly on the subordinates—on what *they* are interested in, how *they* look at things, how *they* feel about them.

When a business leadership is regarded in this way, a number of questions arise. Let us take four of especial importance:

Can a Boss Ever Relinquish His Responsibility by Delegating It to Someone Else?

Our view is that the manager must expect to be held responsible by his superior for the quality of the decisions made, even though operationally these decisions may have been made on a group basis. He should, therefore, be ready to accept whatever risk is involved whenever he delegates decision-making power to his subordinates. Delegation is not a way of "passing the buck." Also, it should be emphasized that the amount of freedom the boss gives to his subordinates cannot be greater than the freedom which he himself has been given by his own superior.

Should the Manager Participate with His Subordinates Once He Has Delegated Responsibility to Them?

The manager should carefully think over this question and decide on his role prior to involving the subordinate group. He should ask if his presence will inhibit or facilitate the problem-solving process. There may be some instances when he should leave the group to let it solve the problem for itself. Typically, however, the boss has useful ideas to contribute, and should function as an additional member of the group. In the latter instance, it is important that he indicate clearly to the

group that he sees himself in a *member* role rather than in an
authority role.

How Important Is It for the Group To Recognize
What Kind of Leadership Behavior the Boss Is Using?

It makes a great deal of difference. Many relationship problems between boss and subordinate occur because the boss
fails to make clear how he plans to use his authority. If, for
example, he actually intends to make a certain decision
himself, but the subordinate group gets the impression that he
has delegated this authority, considerable confusion and
resentment are likely to follow. Problems may also occur
when the boss uses a "democratic" facade to conceal the fact
that he has already made a decision which he hopes the group
will accept as its own. The attempt to "make them think it was
their idea in the first place" is a risky one. We believe that it is
highly important for the manager to be honest and clear in
describing what authority he is keeping and what role he is
asking his subordinates to assume in solving a particular
problem.

Can You Tell How "Democratic" a Manager Is
by the Number of Decisions His Subordinates Make?

The sheer *number* of decisions is not an accurate index of the
amount of freedom that a subordinate group enjoys. More
important is the *significance* of the decisions which the boss
entrusts to his subordinates. Obviously a decision on how to
arrange desks is of an entirely different order from a decision
involving the introduction of new electronic data processing
equipment. Even though the widest possible limits are given
in dealing with the first issue, the group will sense no
particular degree of responsibility. For a boss to permit the
group to decide equipment policy, even within rather narrow
limits, would reflect a greater degree of confidence in them
on his part.

DECIDING HOW TO LEAD

Now let us turn from the types of leadership that are *practical*
and *desirable*. What factors or forces should a manager

consider in deciding how to manage? Three are of particular importance:

- Forces in the manager.
- Forces in the subordinates.
- Forces in the situation.

We should like briefly to describe these elements and indicate how they might influence a manager's action in a decision-making situation.[2] The strength of each of them will, of course, vary from instance to instance, but the manager who is sensitive to them can better assess the problems which face him and determine which mode of leadership behavior is most appropriate for him.

Forces In the Manager

The manager's behavior in any given instance will be influenced greatly by the many forces operating within his own personality. He will, of course, perceive his leadership problems in a unique way on the basis of his background, knowledge, and experience. Among the important internal forces affecting him will be the following:

(1) His value system. How strongly does he feel that individuals should have a share in making decisions which affect them? Or, how convinced is he that the official who is paid to assume responsibility should personally carry the burden of decision making? The strength of his convictions on questions like these will tend to move the manager to one end or the other of the continuum shown in Exhibit I. His behavior will also be influenced by the relative importance that he attaches to organizational efficiency, personal growth of subordinates, and company profits.[3]

(2) His confidence in his subordinates. Managers differ greatly in the amount of trust they have in other people generally, and this carries over to the particular employees they supervise at a given time. In viewing his particular group of subordinates, the manager is likely to consider their knowledge and competence with respect to the problem. A central question he might ask himself is: "Who is best qualified to deal with this problem?" Often he may, justifiably or not, have more confidence in his own capabilities than in those of his subordinates.

(3) *His own leadership inclinations.* There are some managers who seem to function more comfortably and naturally as highly directive leaders. Resolving problems and issuing orders come easily to them. Other managers seem to operate more comfortably in a team role, where they are continually sharing many of their functions with their subordinates.

(4) *His feelings of security in an uncertain situation.* The manager who releases control over the decision-making process thereby reduces the predictability of the outcome. Some managers have a greater need than others for predictability and stability in their environment. This "tolerance for ambiguity" is being viewed increasingly by psychologists as a key variable in a person's manner of dealing with problems.

The manager brings these and other highly personal variables to each situation he faces. If he can see them as forces which, consciously or unconsciously, influence his behavior, he can better understand what makes him prefer to act in a given way. And understanding this, he can often make himself more effective.

Forces In the Subordinate

Before deciding how to lead a certain group, the manager will also want to consider a number of forces affecting his subordinates' behavior. He will want to remember that each employee, like himself, is influenced by many personality variables. In addition, each subordinate has a set of expectations about how the boss should act in relation to him (the phrase "expected behavior" is one we hear more and more often these days at discussions of leadership and teaching). The better the manager understands these factors, the more accurately he can determine what kind of behavior on his part will enable his subordinates to act more effectively.

Generally speaking, the manager can permit his subordinates greater freedom if the following essential conditions exist:

- If the subordinates have relatively high needs for independence. (As we all know, people differ greatly in the amount of direction that they desire.)
- If the subordinates have a readiness to assume responsibility for decision making. (Some see addi-

tional responsibility as a tribute to their ability; others see it as "passing the buck.")

- If they have a relatively high tolerance for ambiguity. (Some employees prefer to have clear-cut directives given to them; others prefer a wider area of freedom.)
- If they are interested in the problem and feel that it is important.
- If they understand and identify with the goals of the organization.
- If they have the necessary knowledge and experience to deal with the problem.
- If they have learned to expect to share in decision making. (Persons who have come to expect strong leadership and are then suddenly confronted with the request to share more fully in decision making are often upset by this new experience. On the other hand, persons who have enjoyed a considerable amount of freedom resent the boss who begins to make all the decisions himself.)

The manager will probably tend to make fuller use of his own authority if the above conditions do *not* exist; at times there may be no realistic alternative to running a "one-man show."

The restrictive effect of many of the forces will, of course, be greatly modified by the general feeling of confidence which subordinates have in the boss. Where they have learned to respect and trust him, he is free to vary his behavior. He will feel certain that he will not be perceived as an authoritarian boss on those occasions when he makes decisions by himself. Similarly, he will not be seen as using staff meetings to avoid his decision-making responsibility. In a climate of mutual confidence and respect, people tend to feel less threatened by deviations from normal practice, which in turn makes possible a higher degree of flexibility in the whole relationship.

Forces In the Situation

In addition to the forces which exist in the manager himself and in his subordinates, certain characteristics of the general situation will also affect the manager's behavior. Among the more critical environmental pressures that surround him are those which stem from the organization, the work group, the nature of the problem, and the pressures of time. Let us look briefly at each of these.

Type of Organization. Like individuals, organizations have values and traditions which inevitably influence the behavior of the people who work in them. The manager who is a newcomer to a company quickly discovers that certain kinds of behavior are approved while others are not. He also discovers that to deviate radically from what is generally accepted is likely to create problems for him.

These values and traditions are communicated in many ways—through job descriptions, policy pronouncements, and public statements by top executives. Some organizations, for example, hold to the notion that the desirable executive is one who is dynamic, imaginative, decisive, and persuasive. Other organizations put more emphasis upon the importance of the executive's ability to work effectively with people—his human relations skills. The fact that his superiors have a defined concept of what the good executive should be will very likely push the manager toward one end or the other of the behavioral range.

In addition to the above, the amount of employee participation is influenced by such variables as the size of the working units, their geographical distribution, and the degree of inter- and intra-organizational security required to attain company goals. For example, the wide geographical dispersion of an organization may preclude a practical system of participative decision making, even though this would otherwise be desirable. Similarly, the size of the working units or the need for keeping plans confidential may make it necessary for the boss to exercise more control than would otherwise be the case. Factors like these may limit considerably the manager's ability to function flexibly on the continuum.

Group Effectiveness. Before turning decision-making responsibility over to a subordinate group, the boss should consider how effectively its members work together as a unit.

One of the relevant factors here is the experience the group has had in working together. It can generally be expected that a group which has functioned for some time will have developed habits of cooperation and thus be able to tackle a problem more effectively than a new group. It can also be expected that a group of people with similar backgrounds and interests will work more quickly and easily than people with dissimilar backgrounds, because the communication problems are likely to be less complex.

The degree of confidence that the members have in their ability to solve problems as a group is also a key consideration. Finally, such group variables as cohesiveness, permissiveness, mutual acceptance, and commonality of purpose will exert subtle but powerful influence[s] on the group's functioning.

The Problem Itself. The nature of the problem may determine what degree of authority should be delegated by the manager to his subordinates. Obviously he will ask himself whether they have the kind of knowledge which is needed. It is possible to do them a real disservice by assigning a problem that their experience does not equip them to handle.

Since the problems faced in large or growing industries increasingly require knowledge of specialists from many different fields, it might be inferred that the more complex a problem, the more anxious a manager will be to get some assistance in solving it. However, this is not always the case. There will be times when the very complexity of the problem calls for one person to work it out. For example, if the manager has most of the background and factual data relevant to a given issue, it may be easier for him to think it through himself than to take the time to fill in his staff on all the pertinent background information.

The key question to ask, of course, is: "Have I heard the ideas of everyone who has the necessary knowledge to make a significant contribution to the solution of this problem?"

The Pressure of Time. This is perhaps the most clearly felt pressure on the manager (in spite of the fact that it may sometimes be imagined). The more that he feels the need for an immediate decision, the more difficult it is to involve other people. In organizations which are in a constant state of "crisis" and "crash programing" one is likely to find managers personally using a high degree of authority with relatively little delegation to subordinates. When the time pressure is less intense, however, it becomes much more possible to bring subordinates in on the decision-making process.

These, then, are the principal forces that impinge on the manager in any given instance and that tend to determine his tactical behavior in relation to his subordinates. In each case his behavior ideally will be that which makes possible the most effective attainment of his immediate goal within the limits facing him.

LONG-RUN STRATEGY

As the manager works with his organization on the problems that come up day by day, his choice of a leadership pattern is usually limited. He must take account of the forces just described and, within the restrictions they impose on him, do the best that he can. But as he looks ahead months or even years, he can shift his thinking from tactics to large-scale strategy. No longer need he be fettered by all of the forces mentioned, for he can view many of them as variables over which he has some control. He can, for example, gain new insights or skills for himself, supply training for individual subordinates, and provide participative experiences for his employee group.

In trying to bring about a change in these variables, however, he is faced with a challenging question: At which point along the continuum *should* he act?

Attaining Objectives

The answer depends largely on what he wants to accomplish. Let us suppose that he is interested in the same objectives that most modern managers seek to attain when they can shift their attention from the pressure of immediate assignments:

1. To raise the level of employee motivation.
2. To increase the readiness of subordinates to accept change.
3. To improve the quality of all managerial decisions.
4. To develop teamwork and morale.
5. To further the individual development of employees.

In recent years the manager has been deluged with a flow of advice on how best to achieve these longer-run objectives. It is little wonder that he is often both bewildered and annoyed. However, there are some guidelines which he can usefully follow in making a decision.

Most research and much of the experience of recent years give a strong factual basis to the theory that a fairly high degree of subordinate-centered behavior is associated with the accomplishment of the five purposes mentioned.[4] This does not mean that a manager should always leave all decisions to his assistants. To provide the individual or the group with greater freedom than they are ready for at any given time may very well tend to generate anxieties and therefore inhibit rather than facilitate the attainment of desired objectives. But this should not keep the manager from making a continuing effort to confront his subordinates with the challenge of freedom.

CONCLUSION

In summary, there are two implications in the basic thesis that we have been developing. The first is that the successful leader is one who is keenly aware of those forces which are most relevant to his behavior at any given time. He accurately understands himself, the individuals and group he is dealing with, and the company and broader social environment in which he operates. And certainly he is able to assess the present readiness for growth of his subordinates.

But this sensitivity or understanding is not enough, which brings us to the second implication. The successful leader is one who is able to behave appropriately in the light of these perceptions. If direction is in order, he is able to direct; if considerable participative freedom is called for, he is able to provide such freedom.

Thus, the successful manager of men can be primarily characterized neither as a strong leader nor as a permissive one. Rather, he is one who maintains a high batting average in accurately assessing the forces that determine what his most appropriate behavior at any given time should be and in actually being able to behave accordingly. Being both insightful and flexible, he is less likely to see the problems of leadership as a dilemma.

RETROSPECTIVE COMMENTARY

Since this HBR Classic was first published in 1958, there have been many changes in organizations and in the world that have affected leadership patterns. While the article's continued popularity attests to its essential validity, we believe it can be reconsidered and updated to reflect subsequent societal changes and new management concepts.

The reasons for the article's continued relevance can be summarized briefly:

- The article contains insights and perspectives which mesh well with, and help clarify, the experiences of managers, other leaders, and students of leadership. Thus it is useful to individuals in a wide variety of organizations—industrial, governmental, educational, religious, and community.
- The concept of leadership the article defines is reflected in a continuum of leadership behavior (see Exhibit I in original article). Rather than offering a choice between two styles of leadership, democratic or authoritarian, it sanctions a range of behavior.
- The concept does not dictate to managers but helps them to analyze their own behavior. The continuum permits them to review their behavior within a context of other alternatives, without any style being labeled right or wrong.

(We have sometimes wondered if we have, perhaps, made it too easy for anyone to justify his or her style of leadership. It may be a small step between being nonjudgmental and giving the impression that all behavior is equally valid and useful. The latter was not our intention. Indeed, the thrust of our endorsement was for the manager who is insightful in assessing relevant forces within himself, others, and the situation, and who can be flexible in responding to these forces.)

In recognizing that our article can be updated, we are acknowledging that organizations do not exist in a vacuum but are affected by changes that occur in society. Consider, for example, the implications for organizations of these recent social developments.

- The youth revolution that expresses distrust and even contempt for organizations identified with the establishment.
- The civil rights movement that demands all minority groups be given a greater opportunity for participation and influence in the organizational processes.
- The ecology and consumer movements that challenge the right of managers to make decisions without considering the interest[s] of people outside the organization.
- The increasing national concern with the quality of working life and its relationship to worker productivity, participation, and satisfaction.

These and other societal changes make effective leadership in this decade a more challenging task, requiring even greater sensitivity and flexibility than was needed in the 1950's. Today's manager is more likely to deal with employees who resent being treated as subordinates, who may be highly critical of any organizational system, who expect to be consulted and to exert influence, and who often stand on the edge of alienation from the institution that needs their loyalty and commitment. In addition, he is frequently confronted by a highly turbulent, unpredictable environment.

In response to these social pressures, new concepts of management have emerged in organizations. Open-system theory, with its emphasis on subsystems' interdependency *and* on the interaction of an organization with its environment, has made a powerful impact on managers' approach[es] to problems. Organization development has emerged as a new behavioral science approach to the improvement of individual, group, organizational, and interorganizational performance. New research has added to our understanding of motivation in the work situation. More and more executives have become concerned with social responsibility and have explored the feasibility of social audits. And a growing number of organizations, in Europe and in the United States, have conducted experiments in industrial democracy.

In light of these developments, we submit the following thoughts on how we would rewrite certain points in our original article.

The article described forces in the manager, subordinates, and the situation as givens, with the leadership pattern a resultant of these forces. We would now give more attention to the *interdependency* of these forces. For example, such interdependency occurs in: (a) the interplay between the manager's confidence in his subordinates, their readiness to assume responsibility, and the level of group effectiveness; and (b) the impact of the behavior of the manager on that of his subordinates, and vice versa.

In discussing the forces in the situation, we primarily identified organizational phenomena. We would now include forces lying outside the organization, and would explore the relevant interdependencies between the organization and its environment.

In the original article, we presented the size of the rectangle in Exhibit I as a given, with its boundaries already determined by external forces—in effect, a closed system. We would now recognize the possibility of the manager and/or his subordinates taking the initiative to change these boundaries through interaction with relevant external forces—both within their own organization and in the larger society.

The article portrayed the manager as the principal and almost unilateral actor. He initiated and determined group functions, assumed responsibility, and exercised control. Subordinates made inputs and assumed power only at the will of the manager. Although the manager might have taken into account forces outside himself, it was *he* who decided where to operate on the continuum—that is, whether to announce a decision instead of trying to sell his idea to his subordinates, whether to invite questions, to let subordinates decide an issue, and so on. While the manager has retained this clear prerogative in many organizations, it has been challenged in others. Even in situations where he has retained it, however, the balance in the relationship between manager and subordinates at any given time is arrived at by interaction—direct or indirect—between the two parties.

Although power and its use by the manager played a role in our article, we now realize that our concern with cooperation and collaboration, common goals, commitment, trust, and mutual caring limited our vision with respect to the realities of power. We did not attempt to deal with unions, other forms of joint worker action, or with individual workers' expressions of resistance. Today, we would recognize much more clearly the power available to *all* parties, and the factors that underlie the interrelated decisions on whether to use it.

In the original article, we used the terms "manager" and "subordinate." We are now uncomfortable with "subordinate" because of its demeaning, dependency-laden connotations and prefer "nonmanager." The titles "manager" and "nonmanager" make the terminological difference functional rather than hierarchical.

We assumed fairly traditional organizational structures in our original article. Now we would alter our formulation to reflect newer organizational modes which are slowly emerging, such as industrial democracy, intentional communities, and "phenomenarchy."[5] These new modes are based on observations such as the following:

- Both manager and nonmanagers may be governing forces in their group's environment, contributing to the definition of the total area of freedom.
- A group can function without a manager, with managerial functions being shared by group members.
- A group, as a unit, can be delegated authority and can assume responsibility within a larger organizational context.

Our thoughts on the question of leadership have prompted us to design a new behavior continuum (see Exhibit II) in which the total area of freedom shared by manager and nonmanagers is constantly redefined by interactions between them and the forces in the environment.

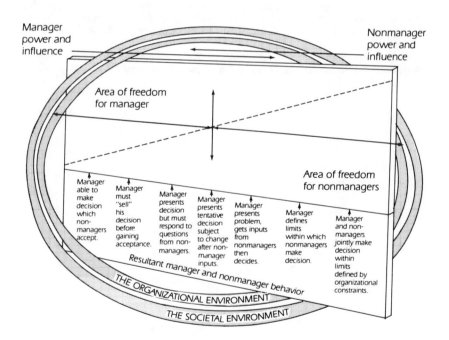

Exhibit II. Continuum of Manager-Nonmanager Behavior.

The arrows in the exhibit indicate the continual flow of interdependent influence among systems and people. The points on the continuum designate the types of manager and nonmanager behavior that become possible with any given amount of freedom available to each. The new continuum is both more complex and more dynamic than the 1958 version, reflecting the organizational and societal realities of 1973.

Notes

[1]For a fuller explanation of this approach, see Leo Moore, "Too Much Management, Too Little Change," *Harvard Business Review*, January-February 1956, p. 41.

[2]See also Robert Tannenbaum and Fred Massarik, "Participation by Subordinates in the Managerial Decision-Making Process," *Canadian Journal of Economics and Political Science*, August 1950, pp. 413-418.

[3]See Chris Argyris, "Top Management Dilemma: Company Needs vs. Individual Development," *Personnel*, September 1955, pp. 123-124.

[4]For example, see Warren H. Schmidt and Paul C. Buchanan, *Techniques that Produce Teamwork* (New London, CT: Arthur C. Croft, 1954); and Morris S. Viteles, *Motivation and Morale in Industry* (New York: W.W. Norton & Company, Inc., 1953).

[5]For a description of phenomenarchy, see Will McWhinney, "Phenomenarchy: A Suggestion for Social Redesign," *Journal of Applied Behavioral Science*, May 1973.

Substitutes for Leadership: Their Meaning and Measurement

Steven Kerr and John M. Jermier

A number of theories and models of leadership exist, each seeking to most clearly identify and best explain the presumedly powerful effects of leader behavior or personality attributes upon the satisfaction and performance of hierarchical subordinates. These theories and models fail to agree in many respects, but have in common the fact that none of them systematically accounts for very much criterion variance. It is certainly true that data indicating strong superior-subordinate relationships have sometimes been reported. In numerous studies, however, conclusions have had to be based on statistical rather than practical significance, and hypothesis support has rested upon the researcher's ability to show that the trivially low correlations obtained were not the result of chance.

Current theories and models of leadership have something else in common: a conviction that hierarchical leadership is always important. Even situational approaches to leadership share the assumption that while the *style* of leadership likely to be effective will vary according to the situation, *some* leadership style will *always* be effective *regardless* of the

Excerpted and reprinted from *Organizational Behavior and Human Performance*, 1978, 22, 375-403. Used with permission of Dr. Steven Kerr and Academic Press, Inc. Copyright © 1978 by Academic Press, Inc.

situation. Of course, the extent to which this assumption is explicated varies greatly, as does the degree to which each theory is dependent upon the assumption. Fairly explicit is the Vertical Dyad Linkage model developed by Graen and his associates (Graen, Dansereau, & Minami, 1972; Dansereau, Cashman, & Graen, 1973), which attributes importance to hierarchical leadership without concern for the situation. The Fiedler (1964, 1967) Contingency Model also makes the general assumption that hierarchical leadership is important in situations of low, medium, and high favorableness, though predictions about relationships between LPC and performance in Octants VI and VII are qualified (Fiedler & Chemers, 1974, p. 82). Most models of decision-centralization (e.g., Tannenbaum & Schmidt, 1958; Heller & Yukl, 1969; Vroom & Yetton, 1973; Bass & Valenzi, 1974) include among their leader decision-style alternatives one whereby subordinates attempt a solution by themselves, with minimal participation by the hierarchical superior. Even in such cases, however, the leader is responsible for initiating the method through delegation of the problem, and is usually described as providing (structuring) information.

The approach to leadership which is least dependent upon the assumption articulated above, and which comes closest to the conceptualization to be proposed in this paper, is the Path-Goal Theory (House, 1971; House & Mitchell, 1974). Under circumstances when both goals and paths to goals may be clear, House and Mitchell (1974) point out that "atttempts by the leader to clarify paths and goals will be both redundant and seen by subordinates as imposing unnecessary, close control." They go on to predict that "although such control may increase performance by preventing soldiering or malingering, it will also result in decreased satisfaction."

This prediction is supported in part by conclusions drawn by Kerr, Schriesheim, Murphy, and Stogdill (1974) from their review of the consideration-initiating structure literature, and is at least somewhat consistent with results from a few recent studies. A most interesting and pertinent premise of the theory, however, is that even unnecessary and redundant leader behaviors will have an impact upon subordinate satisfaction, morale, motivation, performance, and acceptance of the leader (House & Mitchell, 1974; House & Dessler, 1974). While leader attempts to clarify paths and goals are therefore recognized by Path-Goal Theory to be unnecessary and redundant in certain situations, in no situation are they explicitly hypothesized by Path-Goal (or any other leadership theory) to be irrelevant.

This lack of recognition is unfortunate. As has already been mentioned, data from numerous studies collectively demonstrate that in many situations these leader behaviors *are* irrelevant, and hierarchical leadership (as operationalized in these studies) per se does not seem to matter. In fact, leadership variables so often account for very little criterion variance that a few writers have begun to argue that the leadership construct is sterile altogether, that "the concept of leadership itself has outlived its usefulness" (Miner, 1975, p. 200). This view is also unfortunate, however, and fails to take note of accurate predictions by leadership theorists even as such theorists fail to conceptually reconcile their inaccurate predictions.

What is clearly needed to resolve this dilemma is a conceptualization adequate to explain both the occasional successes and frequent failures of the various theories and models of leadership.

SUBSTITUTES FOR LEADERSHIP

A wide variety of individual, task, and organizational characteristics have been found to influence relationships between leader behavior and subordinate satisfaction, morale, and performance. Some of these variables (for example, job pressure and subordinate expectations of leader behavior) act primarily to influence which leadership style will best permit the hierarchical superior to motivate, direct, and control subordinates. The effect of others, however, is to act as "substitutes for leadership," tending to negate the leader's ability to either improve or impair subordinate satisfaction and performance.

Substitutes for leadership are apparently prominent in many different organizational settings, but their existence is not explicated in any of the dominant leadership theories. As a result, data describing formal superior-subordinate relationships are often obtained in situations where important substitutes exist. These data logically ought to be, and usually are, insignificant, and are useful primarily as a reminder that when leadership styles are studied in circumstances where the choice of style is irrelevant, the effect is to replace the potential power of the leadership construct with the unintentional comedy of the "Law of the instrument."[1]

What is needed, then, is a taxonomy of situations where we should not be studying "leadership" (in the formal hierarchical sense) at all. Development of such a taxonomy is still at an early stage, but Woodward (1973) and Miner (1975) have laid important groundwork through their classifications of control, and some effects of nonleader sources of clarity have been considered by Hunt (1975) and Hunt and Osborn (1975). Reviews of the leadership literature by House and Mitchell (1974) and Kerr et al. (1974) have also proved pertinent in this regard, and suggest that individual, task, and organizational characteristics of the kind outlined in Table 1 will help to determine whether or not hierarchical leadership is likely to matter.

Conceptual Domain of Substitutes for Leadership

Since Table 1 is derived from previously-conducted studies, substitutes are only suggested for the two leader behavior styles which dominate the research literature. The substitutes construct probably has much wider applicability, however, perhaps to hierarchical leadership in general.

It is probably useful to clarify some of the characteristics listed in Table 1. "Professional orientation" is considered a potential substitute for leadership because employees with such an orientation typically cultivate horizontal rather than vertical relationships, give greater credence to peer review processes, however informal, than to hierarchical evaluations, and tend to develop important referents external to the employing organization (Filley, House, & Kerr, 1976). Clearly, such attitudes and behaviors can sharply reduce the influence of the hierarchical superior.

"Methodologically invariant" tasks may result from serial interdependence, from machine-paced operations, or from work methods which are highly standardized. In one study (House, Filley, & Kerr, 1971, p. 26), invariance was found to derive from a network of government contracts which "specified not only the performance requirements of the end product, but also many of the management practices and control techniques that the company must follow in carrying out the contract."

Table 1. Substitutes for Leadership

Characteristic	Will tend to neutralize	
	Relationship-Oriented, Supportive, People-Centered Leadership: Consideration, Support, and Interaction Facilitation	Task-Oriented, Instrumental, Job-Centered Leadership: Initiating Structure, Goal Emphasis, and Work Facilitation
Of the subordinate		
1. Ability, experience, training, knowledge		X
2. Need for independence	X	X
3. "Professional" orientation	X	X
4. Indifference toward organizational rewards	X	X
Of the task		
5. Unambiguous and routine		X
6. Methodologically invariant		X
7. Provides its own feedback concerning accomplishment		X
8. Intrinsically satisfying	X	
Of the organization		
9. Formalization (explicit plans, goals, and areas of responsibility)		X
10. Inflexibility (rigid, unbending rules and procedures)		X
11. Highly specified and active advisory and staff functions		X
12. Closely knit, cohesive work groups	X	X
13. Organizational rewards not within the leader's control	X	X
14. Spatial distance between superior and subordinates	X	X

Invariant methodology relates to what Miner (1975) describes as the "push" of work. Tasks which are "intrinsically satisfying" (another potential substitute listed in Table 1) contribute in turn to the "pull" of work. Miner believes that for "task control" to be effective, a force comprised of both the push and pull of work must be developed. At least in theory, however, either type alone may act as a substitute for hierarchical leadership.

Performance feedback provided by the work itself is another characteristic of the task which potentially functions in place of the formal leader. It has been reported that employees with high growth need strength in particular derive beneficial psychological states (internal motivation, general satisfaction, work effectiveness) from clear and direct knowledge of the results of performance (Hackman & Oldham, 1976; Oldham, 1976). Task-provided feedback is often: (1) the most immediate source of feedback given the infrequency of performance appraisal sessions (Hall & Lawler, 1969); (2) the most accurate source of feedback given the problems of measuring the performance of others (Campbell, Dunnette, Lawler, & Weick, 1970); and (3) the most self-evaluation evoking and intrinsically motivating source of feedback given the controlling and informational aspects of feedback from others (DeCharms, 1968; Deci, 1972, 1975; Greller & Herold, 1975). For these reasons, the formal leader's function as a provider of role structure through performance feedback may be insignificant by comparison.

Cohesive, interdependent work groups and active advisory and staff personnel also have the ability to render the formal leader's performance-feedback function inconsequential. Inherent in mature group structures are stable performance norms and positional differentiation (Bales & Strodtbeck, 1951; Borgatta & Bales, 1953; Stogdill, 1959; Lott & Lott, 1965; Zander, 1968). Task-relevant guidance and feedback from others may be provided directly by the formal leader, indirectly by the formal leader through the primary work group members, directly by the primary work group members, by staff personnel, or by the client. If the latter four instances prevail, the formal leader's role may be quite trivial. Cohesive work groups are, of course, important sources of affiliative need satisfaction.

Programming through impersonal modes has been reported to be the most frequent type of coordination strategy employed under conditions of low-to-medium task uncertainty and low task interdependence (Van de Ven, Delbecq, & Koenig, 1976). Thus, the existence of written work goals, guidelines, and ground rules (organizational formalization) and rigid rules and procedures (organizational inflexibility) may serve as substitutes for leader-provided coordination under certain conditions. Personal and group coordination modes involving the formal leader may become important only when less costly impersonal strategies are not suitable.

ELABORATION OF THE CONSTRUCT

Table 1 was designed to capsulize our present knowledge with respect to possible substitutes for hierarchical leadership. Since present knowledge is the product of past research, and since past research was primarily unconcerned with the topic, the table is probably oversimplified and incomplete in a number of respects. Rigorous elaboration of the substitutes construct must necessarily await additional research, but we would speculate that such research would show the following refinements to be important.

Distinguishing Between "Substitutes" and "Neutralizers"

A "neutralizer" is defined by Webster's as something which is able to "paralyze, destroy, or counteract the effectiveness of" something else. In the context of leadership, this term may be applied to characteristics which make it effectively *impossible* for relationship and/or task-oriented leadership to make a difference. Neutralizers are a type of moderator variable when uncorrelated with both predictors and the criterion, and act as suppressor variables when correlated with predictors but not the criterion (Zedeck, 1971; Wherry, 1946).

A "substitute" is defined to be "a person or thing acting or used in place of another." In context, this term may be used to describe characteristics which render relationship and/or task-oriented leadership not only impossible but also *unnecessary*.[2] Substitutes may be correlated with both predictors and the criterion, but tend to improve the validity coefficient when included in the predictor set. That is, they will not only tend to affect which leader behaviors (if any) are influential, but will also tend to impact upon the criterion variable.

The consequences of neutralizers and substitutes for previous research have probably been similar, since both act to reduce the impact of leader behaviors upon subordinate attitudes and performance. For this reason it is not too important that such summaries of previous research as Table 1 distinguish between them. Nevertheless, an important theoretical distinction does exist. It is that substitutes do, but neutralizers do not, provide a "person or thing acting or used in place of" the formal leader's negated influence. The effect of neutralizers is therefore to create an "influence vacuum," from which a variety of dysfunctions may emerge.

As an illustration of this point, look again at the characteristics outlined in Table 1. Since each characteristic has the capacity to counteract leader influence, all 14 may clearly be termed neutralizers. It is *not* clear, however, that all 14 are substitutes. For example, subordinates' perceived "ability, experience, training, and knowledge" tend to impair the leader's influence, but may or may not act as substitutes for leadership. It is known that individuals who are high in task-related self-esteem place high value upon non-hierarchical control systems which are consistent with a belief in the competence of people (Korman, 1970). The problem is that subordinate perceptions concerning ability and knowledge may not be accurate. Actual ability and knowledge may therefore act as a substitute, while false perceptions of competence and unfounded esteem may produce simply a neutralizing effect.

"Spatial distance," "subordinate indifference toward organizational rewards," and "organizational rewards not within the leader's control" are other examples of characteristics which do not render formal leadership unnecessary, but merely create circumstances in which effective leadership may be impossible. If rewards are clearly within the control of some other person this other person can probably act as a substitute for the formal leader, and no adverse consequences (except probably to the leader's morale) need result. When no one knows where control over rewards lies, however, or when rewards are linked rigidly to seniority or to other factors beyond anyone's control, or when rewards are perceived to be unattractive altogether, the resulting influence vacuum would almost inevitably be dysfunctional.

Distinguishing Between Direct and Indirect Leader Behavior Effects

It is possible to conceptualize a *direct effect* of leadership as one which occurs when a subordinate is influenced by some leader behavior *in and of itself*. An *indirect effect* may be said to result when the subordinate is influenced by the *implications* of the behavior for some future consequence. Attempts by the leader to influence subordinates must always produce direct and/or indirect effects or, when strong substitutes for leadership exist, no effect.

This distinction between direct and indirect effects of leader behavior has received very little attention, but its importance to any discussion of leadership substitutes is considerable. For example, in their review of Path-Goal theory, House and Dessler (1974, p. 31) state that "subordinates with high needs for affiliation and social approval would see friendly, considerate leader behavior as an immediate source of satisfaction" (direct effect). As Table 1 suggests, it is conceivable that fellow group members could supply such subordinates with enough affiliation and social approval to eliminate dependence on the leader. With other subordinates, however, the key "may be not so much in terms of what the leader does but may be in terms of how it is *interpreted* by his members" (Graen *et al.*, 1972, p. 235). Graen *et al.* concluded from their data that "consideration is interpreted as the leader's evaluation of the member's role behavior..." (p. 233). For these subordinates, therefore, consideration seems to have been influential primarily because of its perceived implications for the likelihood of receiving future rewards. In this case the effect is an indirect one, for which group member approval and affiliation probably cannot substitute.

In the same vein, we are told by House and Dessler (1974, pp. 31-32) that:

> Subordinates with high needs for achievement would be predicted to view leader behavior that clarifies path-goal relationships and provides goal oriented feedback as satisfying. Subordinates with high needs for extrinsic rewards would be predicted to see leader directiveness or coaching behavior as instrumental to their satisfaction if such behavior helped them perform in such a manner as to gain recognition, promotion, security, or pay increases.

It is apparent from House and Dessler's remarks that the distinction between direct and indirect effects need not be limited to relationship-oriented behaviors. Such characteristics of the task as the fact that it "provides its own feedback" (listed in Table 1 as a potential substitute for task-oriented behavior) may provide achievement-oriented subordinates with immediate satisfaction (direct effect), but fail to negate the superior's ability to help subordinates perform so as to obtain future rewards (indirect effect). Conversely, subordinate experience and training may act as substitutes for the indirect effects of task-oriented leadership, by preventing the leader from improving subordinate performance, but may not offset the direct effects.

Identifying Other Characteristics and Other Leader Behaviors

Any elaboration of the substitutes construct must necessarily include the specification of other leader behaviors, and other characteristics which may act as substitutes for leader behaviors. As was mentioned earlier, most previous studies of leadership were concerned with only two of its dimensions. This approach is intuitively indefensible. Richer conceptualizations of the leadership process already exist, and almost inevitably underscore the importance of additional leader activities. As these activities are delineated in future research, it is likely that substitutes for them will also be identified.

Distinguishing Between Cause and Effect in Leader Behavior

Another area where the substitutes construct appears to have implications for leadership research concerns the question of causality. It is now evident from a variety of laboratory experiments and longitudinal field studies that leader behavior may result from as well as cause subordinate attitudes and performance. It is possible to speculate upon the effect that leadership substitutes would have on the relative causal strength of superior- and subordinate-related variables. This paper has tried to show that such substitutes act to reduce changes in subordinates' attitudes and performance which are *caused* by leader behaviors. On the other hand, there seems no reason why leadership substitutes should prevent changes in leader behavior which *result* from different levels of subordinate performance, satisfaction, and morale. The substitutes for leadership construct may therefore help to explain why the direction of causality is sometimes predominantly from leader behavior to subordinate outcomes, while at other times the reverse is true.

Specification of Interaction Effects Among Substitutes and Neutralizers

From the limited data obtained thus far, it is not possible to differentiate at all among leadership substitutes and neutralizers in terms of relative strength and predictive capability. We have received some indication that the strength of a substitute, as measured by its mean level, is not strongly related to its predictive power. Substitutes for leadership as theoretically important as intrinsic satisfaction, for example, apparently need only be present in moderate amounts to have potent substituting effects. Other, less important substitutes and neutralizers, might have to be present to a tremendous degree before their effects might be felt. Clearly, the data reported in this study are insufficient to determine at what point a particular substitute becomes important, or at what point several substitutes, each fairly weak by itself, might combine to collectively impair hierarchical leader influence. Multiplicative functions involving information on the strength and predictive power of substitutes for leadership should be able to be specified as evidence accumulates.

CONCLUSIONS

The research literature provides abundant evidence that for organization members to maximize organizational and personal outcomes, they must be able to obtain both guidance and good feelings from their work settings. Guidance is usually offered in the form of role or task structuring, while good feelings may stem from "stroking" behaviors,[3] or may be derived from intrinsic satisfaction associated with the task itself.

The research literature does *not* suggest that guidance and good feelings must be provided by the hierarchical superior; it is only necessary that they somehow be provided. Certainly the formal leader represents a potential source of structuring and stroking behaviors, but many other organization members do too, and impersonal equivalents also exist. To the extent that other potential sources are deficient, the hierarchical superior is clearly in a position to play a dominant role. In these situations the opportunity for leader downward influence is great, and formal leadership ought to be important. To the extent that other sources provide structure and stroking in abundance, the hierarchical leader will have little chance to exert downward influence. In such cases it is of small value to gain entree to the organization, distribute leader behavior questionnaires to anything that moves, and later debate about which leadership theory best accounts for the pitifully small percentage of variance explained, while remaining uncurious about the large percentage unexplained.

Of course, few organizations would be expected to have leadership substitutes so strong as to totally overwhelm the leader, or so weak as to require subordinates to rely entirely on him. In most organizations it is likely that, as was true here, substitutes exist for some leader activities but not for others. Effective leadership might therefore be described as the ability to supply subordinates with needed guidance and good feelings which are not being supplied by other sources. From this viewpoint it is inaccurate to inform leaders (say, in management development programs) that they are incompetent if they do not personally provide these things regardless of the situation. While it may (or may not) be necessary that the organization as a whole function in a "9—9" manner (Blake & Mouton, 1964) it clearly is unnecessary for the manager to behave in such a manner unless no substitutes for leader-provided guidance and good feelings exist.

Dubin (1976, p. 33) draws a nice distinction between "proving" and "improving" a theory, and points out that "if the purpose is to prove the adequacy of the theoretical model...data are likely to be collected for values on only those units incorporated in the theoretical model. This usually means that, either experimentally or by discarding data, attention in the empirical research is focused solely upon values measured on units incorporated in the theory."

In Dubin's terms, if we are really interested in improving rather than proving our various theories and models of leadership, a logical first step is that we stop assuming what really needs to be demonstrated empirically. The criticality of the leader's role in supplying necessary structure and stroking should be evaluated in the broader organizational context. Data pertaining to both leadership and possible substitutes for leadership (Table 1) should be obtained, and both main and interaction effects examined. A somewhat different use of information about substitutes for leadership would be as a "prescreen," to assess the appropriateness of a potential sample for a hierarchical leadership study.

What this all adds up to is that, if we really want to know more about the sources and consequences of guidance and good feelings in organizations, we should be prepared to study these things *whether or not* they happen to be provided through hierarchical leadership. For those not so catholic, whose interest lies in the derivation and refinement of theories of formal leadership, a commitment should be made to the importance of developing and operationalizing a *true* situational theory of leadership, one which will explicitly limit its propositions and restrict its predictions *to those situations* where hierarchical leadership theoretically ought to make a difference.

Notes

[1] Abraham Kaplan (1964, p. 28) has observed: "Give a small boy a hammer, and he will find that everything he encounters needs pounding."

[2] This potentially important distinction was first pointed out by M.A. Von Glinow in a doctoral seminar.

[3] "Stroking" is used here, as in transactional analysis, to describe "any type of physical, oral, or visual recognition of one person by another" (Huse, 1975, p. 288).

References

Bales, R., & Strodtbeck, F. Phases in group problem solving. *Journal of Abnormal and Social Psychology*, 1951, *46*, 485-495.

Bass, B., & Valenzi, E. Contingent aspects of effective management styles. In J.G. Hunt & L.L. Larson (Eds.), *Contingency approaches to leadership*. Carbondale, IL: Southern Illinois University Press, 1974.

Blake, R., & Mouton, J. *The managerial grid*. Houston: Gulf, 1964.

Borgatta, E., & Bales, R. Task and accumulation of experience as factors in the interaction of small groups. *Sociometry*, 1953, *16*, 239-252.

Campbell, J.P., Dunnette, M.D., Lawler, E., III, & Weick, K.E., Jr. *Managerial behavior, performance and effectiveness*. New York: McGraw-Hill, 1970.

Dansereau, F., Cashman, J., & Graen, G. Instrumentality theory and equity theory as complementary approaches in predicting the relationship of leadership and turnover among managers. *Organizational Behavior and Human Performance*, 1973, *10*, 184-200.

DeCharms, R. *Personal causation*. New York: Academic Press, 1968.

Deci, E. Intrinsic motivation, extrinsic reinforcement, and inequity. *Journal of Personality and Social Psychology*, 1972, 22, 113-120.

Deci, E. *Intrinsic motivation*. New York: Plenum, 1975.

Dubin, R. Theory building in applied areas. In M. Dunnette (Ed.), *Handbook of industrial and organizational psychology*. Chicago: Rand McNally, 1976.

Fiedler, F.E. A contingency model of leadership effectiveness. In L. Berkowitz (Ed.), *Advances in experimental social psychology*. New York: Academic Press, 1964.

Fiedler, F.E. *A theory of leadership effectiveness*. New York: McGraw-Hill, 1967.

Fiedler, F.E., & Chemers, M.M. *Leadership and effective management*. Glenview, IL: Scott, Foresman, 1974.

Filley, A.C., House, R.J., & Kerr, S. *Managerial process and organizational behavior* (2nd ed.). Glenview, IL: Scott, Foresman, 1976.

Graen, G., Dansereau, F., Jr., & Minami, T. Dysfunctional leadership styles. *Organizational Behavior and Human Performance*, 1972, 7, 216-236.

Greller, M., & Herold, D. Sources of feedback: A preliminary investigation. *Organizational Behavior and Human Performance*, 1975, 13, 244-256.

Hackman, R., & Oldham, G. Motivation through the design of work: Test of a theory. *Organizational Behavior and Human Performance*, 1976, 16, 250-279.

Hall, D., & Lawler, E. Unused potential in R and D labs. *Research Management*, 1969, 12, 339-354.

Heller, F.A., & Yukl, G. Participation, managerial decision-making, and situational variables. *Organizational Behavior and Human Performance*, 1969, 4, 227-234.

House, R.J. A path-goal theory of leader effectiveness. *Administrative Science Quarterly*, 1971, 16, 321-338.

House, R.J., & Dessler, G. The path-goal theory of leadership: Some post hoc and a priori tests. In J.G. Hunt & L.L. Larson (Eds.), *Contingency approaches to leadership*. Carbondale, IL: Southern Illinois University Press, 1974.

House, R.J., Filley, A.C., & Kerr, S. Relation of leader consideration and initiating structure to R and D subordinates' satisfaction. *Administrative Science Quarterly*, 1971, 16, 19-30.

House, R.J., & Mitchell, T.R. Path-goal theory of leadership. *Journal of Contemporary Business*, 1974, 3, 81-97.

Hunt, J. *Different nonleader clarity sources as alternatives to leadership*. Paper presented at the Eastern Academy of Management Conference, 1975.

Hunt, J.G., & Osborn, R.N. An adaptive-reactive theory of leadership: The role of macro variables in leadership research. In J.G. Hunt & L.L. Larson (Eds.), *Leadership frontiers*. Carbondale, IL: Southern Illinois University Press, 1975.

Huse, E.F. *Organization development and change*. St. Paul, MN: West, 1975.

Kaplan, Abraham. *The conduct of inquiry*. San Francisco: Chandler, 1964.

Kerr, S., Schriesheim, C., Murphy, C.J., & Stogdill, R.M. Toward a contingency theory of leadership based upon the consideration and initiating structure literature. *Organizational Behavior and Human Performance*, 1974, 12, 62-82.

Korman, A. Toward a hypothesis of work behavior. *Journal of Applied Psychology*, 1970, 54, 31-41.

Lott, A., & Lott, B. Group cohesiveness as interpersonal attraction: A review of relationships with antecedent and consequent variables. *Psychological Bulletin*, 1965, 64, 259-302.

Miner, J. The uncertain future of the leadership concept: An overview. In J.G. Hunt & L.L. Larson (Eds.), *Leadership frontiers*. Carbondale, IL: Southern Illinois University Press, 1975.

Oldham, G. Job characteristics and internal motivation: The moderating effect of interpersonal and individual variables. *Human Relations*, 1976, 29, 559-570.

Stogdill, R. *Individual behavior and group achievement*. New York: Oxford University Press, 1959.

Tannenbaum, R., & Schmidt, W. How to choose a leadership pattern. *Harvard Business Review*, 1958, *36*, 95-101.

Van de Ven, A., Delbecq, A., & Koenig, R. Determinants of coordination modes within organizations. *American Sociological Review*, 1976, *41*, 322-338.

Vroom, V., & Yetton, P. *Leadership and decision making*. Pittsburgh: University of Pittsburgh Press, 1973.

Wherry, R. Test selection and suppressor variables. *Psychometrika*, 1946, *11*, 239-247.

Woodward, J. Technology, material control, and organizational behavior. In A. Negandhi (Ed.), *Modern organization theory*. Kent, OH: Kent State University, 1973.

Zander, A. Group aspirations. In D. Cartwright & A. Zander (Eds.), *Group dynamics: Research and theory* (3rd ed.). New York: Harper & Row, 1968.

Zedeck, S. Problems with the use of "moderator" variables. *Psychological Bulletin*, 1971, *76*, 295-310.

Styles of Leadership

Florence L. Denmark

INTRODUCTION

Leadership has been defined in many ways, such as: the possession by an individual of personal "leadership" characteristics, possession by an individual of the highest level of skill for a given task, possession by an individual of a leadership office within a group, or the performance of leadership functions within a group. They all deal with different facets of leadership, but have in common the image of an individual who exerts more influence on a group's activities and beliefs than any other single member.

By placing the emphasis on the individual, as in the above, one does not give sufficient attention to the fact that a leader exists, evolves, and functions within some particular group. The group determines leadership—either by conferring it or by accepting the legitimacy of a leader appointed by others or self-chosen. Leadership should not be viewed simply as the qualities or position maintained by an individual, but rather as an interactive process between the individual and the characteristics of a given situation—each affecting the other. In this transactional view, leadership is seen as a reciprocal process of social influence. Leaders both influence and are influenced by their followers.

Reprinted from *Psychology of Women Quarterly,* 1977, 2(2), 99-113. Copyright © 1977 by Human Sciences Press, 72 Fifth Avenue, New York, NY 10011. Used by permission of the author and publisher.

Since leadership varies from situation to situation, what works well with one setting may not work well with another. It is necessary to focus on the relative effectiveness of various styles of leadership in different situations, and to direct increased attention to the way an individual leads or manages. Leaders' styles of exerting influence vary in many ways. Some leaders are depicted as cold, others friendly; some supervise very closely, others allow considerable autonomy.

Several types of leadership styles among males have been investigated (i.e., authoritarianism vs. democratic styles, and task-centered vs. social-emotional leaders). In both instances the more effective style depends on the situation. A survival motive lurks behind a great deal of leadership behavior since a group can immobilize a leader if it is not ready to accept the style of leadership. A style of leadership behavior will be continued to the extent to which the behavior is reinforced from either within or without the group.

MALE AND FEMALE

Most leadership studies have been and are concerned with males, at least male leaders. Gender, as an important aspect of the situation, has rarely been studied. Denmark and Diggory (1966) in a study done 10 years ago found, contrary to their hypotheses, that male leaders exhibit and find approval from followers for more authoritarian behavior than do women leaders. This is especially true when leaders use power to induce individual members to conform to group norms.

The lack of the gender variable in studies of leadership points to the gaps in existing research and theoretical models. In field studies, this deficit may be due to the fact that few women occupy positions of leadership, through appointment by an outside authority, or by assuming a position with the consensus of the group (i.e., as an emergent leader). This paucity however, does not excuse the behavioral scientist from the consideration of gender as an important issue. Small group studies of leadership also have focused primarily on males—no doubt reflecting the real world situation.

There are several reasons that may account for this real life shortage of women in leadership positions. First, it is possible that women need training and/or opportunity in order to develop and exercise their leadership skills. Second, studies of management have shown the importance of similarity in designating leaders. Men, who are usually the ones to make such appointments, tend to pick others who are similar to themselves in status, background, beliefs, and sex (Dalton, 1951; Lipset & Bendix, 1959; Pen, 1966; Wilson & Lupton, 1959).

Sex-role stereotypes, embracing the belief that women do not make good leaders, is a third factor (e.g., Bass, Krusell, & Alexander, 1971). This belief is held by women as well as men. Shein's studies (1973, 1975) show that middle managers are perceived by both male and female managers as having characteristics more similar to those ascribed to men in general than to women in general. Although the female managers viewed women as being more similar to men than did the male managers, the results still imply that women managers are as likely as men to make placement and promotion decisions in favor of men. Thus, stereotypical male characteristics are perceived as a basis for success in management. The *Harvard Business Review* (1965) in a survey of 2,000 executives indicated that 41% of the men in their sample were against women being executives. Many felt women were not "suitable" in this role, and both men and women in the sample felt that women's opportunities for advancement were limited.

Although women obviously will emerge or be perceived as leaders in all-female groups, one can be fairly certain that a man will become the leader in a mixed-sex group. This is true in the real world, but has also been demonstrated in the laboratory. Megargee (1969) paired groups of two Ss each, consisting of one person who scored high on a dominance paper-and-pencil test and one who scored low. The Ss were not aware of the basis for the pairing but had to decide which one would be the leader and which one the follower. Groups were composed of two males, two females, or a female and a male.

In the latter case, half the time a male and half the time a female had the high dominance score. When groups were either all male or all female, in about 70% of the cases the individual with the high dominance score became the leader. In female-male groups, with male dominant, 90% of the males were selected as the leader. However, in female-male groups with the female as the dominant partner, only 20% of the females became the leader. Ironically it was the high dominant female who made this decision to have the male serve as leader. Sex-role norms as to which sex should lead won the day. If women choose not to emerge as leader it may *not* be the result of something like fear of success, but rather fear of visibility (Tresemer, 1974).

REACTIONS TO WOMEN AS LEADERS

But what are the reactions to the women who do attain a position of leadership? Negative attitudes are reported to be found toward women managers in organizations, but the scarcity of women in such positions has precluded many studies (although several will be noted in this paper). It is easier to set up female led, mixed-sex groups in the laboratory.

Jacobson and Effertz (1974) used college students to form three person groups. Half of the groups were all male or all female with a leader randomly selected. The other groups consisted of either two females and one male or two males and one female. In the former situation the male was designated as the leader, and in the latter, the female—although the Ss believed the selection was random. The task given to all groups was to arrange dominoes according to a prepared pattern. Only the leader had access to the pattern and gave verbal instructions to the other group members. However, the task was so difficult that every group experienced failure by being unable to solve the problem. In both same and mixed-sex groups that had a male leader, the leader's performance was rated significantly *worse* than when the female was the leader. The ratings of the followers by the leaders was the exact reverse (i.e., male followers were rated significantly higher than female followers by both male and female leaders). Stereotypes are such that men were expected to be successful leaders and women were expected to be good followers. When these sex-role stereotypes were not fulfilled in this experiment, more negative ratings occurred.

Moving from the laboratory to the field, Kanter (1975) has focused on the sociology of business organizations and the study of women in these organizations, noting that women are most conspicuously absent from positions of influence and prestige. Kanter points out that leadership style and performance by the few women in leadership positions should be studied as a function of membership in a male-dominated group in which the culture of the organization and work behavior is shaped by males. The sex-role stereotyped traits assumed to belong to men are valued and help justify the absence of women from power.

Kanter notes that women in a large business corporation may decide not to strive for promotion into management positions because they might lose their peer relationships with a group of women. The women already in management may not seek promotion into a higher level job because of the difficulties faced in establishing new relationships as well as the threat of interactional isolation. This may be the reason why a male sponsor is so important a factor in the success of female leaders in organizations.

A large-scale study of employment patterns of women in corporate America was carried out in 246 industrial and nonindustrial firms by Lyle and Ross (1973). Women managers tended to be older, have longer service with the firm, and still receive a lower average salary. Women managers were much more optimistic about their own chances for further advancement than were male managers about the same women's chances. Male managers reported that they treated male and female subordinates differently. In contrast, women managers perceived their treatment of subordinates of both sexes to be the same. Perhaps some of these women subordinates miss the special office/wife treatment they received from male bosses and resent a female "boss" who treats them as adults—a behavior they are not used to. One might make a general prediction based on sex-role stereotypes that women leaders should use a style that is more human-relations oriented than that used by their male counterparts.

The women managers in the Lyle and Ross (1973) study fell into four management styles as determined by field research based on interviews with the sample of managers and their subordinates: (1) One-third used a productive but somewhat overcontrolling, task-oriented approach. (2) Another third dealt with subordinates in a permissive manner. They were well-liked and received unanimous praise as managers from their exceptionally loyal subordinates. (3) One-sixth were described as detached, aloof, and under-controlling in their staff relations—the staff solved their own work problems. (4) The final one-sixth attempted to use their job as a stepping stone to a better one and used an exploitative style. They were concerned about looking good to their superiors.

These managers blamed their subordinates for failure, but attributed success to themselves.

The male sample proved to be much more homogeneous. Three-quarters used the exploitative, self-seeking style. The other quarter best fit the productive, over-controlling style. Both the men and the women were reported to display most of the traits associated with management success, such as a desire for achievement and a strong fear of failure, drive for upward mobility, assertiveness, and decisiveness. Interestingly, regardless of leadership style, the women had relied on mentors more than the men. As in Kanter's study, the women had been dependent on male sponsors to break into management.

PERSONAL FACTORS AND LEADERSHIP STYLE

While some studies have focused on behavioral styles of effective leadership, others have been concerned with personal attitudes or demographic variables. A few studies have dealt with birth order. Chemers (1970) found that firstborns tended to be more task-oriented in leadership style, whereas later-borns tended to be more relations-oriented. However, this study did not involve women. Sandler and Scalia (1975) found no relationship between birth order and the attainment of leadership position for men, but reported that firstborn women were more likely to have served in a leadership position (president, vice-president, secretary or treasurer of an organization) than later-born females ($p < .001$).

There has, however, been a lack of research attempting to interrelate leadership style with birth order. A cross-sectional study by Pinder and Pinto (1974) found that managerial style was related to age. The youngest managers (aged 20 to 29 years) in their sample of 200 graduates from the University of Minnesota School of Business Administration were disproportionately autocratic and rated low in human relations. Those aged 40 to 55, the late middle-age managers, were the most efficient. They acted as decisively as the youngest group, but engaged in more information-gathering activities and had the greatest human-relations skills. There was no relationship between leadership style and length of time in present job, but there was a relationship between style and job department. For example, sales and finance personnel were more autocratic, whereas those in more general positions (e.g., general administration, research and development operations) tended to be older and more democratic. Perhaps then, different department demands will promote different style patterns. Thus, context would be important in determining which style is "best." Unfortunately, the Pinder and Pinto sample contained only five women out of 200 subjects. This would be an interesting area to explore, using women as leaders in various settings.

SITUATIONAL FACTORS AND LEADERSHIP EFFECTIVENESS

In all of the studies discussed so far, insufficient attention has been addressed to how situational factors may help determine the effectiveness of different leadership styles. The task itself, its setting, and the personal and demographic characteristics of the participants should moderate to some extent the effectiveness of various leader behaviors. Leadership style and its effectiveness are also influenced by the relation of the leader to her superiors as well as to her subordinates. In fact, the morale of group members relates to their perception of the influence that their leader has with her own superior. Women may have formal authority but be less able to exercise it over subordinates (both male and female) who resent her and are reluctant to "take orders from a woman." They may also have less influence with male supervisors. In general then, we could predict that women are less likely than men to focus on human-relations skills. However, training and skill in sensitivity and human relations won't help a leader's performance if she works in an organization that utilizes and reinforces authoritarian principles. The goals of an organization largely determine the kinds of people who are employed and the style of leadership that is used.

NONVERBAL LEADER BEHAVIOR

In addition to a lack of comparative studies of leadership style in different types of organizations, studies of leadership and leadership style have rarely been concerned with the function of nonverbal communication in the perception of leadership. A study by Gitter, Black, and Goldman (1975) photographed a *male* professional actor, in one instance enacting the role of the "subordinate." The subjects, male and female college students, rated the "superior" nonverbal behavior as bold, dynamic, and strong (i.e., characteristics frequently associated with leadership), while the subordinate nonverbal behavior was perceived as more passive.

Other investigators have analyzed both filmed and live sequences of nonverbal interaction across many modalities and reported sex differences in status-dominance and in affiliation (e.g., Mehrabian, 1971, 1972). Deaux, in a brief summary of research concerning sex differences in nonverbal behavior (1976), notes that women tend to increase affiliation and minimize distance, whereas men use nonverbal behavior that maintains distance and asserts status. Henley (1973a, 1973b) has pointed out that sex differences in touching parallel dominance behavior. Thus, a male's more frequent, non-reciprocal initiation of touching behavior toward a woman indicates a declaration of dominance or higher status. Women are said to adjust their nonverbal responses to that of the male, thus creating equilibrium in the relationship.

Henley (1973c) notes that many nonverbal cues are related to the exercise of power, although the relationship is a complex one. In addition to the clear status differences in touching and the more frequent touching of females by males, Henley summarizes many research investigations and reports that women look more at the other person than do men, perhaps because the listener (woman) tends to look at the speaker (man) more than vice versa. However, in a mutual gaze situation, the woman or subordinate will lower her eyes first. The direct stare, seen as more of a threat, will be used more by men. Smiling, a submissive gesture, is more frequent among women. Men interrupt (as well as talk) more than women. Henley states that if any of these male, higher status behaviors are used by women they then take on sexual connotations, since the use of power is unacceptable if used by the wrong sex (i.e., female) and must be denied.

Weitz (1974) looked at the interactive aspects of sex differences in nonverbal communication and the relationship between nonverbal behaviors and sex-role attitudes. In this experiment, 24 males and 24 females were randomly grouped in same- and opposite-sex pairs, members of each pair were videotaped separately, and the behavior of each subject was rated by five male and five female judges. Weitz reported that men with liberal sex-role attitudes were perceived as being nonverbally warmer in interaction with males and females than was true of men with conservative sex-role attitudes. The reverse tended to be true for more liberal women in same-sex interaction. In addition, nonverbal behaviors of women in opposite sex interactions were significantly related to the test scores of dominance and affiliation of their male partners. Thus, women were perceived as more nonverbally submissive with more dominant male partners, and more dominant if their male partner was more submissive. This adjustment in interaction to the opposite-sexed partner's personality was true only for females. The reverse did not occur for males, nor did it occur for females in the same sex condition.

Nonverbal Leader Behavior: Male and Female

However, none of these nonverbal studies have been concerned with women in *leadership* positions. Sex differences have been examined and reported but there have not been specific investigations of women in high-status leadership positions. Is a woman who behaves nonverbally in a high-status style of manner perceived as the "leader" or "superior"? Will judgments be made on the basis of nonverbal cues or on the basis of sex? Do you get the same results whether her interactant is male or female?

To answer some of these questions, a videotaped study without sound was carried out by McKenna and Denmark (1976) in which subjects made judgments about pairs of actors based on their nonverbal behavior. Pairs were either same sex (female-female and male-male) or cross-sex. Four actors were used, two females and two males, and all possible combinations of interactions between each pair were taped. Each actor behaved nonverbally in both high- and low-status styles depending on the given interaction. Our basic questions were whether the sex of the actor or the nonverbal behavior was used as a cue for power and status, and how both sex and behavior of the actor were related to the sex of the person with whom the actor is interacting. The interaction between each pair resulted in "A" agreeing to work on papers that "B" carried. The independent variables were: Sex of "A", sex of "B", nonverbal behavior ("A" high status, "B" low status; or "A" low status, "B" high status) and sex of subject. Analysis of the results showed the instructions to be effective. When "A" behaved in a high-status style, she/he was perceived as being of higher status. Despite some status by sex interactions, the only variable that influenced judgment about status was nonverbal behavior, and it did so regardless of the other variables including sex. A high-status behaving "A" was seen as voluntarily agreeing with "B" to do the paper work rather than perceived as having to do so, as was true when "A" behaved in a low-status manner (p <.001). Sex was not a factor here.

High-status females were seen as more potent than high-status males, but low-status males were perceived as more potent than low-status females. Low-status agreers (male or female) were more potent when interacting with a male than with a female. Those of high status (both male and female) were rated less positively (i.e., more unpleasant, more impolite, more distant, etc.) than those of lower status. But females of high status were seen as more responsive than males regardless of with whom they interacted. Females were always rated as more "feminine" than males regardless of status (p <.001), but those having low status were also rated as more feminine than those with high status (p <.001).

The jobs ascribed to the actors were influenced somewhat by the actor's sex as well as by the nonverbal behavior. Females were somewhat more likely than males to be perceived as secretaries when they behaved in a low-status manner. But with high-status behavior there was no relationship between sex and job. In those instances the actors were more likely to be perceived as executives.

This study indicated that, despite some sex-by-status interactions and contrary to what might have been predicted, nonverbal behavior rather than sex was basic to the determination of status (or leadership) evaluations. The implications of this study are clear. If women (as well as men) behave a certain way (i.e., smile less, initiate more touching, act more relaxed, etc.), they will be perceived in a high-status or leadership position vis à vis their interactant, regardless of whether the latter is male or female. Perhaps by recognizing and using these nonverbal symbols of power, women can help resolve inequitable power relationships in their environment. If women are perceived as leaders they may be more likely to move into leadership roles. In contrast, those already in positions of leadership may wish to divest themselves of these subtle cues of control in their interactions with others.

A Pilot Field Study

There are issues to be explored regarding women who occupy positions of leadership in the real world. Do they behave nonverbally in accordance with the stereotyped cues of status? Is their nonverbal style the same as that of men in equivalent positions? Does the climate of the organization influence their nonverbal style? In order to begin to answer some of these questions, a pilot study was carried out by Denmark, McKenna, Juran, and Greenberg (1976). Field observations were made by trained observers on the non-verbal interactions of female and male subjects ranging in status from deans to graduate students, with other males and females of differing statuses, in a university setting. The Ss were of higher, equal, or lower status within the university structure than the person with whom she or he [sic] interacted (i.e., the female and male "others"). The nonverbal measures recorded in this study were smiling, arms moving, forward lean, eye contact, head nodding, back lean, straight lean, object manipulation, self-manipulation, and touching. Since only one instance of touching was recorded (a female touching a male), this measure was not included in the study.

Contrary to the results of certain nonverbal studies (Exline, Gray, & Schuette, 1965; Mehrabian, 1971; Beekman, 1974) there were *no* overall differences between male and female subjects on any of the cues measured. Perhaps the particular university setting itself, where individuals work together in a rather informal atmosphere, as compared to many business organizations, may include similar behaviors, regardless of the sex of the actor. The socialization processes involved in bringing persons to a graduate academic facility may also tend to obliterate sex differences in nonverbal mannerisms.

Another unexpected finding was that higher-status subjects showed more affiliative behavior on most of these measures than did the lower-status subjects. Since cues expressing liking, warmth, or affiliation are considered indicators of lower status (Henley, 1973a; Henley, 1973b) this is certainly a surprising result. Perhaps these affiliative cues are *not* status-linked, or perhaps our subject population and their particular organizational climate and setting obliterated conventional status differences on these measures.

The sex of the "other" interactant seemed to be a more important overall determinant of nonverbal behavior than sex of the subject being studied, confirming the importance of studying nonverbal cues within an interactional framework. For higher-status subjects, both male and female, same-sex interactions were quite similar, while cross-sex interactions differed for many of the measures.

Smiling was the only behavior displayed more by higher-status females than males and shown more by lower-status subjects in contrast to higher-status subjects. However, lower-status males engaged in more eye contact than their female counterparts. On three of the measures (eye contact, arms moving, and head nodding), the higher-status males were more affiliative with their own sex than were lower-status males. Conversely higher-status females showed less affiliative behavior with their own sex than did lower-status females.

Contrary to studies relating greater relaxation to higher status, the lower-status subjects in this study showed a non-significant tendency toward greater relaxation as measured by postural indicators. The particular setting may allow for greater freedom for lower-status individuals to appear more "unprofessional" than is true for higher-status faculty and administrators. Subjects, higher-status ones in particular, appeared to be more relaxed when interacting with a male than with a female. This is also contrary to findings in the literature (Mehrabian, 1972). Higher-status females in particular were more relaxed with males than with females on all relevant measures. However, higher-status females were less relaxed generally than lower-status females. Higher-status women showed the least "distress" of all the groups. Males were more "ingratiating" than women, especially those high-status males who interacted with their own sex.

Since this was a pilot study with relatively few subjects, the findings may be considered tentative. It is certainly possible that many nonverbal behaviors have different meanings for various groups in different settings and/or that the meanings attributed to them in the literature are overly simplistic. However, the results do point to the importance of examining leadership style through nonverbal behavior, as well as the necessity of looking at particular settings or organizations when studying leadership style.

In contrast to the pilot study just discussed, most field studies of leadership are found in business or industry. Yet organizations such as large universities differ in climate from large business corporations in that they are more liberal politically, more dynamic, there is more shared decision-making and greater dispersion of power. In large business organizations, most women are clerical workers and most clerical workers are women. There is practically no mobility between clerical workers and management. Each constitutes a separate "caste" with its own separate hierarchy. A management woman's similarity by sex to a clerical "caste" may interfere with her ability to be a successful leader.

In a university there is also little or no mobility between clerical staff and the academic personnel. However, students, especially graduate students, may be considered analogous to management trainees, and therefore in the same hierarchy as faculty and administrators. There are many more female students than female management trainees, there are more (but far from enough) women in academia than in management positions, and there are somewhat more women in higher faculty and academic administrative ranks than in high levels of management.

Additional studies of women in leadership roles in academia should be carried out to compare their styles with those of women leaders in business. Since there are considerable differences among a business firm, a university, a hospital, and/or an advertising agency, effective leadership styles in these diverse organizations should also vary. Some organizations are very innovative and dynamic; others are static (Hage & Aiken, 1972). Dynamic organizations tend to be more complex, decentralized, and to deemphasize stratification. They introduce new programs or new occupational perspectives and face an ever-changing environment. A complex organization requires increased knowledge among its members, thus utilizing occupations that require long periods of training. This should lead to the dispersion of power, shared decision-making, greater individual initiative and autonomy. Hierarchy lines of authority are cut across by informal lines of communication. Status and prestige differences among various occupations and fields in such an organization diminish. Emphasis is on quality and high morale.

The static or unchanging organization is quite different. There is an emphasis on formalization, centralization, rules, and stratification. Power and influence are located in only a few positions. Leadership style should reflect these policies, focusing on efficiency and high quality of production. DiMarco and Whitsitt (1975) found that female supervisors in government differed from those in business. The government group saw their organization as more bureaucratic and to a lesser extent collaborative. The reverse was true for the supervisor in business. The government group had a more formalistic style as well. Universities, research institutes, and welfare agencies are examples of organizations that generally represent a dynamic organizational style. A more participative leadership style would be predicted since it reflects these dynamic systems. This is quite different from the directive leadership style, which is more effective in the more static organizations, such as highly structured businesses, and mass-production industries. Women should be more likely to emerge as leaders in the former as compared to the latter type of organization, since certain characteristics, such as responsiveness and sensitivity to others, although present in both sexes, are socially reinforced in women and fostered in the more dynamic systems.

MALE AND FEMALE LEADERS: CONCLUSIONS

Many of the assumptions that women managers are basically different from men are just not supported by data. The one difference investigators generally agree upon is women's greater concern for relationships among people; this should be considered a plus in terms of leadership effectiveness. Alleged sex differences in ability, attitudes, and personality have been based on sex-role stereotypes, rather than empirical observations of women leaders. Dunlap and Mangelsdorff (1975) note it is commonly assured that male-female leadership teams work better than same-sex teams as facilitators in human relations training groups. According to the sex-role stereotypes that underlie this assumption, the male facilitator will provide a dynamic, assertive, self-assured model, while the female facilitator will model gentleness, acceptance, and emotional sharing. In their study of same and opposite sex group facilitators or leaders, they conclude that sex pairings was not a significant determinant of final evaluations. Individual differences among facilitators may be great, but sex-role stereotypes and male-female combinations are not a basis for leader selection. Women should be judged on the basis of their individual qualifications as men are.

Other studies have shown that female and male leaders who perform similar functions are evaluated as equally effective in terms of performance and skills by their subordinates (Day & Stogdill, 1972; Wexley & Hunt, 1974). One can then question whether it is a good idea to have special training programs to prepare women for leadership positions in management. *Business Week* (1974) notes a new curriculum at Simmons College in Boston especially designed to meet the special needs of women entering the ranks of management. Margaret Hennig, one of the organizers of the program, argues that since women have grown up with different experiences than men, they have a different outlook about strategy, risk-taking, and achievement, and therefore need special preparation—different from that offered men—to enter male-dominated corporations. This program presupposes that women managers need to understand how such corporations work. Pace University in New York City has also launched a special program to train women for management.

One must be careful that such programs do not take on negative connotations and continue to perpetuate the myth that women are less capable of performing effectively in leadership positions. Special training programs for women in management may not be necessary and should be examined more carefully. Special programs should be open to all persons regardless of sex, who need added exposure to a given discipline or area. For example, all employees in an organization should be provided with an early opportunity to have successful experiences working under the leadership of a woman. The importance of prior experience can be seen in work such as that of Koff (1973) who found that two-thirds of successful women managers in her study had four or more years of prior work experience before attempting supervision of others. In contrast, women recruited from nonbusiness college majors simply to meet affirmative action goals found it hard to be suddenly cast in the role of supervisor. They lacked the background, skills, and language of the business field they entered, as well as the leadership or supervisory experience. In such cases an internship or similar training program would be helpful. It might also be much more effective to design programs to modify the negative beliefs held by some about women's capabilities for leadership.

Women can be effective leaders. Their styles may or may not be different from those of men. Only by serving as leaders can women hope to overcome debilitating sex-role stereotypes.

References

Are women executives people? *Harvard Business Review*, 1965, *43*, 14-16+.

Bass, B., Krusell, J., & Alexander, R.A. Male managers' attitudes toward working women. *American Behavioral Scientist*, November 1971, 221-236.

Beekman, S.J. *Sex differences in nonverbal behavior*. Unpublished doctoral dissertation, University of Chicago, 1974.

Chemers, M.M. The relationship between birth order and leadership style. *Journal of Social Psychology*, 1970, *80*(2), 243-244.

Dalton, M. Informal factors in career achievement. *American Journal of Sociology*, 1951, *56*, 407-415.

Day, D., & Stogdill, R. Leader behavior of male and female supervisors: A comparative study. *Personnel Psychology*, 1972, *25*(2), 353-360.

Deaux, K. *The behavior of women and men*. Monterey, CA: Brooks/Cole, 1976.

Denmark, F.L., & Diggory, J.C. Sex differences in attitudes toward leaders' display of authoritarian behavior. *Psychological Reports*, 1966, *18*, 863-872.

Denmark, F.L., McKenna, W., Juran, S., & Greenberg, H.M. Status and sex differences in nonverbal behavior. Unpublished research, 1976.

DiMarco, N., & Whitsitt, S.E. A comparison of female supervisors in business and government organizations. *Journal of Vocational Behavior*, 1975, *6*, 185-196.

Dunlap, S.M., & Mangelsdorff, A.D. Male-female coleadership: Testing the Adam and Eve myth. Paper presented at the Southwestern Psychological Association, Houston, 1975.

Exline, R., Gray, D., & Schuette, D. Visual behavior in a dyad as affected by interview content and sex of respondent. *Journal of Personality and Social Psychology*, 1965, *1*, 201-209.

Gitter, A.G., Black, H., & Goldman, A. Role of nonverbal communication in the perception of leadership. *Perceptual and Motor Skills*, 1975, *40*, 463-466.

Hage, J., & Aiken, M. Styles of organizational change: The problems of change of the system. In L. Marlowe (Ed.), *Basic topics in social psychology*. Boston: Holbrook Press, 1972.

Henley, N.M. The politics of touch. In P. Brown (Ed.), *Radical psychology*. New York: Harper & Row, 1973a.

Henley, N.M. Status and sex: Some touching observations. *Bulletin of the Psychonomic Society*, 1973b, *2*, 91-93.

Henley, N.M. Power, sex, and nonverbal communication. *Berkeley Journal of Sociology*, 1973c, *18*, 1-26.

Jacobson, M.B., & Effertz, J. Sex roles and leadership: Perceptions of the leaders and the led. *Organizational Behavior and Human Performance*, 1974, *12*, 383-396.

Kanter, R.M. Women and the structure of organization: Explanations in theory and behavior. In Millman & Kanter (Eds.), *Another voice*. New York: Doubleday, 1975.

Koff, L.A. Age, experience, and success among women managers. *Management Review*, November 1973, 65-66.

Lipset, S., & Bendix, R. *Social mobility in industrial society*. Berkeley, CA: University of California Press, 1959.

Lyle, J.R., & Ross, J.L. *Women in industry*. Lexington, MA: D.C. Heath & Co., 1973.

McKenna, W., & Denmark, F.L. The interaction of nonverbal behaviors and sex-role stereotypes in the attribution of status. Unpublished research, 1976.

Megargee, E.I. Influence of sex roles on the manifestation of leadership. *Journal of Applied Psychology*, 1969, *53*, 377-382.

Mehrabian, A. Nonverbal communication. In J.K. Cole (Ed.), *Nebraska symposium on motivation*. Lincoln, NE: University of Nebraska Press, 1971.

Mehrabian, A. *Nonverbal communication*. Chicago: Aldine-Atherton, 1972.

Pen, J. *Harmony and conflict in modern society*. New York: McGraw-Hill, 1966.

Pinder, C.C., & Pinto, P.R. Demographic correlates of managerial style. *Personnel Psychology*, 1974, *27*, 257-270.

Sandler, B.E., & Scalia, F.A. The relationship between birth order, sex, and leadership in a religious organization. *Journal of Social Psychology*, 1975, *95*, 279-280.

Shein, V.E. The relationship between sex-role stereotypes and requisite management characteristics. *Journal of Applied Psychology*, 1973, *57*, 95-100.

Shein, V.E. Relationships between sex-role stereotypes and requisite management characteristics among female managers. *Journal of Applied Psychology*, 1975, *60*, 340-344.

Tresemer, D. Fear of success: Popular, but unproven. *Psychology Today*, 1974, 7(10), 82-85.

Weitz, S. Sex differences in non-verbal communication. Paper presented at Eastern Psychological Association annual convention, Philadelphia, 1974.

Wexley, K., & Hunt, P. Male and female leaders: Comparison of performance and behavior patterns. *Psychological Reports*, 1974, *35*, 867-872.

Why women need their own MBA programs. *Business Week*, February 23, 1974, p. 102.

Wilson, C., & Lupton, T. The social background and connections of top decision makers. *Manchester School of Economics and Social Studies*, 1959, *27*, 33-51.

Theories of Leadership:
A Review of Useful Research

Marshall Sashkin and William R. Lassey

What does a leader contribute to a group, business, organization, voluntary community, educational institution, or in politics and government? What does a leader do to increase effectiveness and productivity? How can a leader generate improved performance among those who are led? What specific roles does a leader perform that are unique and critical to effective leadership? These and other issues related to leadership have been the subject of investigation by social scientists for more than fifty years. Although answers to the questions posed are not definitive, progress in the advancement of knowledge is clearly evident.

Leadership research is examined here under four major headings: (a) leadership traits, or the "great man" approach, (b) leadership behavior, (c) contingency theories, and (d) the situational-control approach. Research focused on each approach has provided partial answers to the basic questions, but none of these approaches provides complete answers. This article focuses on the practical value of research findings while making specific suggestions for improving leadership effectiveness.

Adapted from an original chapter prepared by Marshall Sashkin and William C. Morris. Adapted especially for this volume and used by permission.

LEADERSHIP TRAITS AND THE "GREAT MAN"

The characteristics of leaders were the primary focus of investigators during the period from 1920 through the 1940s. An array of studies examines evidence of greater intelligence, more creativeness, deeper curiosity, wider insight, and other "traits" that distinguish leaders from their followers. A classic review of more than one hundred such studies by Stogdill (1948) suggests that these inquiries may have been addressing the wrong question. While leaders tend to have marginal advantages over "nonleaders" in many traits such as intelligence and physical dimensions, there were no characteristics in which leaders were consistently identified as being superior.

This does not necessarily imply that the study of traits is altogether worthless. Charismatic leaders such as Churchill, Roosevelt, Bonaparte, Hitler, and others appeared able to recognize basic human fears, fantasies, and aspirations to which they could appeal eloquently (Schiffer, 1973). Although there is no entirely satisfying explanation of how this "great man" charisma operates, it is nonetheless clear that many national leaders have attracted large and devoted followings, even though they had relatively few "traits" in common.

Borgatta and his associates (1954) used small group experiments to demonstrate the tendency of certain members to consistently emerge as leaders by demonstrating exceptional abilities. However, over the course of 166 group discussion sessions, only 5 percent of the participants were judged sufficiently consistent to qualify as "great" leaders. This small proportion would not satisfy the need for the large numbers of leaders required by organizations, communities, social movements, and the range of other social settings. Hence, the use of "traits" or characteristics of "greatness" in leaders provides an insufficient basis for understanding leadership.

LEADERSHIP BEHAVIOR

Research on behaviors associated with leadership began in the 1930s and was given impetus because of disillusionment with attempts to identify leaders on the basis of traits. A broad range of behavioral theories has been tested; these various approaches contain some essential common elements.

A One-Dimensional Approach: The Early Michigan Studies

A series of studies made at the University of Michigan's Survey Research Center in the late 1940s and early 1950s (Katz, Maccoby, & Morse, 1950; Katz, Maccoby, Gurin, & Floor, 1951) led the researchers to suggest that leadership behavior could be described along a dimension of employee-centered behavior to production-centered behavior, as illustrated in Figure 1. Supervisors who were more employee-centered and less production-centered had more productive work crews. Employee-centeredness was therefore defined as a leadership style that should result in improved performance and productivity. However, further studies at the University of Michigan (Kahn, 1956), as well as the early studies conducted at Ohio State University, soon demonstrated that the employee-centered and production-centered leadership styles were not opposite ends of a single dimension but were, instead, two independent dimensions of leader behavior.

Neutral

Employee-Centered (Supportive, friendly, concerned for subordinates' welfare) ◄─┼─┼─┼─┼─┼─┼─► Task-Centered (Directive, distant, concerned that the work be accomplished)

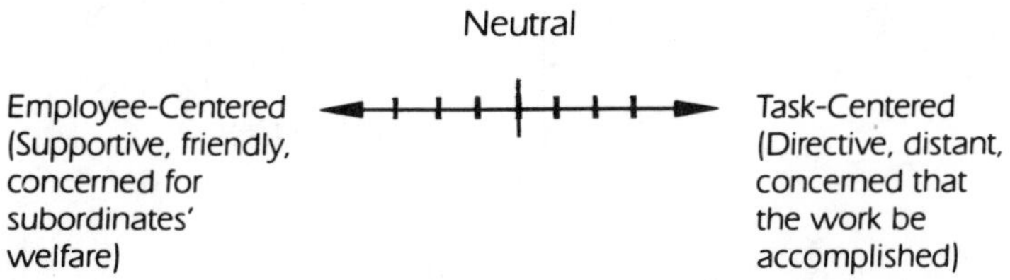

Figure 1. The Single Dimension of Leader Behavior as Defined in the Early Michigan Studies

Two Dimensions of Leadership Behavior: The Ohio State Studies

Investigators at Ohio State University (Fleishman, Harris, & Burtt, 1955; Stogdill & Coons, 1957) attempted to identify and describe dimensions of leader behavior through empirical measurement of the behavior of leaders in organizations. The early studies were undertaken with the cooperation of International Harvester Company (a manufacturer of farm equipment); later work included other organizations.

Although fourteen dimensions of leadership were initially identified (Stogdill, 1963), only two were actually found to be very common or typical of leader behavior (see Figure 2). The dimensions have since been identified by various labels, but the original researchers called them "consideration" for subordinates and "initiating structure" through directions and orders. Other polar terms often used include "task orientation" versus "maintenance orientation," and "production orientation" versus "people orientation." These are similar to the end points of the continuum in the one-dimensional approach noted earlier. The key difference here is that a leader is likely to engage in both types of behavior to various degrees (see Figure 2).

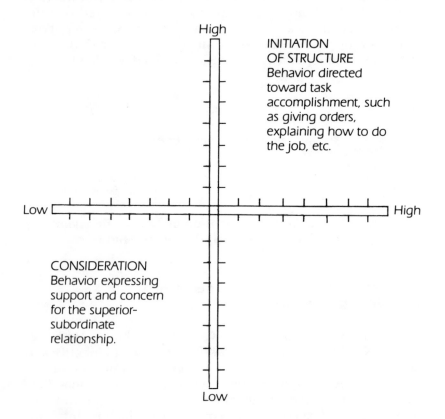

Figure 2. The Two Major Dimensions of Leader Behavior Identified in the Ohio State Studies

Early research on the two-dimensional approach seemed to indicate that the most effective leadership would usually consist of strong performance in both dimensions. Fleishman and Harris (1962), for example, were able to demonstrate that supervisors with high scores for both factors had fewer employee grievances and lower turnover rates. More recent research (Hall & Donnell, 1979) showed that high-achieving managers use a participative leadership style that emphasizes both dimensions.

In the thirty years since the first publication of the Ohio State leadership studies, a variety of training programs have been developed to teach managers how to maximize their behavior on both dimensions. The most widely used of these two-dimensional approaches is probably the Managerial Grid® program developed by Blake and Mouton (1964) and detailed in their article in Part II of this book.

The two-dimensional paradigm represents the most widely used approach to leadership theory, research, and training. The two behavioral dimensions are observable and account for a large proportion of actual behavior. They also, however, have served as a basis for the following, more complex, theories.

Three-Dimensional Theory

Lewin, Lippitt, and White (1939) were early investigators of three leadership dimensions or styles: "autocratic," "democratic," and "laissez-faire." Autocratic corresponds to extreme directiveness or task orientation, as discussed above, while democratic is similar to a participative or relationship style. Laissez-faire is a French word meaning, essentially, "leave them alone."

Lewin and his colleagues undertook an experiment with boys clubs to test the consequences of the three leadership styles. Levels of hostility, aggression, and productivity (in the boys' activities) were evaluated. They found the democratically led groups to be most productive and the least hostile or aggressive. The autocratically led groups were productive only while the leader was present; hostility was exhibited in the absence of the leader. The laissez-faire groups were left to their own devices and demonstrated neither productivity nor hostility. Nearly thirty years later, similar experiments with college students produced comparable results (Litwin & Stringer, 1968). An achievement-oriented democratic leadership style was found to be most productive.

The three-dimensional studies demonstrated that real or simulated organizations could be created to illustrate the operation and effects of the three styles of leadership behavior. The three theoretical dimensions "held up" in real-life tests.

Four Factors

Bowers and Seashore (1966) were able to empirically identify four factors in leader behavior: (a) supportiveness, (b) interaction facilitation, (c) work facilitation, and (d) goal emphasis. The measurements were based on variables in Likert's (1961, 1967) theory of organization and were undertaken at the University of Michigan's Institute for Social Research. The factors represent an elaboration of the two Ohio State dimensions of "consideration" and "structure."

Supportiveness is basically comparable to consideration, while interaction facilitation adds concern for smoother and more effective interactions among workers. Goal emphasis is similar to establishing structure, while work facilitation adds a focus on task achievement through the provision of information and materials.

The Likert (1967) theory suggests that leadership behavior does not necessarily lead directly to increases in subordinate performance. Rather, leadership as represented by the four factors determines the "organizational climate"—communication patterns, goal-setting activities, involvement in decisions, and opportunities for influence. These climate factors act directly to increase or decrease performance (Franklin, 1975).

Key Elements of Leader-Behavior Theory

Each of the behavioral theories is based on the categories of relationship orientation and task orientation. High levels of performance in both categories are deemed critical to effective leadership. These findings are consistent with earlier work by Borgatta, Couch, and Bales (1954) and Bales (1958), which concluded that "great man" leaders performed well in both categories.

Fleishman and Harris (1962) showed that leaders who were strong in both dimensions had fewer grievances and lower turnover, but could not relate the leaders' behaviors directly to subordinate performance. Other studies by Fleishman and his colleagues (Fleishman & Ko, 1962; Fleishman & Peters, 1962; Fleishman & Simmons, 1970) showed clearly that supervisors who scored high on both dimensions are rated higher by their bosses than are other supervisors. This is strongly confirmed by Hall and Donnell (1979) who showed that managers who were promoted at younger ages—high achievers—also rated high on both dimensions of leader behavior. Still, none of these findings tell us that these leaders are more *effective* in terms of subordinate performance; they are only more "successful," recalling Bass' distinction between successful and effective leadership.

In order to show how leadership affects subordinate performance, Likert (1967) argued that the relation is indirect, as outlined earlier. Other researchers turned to new, more complex theories that they hoped would show that the most effective leader behavior is *contingent* on certain factors associated with subordinates or with situations. The most effective leader behavior would then vary, depending on these contingencies.

CONTINGENCY THEORIES

Tannenbaum and Schmidt (1958) suggested that leaders need to vary their leadership styles in terms of the balance between task-directed and relationship-oriented activity. The appropriate balance depends on the situation or context in which tasks are performed. Tannenbaum and Schmidt did not, however, define the varying contexts in much detail. Contingency theories attempt to illuminate the contexts and suggest appropriate leader-behavior adaptations.

Contingency Theory: Fiedler

The research that resulted in Fiedler's (1967) contingency model began in the early 1950s. The initial focus was on military leadership. Fiedler and his colleagues attempted to measure leaders' sentiments about least-preferred co-workers (Fiedler, 1955; Fiedler & Meuwese, 1963). Later, basketball teams, dairy cooperatives, and many other organizations were studied. Some of this research is summarized in Fiedler's article in Part II. The eventual conclusion was that leaders who disliked their least-preferred co-worker were motivated primarily by a need for task accomplishment, while leaders who were more positive about their least preferred co-worker were motivated by a need for good interpersonal relationships.

The contingency model is based on the premise that situational conditions determine whether task-oriented behavior or relationship-oriented behavior is more appropriate. Situational variables are differentiated into three major categories: (a) leader-member relations, which can vary from very good to very poor; (b) task structure, which can vary from high to low; and (c) leader position power or legitimate authority, which can be strong or weak. Eight combinations are then identified along a dimension of "favorableness for the exercise of leadership" (Figure 3).

Type of Situation	I	II	III	IV	V	VI	VII	VIII
Favorableness	High ⟵					⟶ Low		
Leader-Member Relations	Good				Poor			
Task Structure	High		Low		High		Low	
Leader Position Power	Strong	Weak	Strong	Weak	Strong	Weak	Strong	Weak

Figure 3. Fiedler's Primary Situational Variables Define Eight Types of Situations Along a Dimension of "Favorableness for the Exercise of Leadership"

Situations I, II, and III are the most favorable. It is much easier to exercise leadership in these situations than situations VI, VII, or VIII. Research has demonstrated that task-motivated leaders (negative toward least-preferred co-worker) are generally more effective in the first three, very favorable, situations; relationship-motivated leaders (positive toward least-preferred co-worker) are more effective in moderately difficult situations (IV, V); and task-motivated leaders, again, are more effective in the very negative (VI, VII, VIII) situations (Fiedler, 1967, 1971; Maier & Sashkin, 1971; Sashkin, 1972; Sashkin, Taylor, & Tripathi, 1974).

Although the contingency model does predict which leaders will be effective in which situations, the prediction is far from perfect. The reason why the model works has never been resolved. Fiedler has suggested a variety of possible explanations, all of which are rather complicated. Fiedler argues, however, that in a "pretzel-shaped world," we need pretzel-shaped theories.

The most recent research by Fiedler and his colleagues shows that leaders can be trained to recognize the nature of the situation and modify conditions to make their style of leadership applicable (Fiedler, Chemers, & Mahar, 1976). This can mean changing the task structure, sharing more power with subordinates, or assuming *more* authority. The focus also can be on creating more positive interpersonal relationships with subordinates. Trained leaders can improve their own effectiveness and increase the performance of their subordinates (Fiedler & Mahar, 1979).

Situational Leadership™ Theory: Hersey and Blanchard

The Hersey and Blanchard (1969, 1982) approach differs from Fiedler's model in at least two important ways. First, it is based on the assumption that leaders can change their behavior to fit the situation, rather than deliberately rearranging situations to fit their particular approaches. Second, the subordinate's level of "task maturity" is the primary situational variable. Maturity is defined as (a) job maturity—the *ability* to do a particular job and (b) psychological maturity—the *willingness or confidence* to do the work (Figure 4).

Ability	to do a job:	Does the person have the knowledge, skill, and experience required to successfully carry out the task?
+		
Willingness	to do a job:	Does the person have the motivation, commitment, and confidence to carry out the task?
=		
Task Maturity		

Figure 4. The Components of Task Maturity

There are four possible combinations of the two maturity factors. Each is best dealt with by one of the four primary combinations of leader task and relationship behavior: high-high, high-low, low-high, or low-low. The format for this approach is outlined in Figure 5. Further explanation can be found in the Hersey and Blanchard article in Part II of this book and in the Hersey et al. paper in Part III.

It is important to remember that the Situational Leadership™ term "maturity" does not mean emotional or psychological maturity in the usual sense. It refers strictly to the two factors described in Figure 4. Moreover, the maturity level is diagnosed only for one specific task at a time, not for the person's overall job performance.

	SITUATION THREE	SITUATION TWO
HIGH	The subordinate is moderately high on task maturity, able but not fully willing to do the job. Often this is because of a lack of self-confidence, a feeling of low organizational support, or lack of awareness of the rewards for effective task accomplishment. The most effective leader behavior, "participating," involves high levels of support, attempts to improve the subordinate's faith in himself, and assurance of positive rewards for achievement. No directive behavior is needed, because the subordinate already knows how to do the job.	The subordinate is moderately low on task maturity, willing but not really able to do the task. The most effective leader behavior is "selling," both task-directive and explicitly, openly considerate and relationship oriented. The leader must be a guide, showing the subordinate how to accomplish the task while keeping the subordinate enthusiastic by expressing support for the subordinate's willingness to tackle a new challenge.
	SITUATION FOUR	SITUATION ONE
LOW	The subordinate has high task maturity and needs almost no direction and very little support. The most effective leader behavior is "delegating," low on both dimensions, but the leader does engage in some interpersonal relationship behavior in order to maintain the quality of the supervisor-subordinate relationship.	The subordinate has low task maturity and needs to have clearly detailed and specific instructions in order to learn to do the job. The most effective leader behavior is "telling," which is highly directive with low relationship focus. The fact that the leader takes the time and effort to show the subordinate what to do in such detail is itself evidence of sincere concern for the subordinate if the leader is directive in a way that shows caring and concern, not an impersonal or degrading attitude.

Relationship-Oriented Behavior: Considerate, Interpersonal

LOW   HIGH

Task-Oriented Behavior: Directive, Initiating Structure

Figure 5. Situational Leadership™ Theory

A study in a large division of the Xerox Corporation seems to confirm the relevance of Situational Leadership™ theory for managerial behavior (Hambleton & Gumpert, 1982). When managers could correctly assess subordinates' maturity levels and identify the appropriate leadership style to use, subordinates were rated as performing better (compared to subordinates whose maturity levels were not correctly identified). An experimental study by Hersey and his colleagues that adds further support to the theory is reprinted in Part III.

Contingency Theories: Summary and Conclusions

It eventually became clear that certain behavioral approaches to leadership were not effective in terms of the performance and productivity of subordinates. Contingency theorists then attempted to identify situational characteristics that would determine the success of behavioral approaches. Research supporting both of the contingency approaches discussed here does not prove that either approach is essentially correct; improved performance following leadership training of any kind may occur simply as a result of the trainees' increased self-understanding of their own behaviors and of the important factors in the effective exercise of leadership. However, contingency approaches are important because they identify important situational factors, such as the way a task is structured, the leader's power, the basic atmosphere of friendship and support for the leader from the subordinates, the ability of the subordinates to do a task, and the willingness of subordinates to carry out the task. These factors exist aside from the particular behavioral style of the leader. Being able to recognize these factors and deal with them in a practical, direct manner probably results in improvements in leadership effectiveness.

SITUATIONAL-CONTROL THEORY

The approaches to leadership discussed so far have centered, in one way or another, on the behavior of the person in charge. In contrast, "situational control" implies adjusting the environment in order to improve long-term performance or motivation among subordinates. "Substitutes" for leadership are identified, and these make the behavior or character of the leader less significant.

Path-Goal Theory

The "expectancy" theory of motivation is the primary basis for the Path-Goal Theory (House, 1971; House & Dessler, 1974; House & Mitchell, 1974). The Path-Goal Theory rests primarily on the workers' expectancy that efforts will lead to successful task results. This expectancy may be unclear when the task is uncertain, when required work activities are ambiguous, or when participants are inexperienced at the job to be done. Role clarification is therefore needed to specify expected behavior. Task-directive behavior by leaders is needed to establish structure in the work situation. Very specific "coaching" may be required until each worker learns the necessary behaviors that will lead to expected results and rewards.

In the case of tasks that are highly structured with little uncertainty or ambiguity, the primary role of the leader may be to express support as a reward for effective performance. If intrinsic motivation is missing because of a repetitive and highly structured task, leader behavior can help to reward workers who might otherwise feel little satisfaction with achievement (Sims, 1977; Keller & Szilagyi, 1976).

Behaviorism

Behaviorism—sometimes referred to as stimulus-response theory—complements the path-goal concept by focusing on another form of expectancy: a clearly defined relationship between achievements and rewards. The leader must, of course, have the resources to provide rewards as a direct consequence of desirable subordinate performance (Pelz, 1952; Sims & Szilagyi, 1975). When achievement is consistently followed by reward, performance persistently improves.

Substitutes for Leadership

As Kerr and Jermier (1978) note in their article in this volume, a leader's efforts may be neutralized by characteristics of subordinates, attributes of the task, or organizational features. For example, when subordinates enter a position with high degrees of skill, experience, and training, there is little need for directive behavior by a leader. Such attempts at leadership may in fact lead to lowered performance and resentment. Similarly, when strong organizational norms are clear with respect to expected performance, there is little need for additional structure to be initiated by the unit leader. When subordinates desire rewards that the leader cannot directly provide, attempts at leadership may be ineffective. Coercion through threats of punishment or withholding of rewards may produce lowered rather than increased task performance (Kerr & Jermier, 1978). Finally, when an organization is structured so as to continuously clarify the means to achieve desired goals (i.e., through formalized planning and clear rules associated with expected activities), the need for directive leader behavior is reduced.

Central Elements of Situational Control

Situational control focuses on the management of the work situation to minimize the need for strong leader activity. Clear expectations and a strong relationship between achievements and rewards may be "substitutes" for ongoing leadership direction. Leadership activities that negate effectiveness (threats of punishment) are minimized or eliminated. The worker and leader function in tandem to achieve clearly perceived and jointly desired goals.

CONCLUSIONS

The trait or "great man" approach to leadership research has produced few clear indications of consistent characteristics of leaders, although high need for power has been shown to be related to effective management (McClelland & Burnham, 1976). Two primary dimensions of leader behavior are clear: task-directive and relationship-oriented behavior. These two classes of behaviors can be further subdivided to increase the specificity of appropriate leader actions.

The contingency theories have been sufficiently tested to demonstrate that different leader behaviors may be appropriate in different situations. Situational control theory clarifies the means through which "settings" can be designed and controlled to achieve productivity and satisfaction. Collectively, these theories increase our understanding of the leader as active designer and initiator of actions. An understanding of key human behavioral patterns, skill in the design of work situations, and an appreciation of organizational or community dynamics are central elements of the leadership role.

Integration of the knowledge achieved from fifty years of research remains to be completed. Nonetheless, current management development and leadership training efforts can take advantage of many research findings. As we learn more about leadership, the "theories" begin more to resemble "reality": Greater numbers of leaders do not simply react to people or situations, but ign and initiate actions, based on some understanding of human motivation, the design of jobs, the nature of organizations, and the dynamics of a wide range of social units.

References

Bales, R.F. Task roles and social roles in problem-solving groups. In E.E. Maccoby, T.M. Newcomb, & E.L. Hartley (Eds.), *Readings in social psychology* (3rd ed.). New York: Holt, Rinehart and Winston, 1958.

Blake, R.R., & Mouton, J.S. *The managerial grid.* Houston, TX: Gulf, 1964.

Borgatta, E.F., Couch, A.S., & Bales, R.F. Some findings relevant to the great man theory of leadership. *American Sociological Review*, 1954, *19*, 755-759.

Bowers, D.G., & Seashore, S.E. Predicting organizational effectiveness with a four-factor theory of leadership. *Administrative Science Quarterly*, 1966, *11*, 238-263.

Fiedler, F.E. The influence of leader-key man relations on combat crew effectiveness. *Journal of Abnormal and Social Psychology*, 1955, *51*, 227-235.

Fiedler, F.E. *A theory of leadership effectiveness.* New York: McGraw-Hill, 1967.

Fiedler, F.E. Validation and extension of the contingency model of leadership effectiveness: A review of empirical findings. *Psychological Bulletin*, 1976, *76*, 128-148.

Fiedler, F.E., Chemers, M.M., & Mahar, L. *Improving leadership effectiveness.* New York: John Wiley, 1976.

Fiedler, F.E., & Mahar, L. The effectiveness of contingency model training: A review of the validation of leader match. *Personnel Psychology*, 1979, *32*, 45-62.

Fiedler, F.E., & Meuwese, W.A.T. Leader's contribution to task performance in cohesive and uncohesive groups. *Journal of Abnormal and Social Psychology*, 1963, *67*, 83-87.

Fleishman, E.A., & Harris, E.F. Patterns of leadership behavior related to employee grievances and turnover. *Personnel Psychology*, 1962, *15*, 43-56.

Fleishman, E.A., Harris, E.F., & Burtt, H.E. *Leadership and supervision in industry.* Columbus, OH: Bureau of Educational Research, Ohio State University, 1955.

Fleishman, E.A., & Ko, I. Leadership patterns associated with managerial evaluation of effectiveness. Unpublished report, Yale University, 1962.

Fleishman, E.A., & Peters, D.R. Interpersonal values, leadership attitudes, and managerial "success." *Personnel Psychology*, 1962, *15*, 127-143.

Fleishman, E.A., & Simmons, J. Relationship between leadership patterns and effectiveness ratings among Israeli foremen. *Personnel Psychology*, 1970, *23*, 169-172.

Franklin, J.L. Relations among four social-psychological aspects of organizations. *Administrative Science Quarterly*, 1975, *20*, 422-433.

Hall, J., & Donnell, S.M. Managerial achievement: The personal side of behavioral theory. *Human Relations,* 1979, *32,* 77-101.

Hambleton, R.K., & Gumpert, R. The validity of Hersey and Blanchard's theory of leader effectiveness. *Group & Organization Studies,* 1982, *7,* 225-242.

Hersey, P., & Blanchard, K.H. Life cycle theory of leadership. *Training and Development Journal,* 1969, *23*(5), 26-34.

Hersey, P., & Blanchard, K.H. *Management of organizational behavior: Utilizing human resources* (4th ed.). Englewood Cliffs, NJ: Prentice-Hall, 1982.

House, R.J. A path-goal theory of leader effectiveness. *Administrative Science Quarterly,* 1971, *16,* 321-339.

House, R.J., & Dessler, G. The path goal theory of leadership. In J.G. Hunt and L.L. Larson (Eds.), *Contingency approaches to leadership.* Carbondale, IL: Southern Illinois University Press, 1974.

House, R.J., & Mitchell, T.R. Path-goal theory of leadership. *Journal of Contemporary Business,* 1974, *3*(4), 81-98.

Kahn, R.L. The prediction of productivity. *Journal of Social Issues,* 1956, *12*(2), 41-49.

Katz, D., Maccoby, N., Gurin, G., & Floor, L.G. *Productivity, supervision, and morale among railroad workers.* Ann Arbor, MI: Institute for Social Research, The University of Michigan, 1951.

Katz, D., Maccoby, N., & Morse, N.C. *Productivity, supervision, and morale in an office situation.* Ann Arbor, MI: Institute for Social Research, The University of Michigan, 1950.

Keller, R.T., & Szilagyi, A.D. Employee reactions to leader reward behavior. *Academy of Management Journal,* 1976, *19,* 619-627.

Kerr, S., & Jermier, J.M. Substitutes for leadership: Their meaning and measurement. *Organizational Behavior and Human Performance,* 1978, *22,* 375-403.

Lewin, K., Lippitt, R., & White, R.K. Patterns of aggressive behavior in experimentally created social climates. *Journal of Social Psychology,* 1939, *10,* 271-301.

Likert, R. *New patterns of management.* New York: McGraw-Hill, 1961.

Likert, R. *The human organization.* New York: McGraw-Hill, 1967.

Litwin, G.H., & Stringer, R.A. *Motivation and organizational climate.* Boston: Graduate School of Business Administration, Harvard University, 1968.

Maier, N.R.F., & Sashkin, M. Specific leadership behaviors that promote problem solving. *Personnel Psychology,* 1971, *24,* 35-44.

McClelland, D.C., & Burnham, D.H. Power is the great motivator. *Harvard Business Review,* 1976, *62*(2), 100-110.

Pelz, D.C. Influence: A key to effective leadership in the first-line supervisor. *Personnel,* 1952, *29,* 209-217.

Sashkin, M. Leadership style and group decision effectiveness. *Organizational Behavior and Human Performance,* 1972, *8,* 347-362.

Sashkin, M., Taylor, F.C., & Tripathi, R.C. An analysis of situational moderating effects on the relationships between least preferred co-worker and other psychological measures. *Journal of Applied Psychology,* 1974, *59,* 731-740.

Schiffer, I. *Charisma: A psychoanalytic look at mass society.* Toronto: University of Toronto Press, 1973.

Sims, H.P., Jr. The leader as a manager of reinforcement contingencies. In J.G. Hunt and L.L. Larson (Eds.), *Leadership: The cutting edge.* Carbondale, IL: Southern Illinois University Press, 1977.

Sims, H.P., Jr., & Szilagyi, A.D. Leader reward behavior and subordinate satisfaction and performance. *Organizational Behavior and Human Performance,* 1975, *14,* 426-437.

Stogdill, R.M. Personal factors associated with leadership: A survey of the literature. *Journal of Psychology*, 1948, 25, 37-71.

Stogdill, R.M. *Manual for the Leader Behavior Description Questionnaire—Form XII*. Columbus, OH: Bureau of Business Research, Ohio State University, 1963.

Stogdill, R.M., & Coons, A.E. *Leader behavior: Its description and measurement*. Columbus, OH: Bureau of Business Research, Ohio State University, 1957.

Tannenbaum, R., & Schmidt, W.H. How to choose a leadership pattern. *Harvard Business Review*, 1958, 36(2), 95-101.

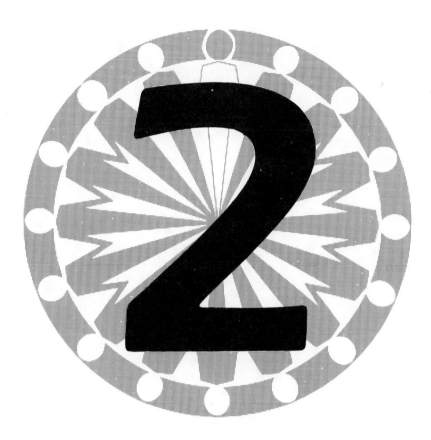

Leadership in
Complex Organizations

Introduction to Part 2: Leadership in Complex Organizations

The work of Douglas McGregor, an educational administrator and social scientist, is probably as widely recognized, almost twenty years after his death, as that of any other management scholar. McGregor was deeply influenced by Abraham Maslow (1943), who developed a theory of human motivation that emphasized the positive, growth-directed forces in human behavior. McGregor applied Maslow's theory to the management of organizations in a 1957 paper, "The Human Side of Enterprise," in which his elegantly simple "Theory X" and "Theory Y" were first defined. In Part I of this book, the stimulus-response or behaviorist approach was noted only briefly; yet this carrot-and-stick, reward or punishment style represented for McGregor the primary thrust of existing organizational leadership theory. His alternative might not only be more accurate but also may have more positive results for both individuals and organizations. McGregor believed that all organizational members could benefit through greater participation in managing the organization.

In McGregor's time, most organizations operated on authoritarian ("Theory X") assumptions, and this remains the norm despite considerable evidence that the participative model ("Theory Y") is more effective for accomplishing organizational goals and satisfying the emotional needs of organizational members.

The participative, "Theory Y" approach, McGregor argues (and research supports), provides organizational members with (a) the autonomy that mature human beings require (Argyris, 1957), (b) more meaningful work through personal achievement (Blauner, 1964; Hackman & Oldham, 1980), and (c) an opportunity to work with other people to accomplish a task, thus fulfilling the social need for interpersonal contact (Sashkin, 1982). Because organizations tend to operate on the authoritarian, Theory X model, they often fail to take advantage of the creativity and potential contribution of organizational members while preventing the satisfaction of social needs.

Blake and Mouton (1974) are among those who have applied and further popularized the ideas of McGregor. The Managerial Grid® training program has been used widely throughout the world for more than twenty years and incorporates many concepts of Theory Y. The focus is on jointly maximizing two primary dimensions, "initiating structure" and "consideration." Blake and Mouton (1981) argue that by correctly combining the two leader-behavior dimensions, one achieves an outcome that is more than the sum of two parts. The Managerial Grid® training program is designed to build management skills that maximize both human satisfaction and task productivity.

Hall and Donnell add support to Blake and Mouton's approach, showing that leaders who are personally successful in their organizations (in terms of achieving promotions at an early age) engage in participative management practices *and* utilize the Managerial Grid® approach to a much greater extent than their less successful organizational colleagues. Hall and Donnell draw their conclusions from an unusually extensive data base. Despite the highly significant results obtained, they deal only with what Bass (refer to Part I) calls "successful leadership"—leadership that is attempted and accepted. This is not necessarily the same as *effective* leadership.

The article by Hersey and Blanchard is an early formulation of "Situational Leadership™ Theory." It continues to be among the clearest and most succinct summaries of the Situational Leadership™ concept.

Blake and Mouton (1981, 1982) have challenged the Hersey-Blanchard approach, and vice versa, but neither approach has been subjected to the kind of scientific tests in organizations that could provide clear-cut support or demonstrate failure. Hersey and Blanchard (1982) argue that the Managerial Grid® approach centers on attitudes while their theory is behavior-focused. An alternative way to resolve this apparent inconsistency is to view Blake and Mouton's approach as concentrating on overarching leadership *strategy*, while the Hersey-Blanchard theory focuses on more concrete *tactics* of leader behavior. Indeed, Blake and Mouton (1980) speak of the "versatile manager" as one who keeps in mind the principles inculcated through Managerial Grid® training while varying specific behaviors to fit *situational* needs.

Fiedler's approach is quite a different enterprise. It has been the subject of acrimonious debate among academic researchers for the past twenty years. Much of the conflict has to do with uncertainty about what the "esteem for least-preferred co-worker" (LPC) questionnaire actually measures. Fiedler argues that it measures a motivational pattern, the predisposition to derive satisfaction from either task achievement *or* interpersonal relationships. The LPC measure, however, does not seem to be related to any of the accepted and validated motivational measures. Furthermore, Fiedler makes strong assertions about how the two polar "types" of leaders behave in various situations, but no one has yet tried to observe or measure this behavior in the context of the contingency model. However, there are two arguments in Fiedler's favor. First, there is ample evidence that his theory does predict leadership effectiveness, even though the outcomes are imperfect. Second, Fiedler and his associates have clearly shown that leaders trained in the contingency model are rated as superior to comparable but untrained leaders. Studies demonstrating that subordinates of the trained leaders outperform the subordinates of untrained leaders are even more convincing. Thus, there is evidence that Fiedler's approach leads to *effective* (in Bass' terms) rather than simply "successful" leadership.

Despite these findings, Fiedler's view that leaders cannot learn to change their own behavior (but are limited to altering situations to fit their own styles) contradicts results from other leader training. Furthermore, most leaders are unlikely to engage in only one of the two primary behavioral dimensions. Thus, Fiedler's theory is something of a puzzle: it works (though not always well), but we do not know precisely why. Perhaps the training simply "raises the consciousness" of the leader, who is then able to take important situational variables into account and act appropriately. There is some evidence that this was true for a Managerial Grid® training experiment reported by Beer and Kleisath (1967). Managers gained a new "language" of leadership based on knowledge of behavioral science. This allowed them to communicate better and to work together more effectively.

We do not know whether managers know how to engage in participative leadership without training. Even if they do know how to elicit participation, we do not know how effective they are as leaders. To examine this issue, we must return to a study of the behavioral aspects of leadership, with the aim of defining *effective* leader behavior, not just attempted or even "successful" leadership.

Finch suggests that the task-centered aspect of leadership behavior be redefined. He argues that true participative leadership can be attained only if the leader moves away from the role of task-focused decision maker toward the role of *coordinator* of group and intergroup activities. Although this may seem to be a radical change, it may be just a logical extension of the relationship dimension of leadership behavior. That is, the effect may achieve more of a *balance* between the two behavioral dimensions by making the relationship dimension more explicit. Finch's ideas are fully consistent with Likert's "System 4" theory of organizations, which specifies that leadership is group centered, that the leader shares decision-making authority with the group, and that leaders act as representatives of the group (Likert, 1961, 1967).

Finch extends the Likert emphasis to a broader "sociotechnical systems" perspective (Pasmore & Sherwood, 1978), introducing the important element of *group* operation. This element has, until very recently, been neglected in organizational leadership research (Sashkin, 1982).

Application of leadership theories in complex organization has presented a dilemma. What we know to be valid (such as Fiedler's research data) does not seem very applicable, and that which seems very applicable (such as the Managerial Grid® or Situational Leadership™) has not yet been adequately validated. Perhaps we can take some comfort in Bennis' (1972) observation that McGregor believed not so much in the absolute truth of Theory X or Theory Y, but in the effects of managers' beliefs in—and behaviors consistent with—one or the other. That is, we often create "self-fulfilling prophecies." People behave as we expect. If we expect laziness and avoidance of work, that is what may result, just as responsible, achievement-centered performance may result if *that* is our expectation. Thus, the participative, Theory Y approach may work, *if* we believe it will and *act consistently* with that belief.

The authors in Part 2 repeatedly emphasize the participative approach. The articles about organizational leadership that have become increasingly crucial for the effective functioning of our society. Unless we can learn to do better at the basic tasks of leadership—organizing, developing, managing, and changing complex organizations—we may become incapable of meeting the human emotional and the rational productive needs of society.

References

Argyris, C. *Personality and organization*. New York: Harper & Row, 1957.

Bales, R.F. Task roles and social roles in problem-solving groups. In E.E. Maccoby, T.M. Newcomb, & E.L. Hartley (Eds.), *Readings in social psychology* (3rd ed.). New York: Holt, Rinehart & Winston, 1958.

Beer, M., & Kleisath, S. The effects of the Managerial Grid on organizational and leadership dimensions. Paper presented as part of a symposium, Research on the Impact of Using Different Laboratory Methods for Interpersonal and Organizational Change (S.S. Zalkind, Chairperson), presented at the annual meeting of the American Psychological Association, Washington, DC, September 1967.

Bennis, W. Chairman Mac in perspective. *Harvard Business Review*, September-October, 1972, 140-142, 144-145.

Blake, R.R., & Mouton, J.S. *The managerial grid*. Houston, TX: Gulf, 1964.

Blake, R.R., & Mouton, J.S. *The versatile manager*. Homewood, IL: Irwin, 1980.

Blake, R.R., & Mouton, J.S. Grid principles versus situationalism. *Group & Organization Studies*, 1982, 7, 211-215.

Blake, R.R., & Mouton, J.S. Management by Grid principles or situationalism: Which? *Group & Organization Studies*, 1981, 6, 439-455.

Blauner, R. *Alienation and freedom*. Chicago: University of Chicago Press, 1964.

Hackman, J.R., & Oldham, G.R. *Work redesign*. Reading, MA: Addison-Wesley, 1980.

Hersey, P., & Blanchard, K.H. Grid principles and situationalism: Both! *Group & Organization Studies*, 1982, 7, 207-210.

Likert, R. *New patterns of management*. New York: McGraw-Hill, 1961.

Likert, R. *The human organization*. New York: McGraw-Hill, 1967.

Maslow, A.H. A theory of human motivation. *Psychological Review*, 1943, 50, 370-396.

McGregor, D.M. The human side of enterprise. In *Adventures in thought and action* (Proceedings of the Fifth Anniversary Convocation of the School of Industrial Management, Massachusetts Institute of Technology, Cambridge, MA, April 9, 1957).

Pasmore, W., & Sherwood, J.J. *Sociotechnical systems*. San Diego, CA: University Associates, 1978.

Sashkin, M. *A manager's guide to participative management*. New York: American Management Associations, 1982.

Theory Y: The Integration of Individual and Organizational Goals

Douglas McGregor

To some, the...analysis [of Theory X] will appear unduly harsh. Have we not made major modifications in the management of the human resources of industry during the past quarter century? Have we not recognized the importance of people and made vitally significant changes in managerial strategy as a consequence? Do the developments since the twenties in personnel administration and labor relations add up to nothing?

There is no question that important progress has been made in the past two or three decades. During this period the human side of enterprise has become a major preoccupation of management. A tremendous number of policies, programs, and practices which were virtually unknown thirty years ago have become commonplace. The lot of the industrial employee—be he worker, professional, or executive—has improved to a degree which could hardly have been imagined by his counterpart of the nineteen twenties. Management has adopted generally a far more humanitarian set of values; it has successfully striven to give more equitable and more generous treatment to its employees. It has significantly reduced economic hardships, eliminated the more extreme forms of industrial warfare, provided a generally safe and pleasant working environment, *but it has done all these things without changing its fundamental theory of management.* There are exceptions here and there, and they are important; nevertheless, the assumptions of Theory X remain predominant throughout our economy.

Management was subjected to severe pressures during the Great Depression of the thirties. The wave of public antagonism, the open warfare accompanying the unionizations of the mass production industries, the general reaction against authoritarianism, the legislation of the New Deal produced a wide "pendulum swing." However, the changes in policy and practice which took place during that and the next decade were primarily adjustments to the increased power of organized labor and to the pressures of public opinion.

Some of the movement was away from "hard" and toward "soft" management, but it was short-lived, and for good reasons. It has become clear that many of the initial strategic interpretations accompanying the "human relations approach" were as naive as those which characterized the early stages of progressive education. We have now discovered that there is no answer in the simple removal of control— that abdication is not a workable alternative to authoritarianism. We have learned that there is no direct correlation between employee satisfaction and productivity. We recognize today that "industrial democracy" cannot consist in permitting everyone to decide everything, that industrial health does not flow automatically from the elimination of dissatisfaction, disagreement, or even open conflict. Peace is not synonymous with organizational health; socially responsible management is not co-extensive with permissive management.

Now that management has regained its earlier prestige and power, it has become obvious that the trend toward "soft" management was a temporary and relatively superficial reaction rather than a general modification of fundamental assumptions or basic strategy. Moreover, while the progress we have made in the past quarter century is substantial, it has reached the point of diminishing returns. The tactical possibilities within conventional managerial strategies have been pretty completely exploited, and significant new developments will be unlikely without major modifications in theory.

THE ASSUMPTIONS OF THEORY Y

There have been few dramatic break-throughs in social science theory like those which have occurred in the physical sciences during the past half century. Nevertheless, the accumulation of knowledge about human behavior in many specialized fields has made possible the formulation of a number of generalizations which provide a modest beginning for new theory with respect to the management of human resources.

1. *The expenditure of physical and mental effort in work is as natural as play or rest.* The average human being does not inherently dislike work. Depending upon controllable conditions, work may be a source of satisfaction (and will be voluntarily performed) or a source of punishment (and will be avoided if possible).

2. *External control and the threat of punishment are not the only means for bringing about effort toward organizational objectives. Man will exercise self-direction and self-control in the service of objectives to which he is committed.*

3. *Commitment to objectives is a function of the rewards associated with their achievement.* The most significant of such rewards, e.g., the satisfaction of ego and self-actualization needs, can be direct products of effort directed toward organizational objectives.

4. *The average human being learns, under proper conditions, not only to accept but to seek responsibility.* Avoidance of responsibility, lack of ambition, and emphasis on security are generally consequences of experience, not inherent human characteristics.

5. *The capacity to exercise a relatively high degree of imagination, ingenuity, and creativity in the solution of organizational problems is widely, not narrowly, distributed in the population.*

6. *Under the conditions of modern industrial life, the intellectual potentialities of the average human being are only partially utilized.*

These assumptions involve sharply different implications for managerial strategy than do those of Theory X. They are dynamic rather than static: They indicate the possibility of human growth and development; they stress the necessity for selective adaptation rather than for a single absolute form of control. They are not framed in terms of the least common denominator of the factory hand, but in terms of a resource which has substantial potentialities.

Above all, the assumptions of Theory Y point up the fact that the limits on human collaboration in the organizational setting are not limits of human nature but of management's ingenuity in discovering how to realize the potential represented by its human resources. Theory X offers management an easy rationalization for ineffective organizational performance: It is due to the nature of the human resources with which we must work. Theory Y, on the other hand, places the problems squarely in the lap of management. If employees are lazy, indifferent, unwilling to take responsibility, intransigent, uncreative, uncooperative, Theory Y implies that the causes lie in management's methods of organization and control.

The assumptions of Theory Y are not finally validated. Nevertheless, they are far more consistent with existing knowledge in the social sciences than are the assumptions of Theory X. They will undoubtedly be refined, elaborated, modified as further research accumulates, but they are unlikely to be completely contradicted.

On the surface, these assumptions may not seem particularly difficult to accept. Carrying their implications into practice, however, is not easy. They challenge a number of deeply ingrained managerial habits of thought and action.

THE PRINCIPLE OF INTEGRATION

The central principle of organization which derives from Theory X is that of direction and control through the exercise of authority—what has been called "the scalar principle." The central principle which derives from Theory Y is that of integration: The creation of conditions such that the members of the organization can achieve their own goals *best* by directing their efforts toward the success of the enterprise. These two principles have profoundly different implications with respect to the task of managing human resources, but the scalar principle is so firmly built into managerial attitudes that the implications of the principle of integration are not easy to perceive.

Someone once said that fish discover water last. The "psychological environment" of industrial management—like water for fish—is so much a part of organizational life that we are unaware of it. Certain characteristics of our society, and of organizational life within it, are so completely established, so pervasive, that we cannot conceive of their being otherwise. As a result, a great many policies and practices and decisions and relationships could only be—it seems—what they are.

Among these pervasive characteristics of organizational life in the United States today is a managerial attitude (stemming from Theory X) toward membership in the industrial organization. It is assumed almost without question that organizational requirements take precedence over the needs of individual members. Basically, the employment agreement is that in return for the rewards which are offered, the individual will accept external direction and control. The very idea of integration and self-control is foreign to our way of thinking about the employment relationship. The tendency, therefore, is either to reject it out of hand (as socialistic, or anarchistic, or inconsistent with human nature) or to twist it unconsciously until it fits existing conceptions.

The concept of integration and self-control carries the implication that the organization will be more effective in achieving its economic objectives if adjustments are made, in significant ways, to the needs and goals of its members.

A district manager in a large, geographically decentralized company is notified that he is being promoted to a policy level position at headquarters. It is a big promotion with a large salary increase. His role in the organization will be a much more powerful one, and he will be associated with the major executives of the firm.

The headquarters group who selected him for this position have carefully considered a number of possible candidates. This man stands out among them in a way which makes him the natural choice. His performance has been under observation for some time, and there is little question that he possesses the necessary qualifications, not only for this opening but for an even higher position. There is genuine satisfaction that such an outstanding candidate is available.

The man is appalled. He doesn't want the job. His goal, as he expresses it, is to be the "best damned district manager in the company." He enjoys his direct associations with operating people in the field, and he doesn't want a policy level job. He and his wife enjoy the kind of life they have created in a small city, and they dislike actively both the living conditions and the social obligations of the headquarters city.

He expresses his feelings as strongly as he can, but his objections are brushed aside. The organization's needs are such that his refusal to accept the promotion would be unthinkable. His superiors say to themselves that of course when he has settled in to the new job, he will recognize that it was the right thing. And so he makes the move.

Two years later he is in an even higher position in the company's headquarters organization, and there is talk that he will probably be the executive vice-president before long. Privately he expresses considerable unhappiness and dissatisfaction. He (and his wife) would "give anything" to be back in the situation he left two years ago.

Within the context of the pervasive assumptions of Theory X, promotions and transfers in large numbers are made by unilateral decision. The requirements of the organization are given priority automatically and almost without question. If the individual's personal goals are considered at all, it is assumed that the rewards of salary and position will satisfy him. Should an individual actually refuse such a move without a compelling reason, such as health or a severe family crisis, he would be considered to have jeopardized his future because of this "selfish" attitude. It is rare indeed for management to give the individual the opportunity to be a genuine and active partner in such a decision, even though it may affect his most important personal goals. Yet the implications following from Theory Y are that the organization is likely to suffer if it ignores these personal needs and goals. In making unilateral decisions with respect to promotion, management is failing to utilize its human resources in the most effective way.

The principle of integration demands that both the organization's and the individual's needs be recognized. Of course, when there is a sincere joint effort to find it, an integrative solution which meets the needs of the individual *and* the organization is a frequent outcome. But not always—and this is the point at which Theory Y begins to appear unrealistic. It collides head on with pervasive attitudes associated with management by direction and control.

The assumptions of Theory Y imply that unless integration is achieved *the organization will suffer*. The objectives of the organization are *not* achieved best by the unilateral administration of promotions, because this form of management by direction and control will not create the commitment which would make available the full resources of those affected. The lesser motivation, the lesser resulting degree of self-direction and self-control are costs which, when added up for many instances over time, will more than offset the gains obtained by unilateral decisions "for the good of the organization."

One other example will perhaps clarify the sharply different implications of Theory X and Theory Y.

It could be argued that management is already giving a great deal of attention to the principle of integration through its efforts in the field of economic education. Many millions of dollars and much ingenuity have been expended in attempts to persuade employees that their welfare is intimately connected with the success of the free enterprise system and of their own companies. The idea that they can achieve their own goals best by directing their effort toward the objectives of the organization has been explored and developed and communicated in every possible way. Is this not evidence that management is already committed to the principle of integration?

The answer is a definite no. These managerial efforts, with rare exceptions, reflect clearly the influence of the assumptions of Theory X. The central message is an exhortation to the industrial employee to work hard and follow orders in order to protect his job and his standard of living. Much has been achieved, it says, by our established way of running industry, and much more could be achieved if employees would adapt themselves to management's definition of what is required. Behind these exhortations lies the expectation that of course the requirements of the organization and its economic success must have priority over the needs of the individual.

Naturally, integration means working together for the success of the enterprise so we all may share in the resulting rewards. But management's implicit assumption is that working together means adjusting to the requirements of the organization as management perceives them. In terms of existing views, it seems inconceivable that individuals, seeking their own goals, would further the ends of the enterprise. On the contrary, this would lead to anarchy, chaos, irreconcilable conflicts of self-interest, lack of responsibility, inability to make decisions, and failure to carry out those that were made.

All these consequences, and other worse ones, would be inevitable unless conditions could be created such that the members of the organization perceived that they could achieve their own goals best by directing their efforts toward the success of the enterprise. If the assumptions of Theory Y are valid, the practical question is whether, and to what extent, such conditions can be created.

THE APPLICATION OF THEORY Y

In the physical sciences there are many theoretical phenomena which cannot be achieved in practice. Absolute zero and a perfect vacuum are examples. Others, such as nuclear power, jet aircraft, and human space flight, are recognized theoretically to be possible long before they become feasible. This fact does not make theory less useful. If it were not for our theoretical convictions, we would not even be attempting to develop the means for human flight into space today. In fact, were it not for the development of physical science theory during the past century and a half, we would still be depending upon the horse and buggy and the sailing vessel for transportation. Virtually all significant technological developments wait on the formulation of relevant theory.

Similarly, in the management of the human resources of industry, the assumptions and theories about human nature at any given time limit innovation. Possibilities are not recognized, innovating efforts are not undertaken, until theoretical conceptions lay a groundwork for them. Assumptions like those of Theory X permit us to conceive of certain possible ways of organizing and directing human effort, but not others. Assumptions like those of Theory Y open up a range of possibilities for new managerial policies and practices. As in the case of the development of new physical science theory, some of these possibilities are not immediately feasible, and others may forever remain unattainable. They may be too costly, or it may be that we simply cannot discover how to create the necessary "hardware."

There is substantial evidence for the statement that the potentialities of the average human being are far above those which we typically realize in industry today. If our assumptions are like those of Theory X, we will not even recognize the existence of those potentialities and there will be no reason to devote time, effort, or money to discovering how to realize them. If, however, we accept assumptions like those of Theory Y, we will be challenged to innovate, to discover new ways of organizing and directing human effort, even though we recognize that the perfect organization, like the perfect vacuum, is practically out of reach.

We need not be overwhelmed by the dimensions of the managerial task implied by Theory Y. To be sure, a large mass production operation in which the workers have been organized by a militant and hostile union faces management with problems which appear at present to be insurmountable with respect to the application of the principle of integration. It may be decades before sufficient knowledge will have accumulated to make such an application feasible. Applications of Theory Y will have to be tested initially in more limited ways and under more favorable circumstances. However, a number of applications of Theory Y in managing managers and professional people are possible today. Within the managerial hierarchy, the assumptions can be tested and refined, techniques can be invented and skill acquired in their use. As knowledge accumulates, some of the problems of application at the worker level in large organizations may appear less baffling than they do at present.

Perfect integration of organizational requirements and individual goals and needs is, of course, not a realistic objective. In adopting this principle, we seek that degree of integration in which the individual can achieve his goals best by directing his efforts toward the success of the organization. "Best" means that this alternative will be more attractive than the many others available to him: indifference, irresponsibility, minimal compliance, hostility, sabotage. It means that he will continuously be encouraged to develop and utilize voluntarily his capacities, his knowledge, his skill, his ingenuity in ways which contribute to the success of the enterprise.[1]

Acceptance of Theory Y does not imply abdication or "soft" management, or "permissiveness." As was indicated above, such notions stem from the acceptance of authority as the single means of managerial control, and from attempts to minimize its negative consequences. Theory Y assumes that people will exercise self-direction and self-control in the achievement of organizational objectives to the degree that they are committed to those objectives. If that commitment is small, only a slight degree of self-direction and self-control will be likely, and a substantial amount of external influence will be necessary. If it is large, many conventional external controls will be relatively superfluous, and to some extent self-defeating. Managerial policies and practices materially affect this degree of commitment.

Authority is an inappropriate means for obtaining commitment to objectives. Other forms of influence—help in achieving integration, for example—are required for this purpose. Theory Y points to the possibility of lessening the emphasis on external forms of control to the degree that commitment to organizational objectives can be achieved. Its underlying assumptions emphasize the capacity of human beings for self-control, and the consequent possibility of greater managerial reliance on the other means of influence. Nevertheless, it is clear that authority is an appropriate means for control under certain circumstances—particularly where genuine commitment to objectives cannot be achieved. The assumptions of Theory Y do not deny the appropriateness of authority, but they do deny that it is appropriate for all persons and under all circumstances.

Many statements have been made to the effect that we have acquired today the know-how to cope with virtually any technological problems which may arise, and that the major industrial advances of the next half century will occur on the human side of enterprise. Such advances, however, are improbable so long as management continues to organize and direct and control its human resources on the basis of assumptions—tacit or explicit—like those of Theory X. Genuine innovation, in contrast to a refurbishing and patching of present managerial strategies, requires first the acceptance of less limiting assumptions about the nature of the human resources we seek to control, and second the readiness to adapt selectively to the implications contained in those new assumptions. Theory Y is an invitation to innovation.

Note

[1] A recent, highly significant study of the sources of job satisfaction and dissatisfaction among managerial and professional people suggests that these opportunities for "self-actualization" are the essential requirements of both job satisfaction and high performance. The researchers find that "the wants of employees divide into two groups. One group revolves around the need to develop in one's occupation as a source of personal growth. The second group operates as an essential base to the first and is associated with fair treatment in compensation, supervision, working conditions, and administrative practices. *The fulfillment of the needs of the second group does not motivate the individual to high levels of job satisfaction and...to extra performance on the job.* All we can expect from satisfying (this second group of needs) is the prevention of dissatisfaction and poor job performance." Frederick Herzberg, Bernard Mausner, and Barbara Bloch Snyderman, *The Motivation to Work.* New York: John Wiley, 1959, pp. 114-115. (Italics mine.)

An Overview of the Grid®

Robert R. Blake and Jane Srygley Mouton

Dramatic changes are occurring in the way Americans handle their affairs. This is true across the spectrum, from commercial firms to government agencies, to schools and universities. What these are, and how they can be met and brought under management is discussed below.

BREAKDOWN OF AUTHORITY AND OBEDIENCE

In the past, bosses could exercise work-or-starve authority over their subordinates. They expected and got obedience from them. Authority-obedience was the basis for supervision that built pyramids, big ships, great armies and that made Prussia famous.

But authority-obedience as a way of life has been under greater and greater attack for the past hundred years. Though wars tended to bring it back, during peacetime it became more and more objectionable as a basis for getting people to cooperate. But today, in an environment of vastly improved education and of relative affluence, many are rejecting traditional authority and trying to set up and act upon their own.

Reprinted from R.R. Blake and J.S. Mouton, "An Overview of the Grid®," *Training and Development Journal*, 1975, 29(5), 29-37. Used by permission of the authors and publisher. Copyright © 1975 by Robert R. Blake and Jane Srygley Mouton.

The year 1968 might be taken as the beginning of the end for authority-obedience as the control mechanism of American society. That was the year when Detroit and Watts burned. It was when young people were burning their draft cards and dodging the draft by heading for Canada, Sweden and elsewhere. And it was when several universities' presidents were held as hostages in their offices. Furthermore, truancy, runaways and drug problems tell us that the old family pattern where father was boss and the children complied with his authority has crumbled too.

The 1964 Civil Rights Act put society on notice that equality, not authority and obedience, was to be the basis for race relations in the future. Other federal legislation established standards for organizations to be more responsible for the safety of their employees, for their customers and for the everyday citizen as well. Understanding all this new-found and partly enforced equality and social justice and the motivations that underlie it is important for comprehending the new day that is emerging.

These many influences tell us as far as bosses and subordinates are concerned that authority and obedience is no longer the name of the game.

The new relationship between a "boss" and a "subordinate" is such that they seek to reach mutual understanding and agreement as to the course of action to be taken, as well as how to go about it. Before coming to any conclusion on the "how," though, the *main* alternative ways of managing will be presented. First examined is how management occurs under an authority-obedience system and its strengths and weaknesses. Then the "love conquers all" proposition will be considered. This is where the boss says, "If my subordinates love me, they'll do what I want without me having to tell them."

Then those hard-to-notice managers who are doing the least amount to get by on a "see no evil, speak no evil, hear no evil" basis will be viewed. Next to be described is the "halfway is far enough" manager who deals with problems by compromise, adjustment, and accommodation of differences, by being willing to do what's "practical." Finally the possibility already introduced, seeking for excellence through getting the highest possible involvement-participation-com-mitment to organization purpose up and down the line, is evaluated.

THE GRID®

The Grid is a way of sorting out all these possibilities and seeing how each compares with the others. What is involved is this:

The Grid, shown in Figure 1, clarifies and crystallizes many of the different possible ways of supervision. Here is the basis of it. Any person who is working has some assigned responsibilities. This is true whether he or she works very low on the job ladder or high up in the organization. There are two

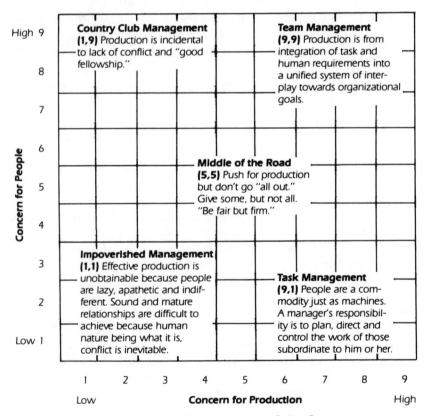

Figure 1. The Managerial Grid

matters on his or her mind whenever acting as a manager. One is production—getting results, or accomplishing the mission. How intensely he or she thinks about results can be described as a degree of concern for production. On the Grid, the horizontal axis stands for concern for production. It is a nine-point scale where 9 shows high concern for production and 1, low concern.

A manager is also thinking about those whose work he or she directs, because he or she has to get results through people. The Grid's vertical axis represents this concern for people. This, too, is on a nine-point scale with 9 a high degree and 1 a low degree.

The Grid identifies these two concerns. It does so in a way that enables a person to see how the two concerns interact. Various "theories" are found at points of intersection of the two scales. Whether he or she realizes it or not, these are theories that different managers use when they think about how to get results through people. Five of the many possible theories or styles of management mentioned earlier stand out clearly. They appear in the four corners and in the center of the Grid.

Going Around the Grid

As can be seen from the Grid figure, in the lower right corner, 9,1 represents a great deal of concern for output but little for the people who are expected to produce. 9,1 is the authority-obedience theory. At the opposite corner of the Grid, the top left, is the 1,9 theory. It's the "love conquers all" approach. In the lower left Grid corner is 1,1. It might seem odd that a manager could have almost no concern for either production or people. He or she goes through the motions of being part of the organization but is not really contributing to it. But such managers do exist, even though they may not be easy to notice until you know their theory. They are not doers but free-loaders, getting by on a "speak no, hear no, see no evil" basis. They have not physically quit the firm, but they walked out mentally, perhaps many years ago.

In the center is the 5,5 style. The manager with this approach is going up the middle of the road. His or her attitude is "Get results but don't kill yourself! Don't push too much or you will be seen as a 'hard nose.' Don't let people off too easily or they will think you are soft. Be fair but firm. Do the job but find a comfortable tempo." The 5,5 manager is an "organization man."

The upper right corner, the 9,9 position, is high concern for production united with high concern for people. A person who manages according to this theory stresses understanding and agreement through involvement-participation-commitment as the key to solving boss-subordinate problems. Whenever disagreements arise, he or she sees to it that facts are examined. The problem is thrashed through to solution in an open and aboveboard way that can result in mutual understanding with full commitment to conclusions reached. People working together in a 9,9 manner know that they have a common stake in the outcome of their endeavors. They mesh effort in an interdependent way. The 9,9 theory doesn't abide by the laws of simple arithmetic. On the joining of contributions, "one" plus "one" can add up to "three."

You may have figured out that there are 81 combinations of concerns represented on the Grid. Adjacent to 9,1 are 8,2 and 7,3. And 1,9 has 2,8 and 3,7 near it. There are 3,3, 4,4, 6,6, 7,7 along the diagonal between 1,1 and 9,9 and so on. But our main emphasis is on the theories in the corners and at the middle of the Grid. These are the most distinct styles. They're the ones you see most often. But you might think of a Grid style as you do shades of hair—black, brown, red, blond and white.

Within each hair shade there's a variety—for example, twenty-seven different ways to be blond—yet on your driver's license the outstanding feature is enough for identification. The five main Grid styles, too, are broadly descriptive. We'll use them in much the same way. While talking about 9,1, remember it's just a tinge away to 8,2 or 7,3, or a halftone or so to 6,4, but all these neighboring combinations describe behavior in broadly similar ways.

Basic Assumptions

Grid theories describe sets of basic assumptions under which people deal with one another. An *assumption* is what you take for granted as being true or reliable. Maybe you learned most of your present-day assumptions as you grew up. "I have to be...(a tough character or nice person)...to get what I want," illustrates some assumptions from childhood that persist. In supervision they lay down the pathway of the boss' everyday approach. Managers act on the assumptions they hold even though it may be rare for you to put them into words. The same set of assumptions usually underlies a whole range of attitudes and activities.

For example, a 1,9-oriented boss who wants to please subordinates may be quite inventive in finding all sorts of ways to show personal warmth. His or her behavior may not be so simple as to say "I appreciate you and everything you do" 25 times a day, but, nonetheless, the subordinate dominates his or her thoughts and concerns. His or her subordinate might say, "I never know what nice surprise the boss will think up next," and yet the manager's core assumptions are remarkably consistent—to please his or her subordinate and win their appreciation.

Were persons to act without assumptions, their behavior would be random, purposeless; it would make no sense in any predictable way. Even so, it is not enough just to have a set of assumptions—any old set. Faulty assumptions can ruin a manager. More reliable ones can enhance his or her work and enrich his or her life on the job, not to mention elsewhere. When a person acting under any set of assumptions understands them, this Grid knowledge can aid him or her to predict what the impact of his or her behavior will be on colleagues and subordinates. Thus, learning the Grid framework will help you understand what kinds of actions are likely to lead to what kinds of results.

"Dominants" and "Backups"

Does a manager have just one Grid style strategy or does he or she skip over the surface of the Grid, shifting and adapting according to how he or she sees the situation?

All but a very few do have characteristic styles which, presently, they are using most of the time. Let's call this the manager's *dominant* style. Each boss' basic approach resembles one that is founded on either 9,1; 1,9; 5,5; 1,1; or 9,9 assumptions. How can the idea that a person has a dominant Grid style be squared with the fact that people observably do shift and change? It can be understood in the following way. Not only does a supervisor have a dominant style, he or she also has a back-up strategy, and sometimes a third strategy to fall back on even beyond the second way of operating.

The back-up strategy is likely to show when a manager runs up against difficulty in using the dominant strategy. A back-up Grid strategy is the one he or she falls back on, particularly when feeling the strain of tension, frustration or conflict. This can happen when initial efforts meet nothing but resistance or when, at the point of getting down to working on a project the subordinate's enthusiasm turns to stubborn reluctance.

Apparent complexity, when you first encounter it, can be confusing. Maybe you have played with a kaleidoscope. It contains bits of glass, not many, of different shapes and colors, and these can arrange themselves in an endless variety of patterns that you see reflected from its mirrors. Children are fascinated yet bewildered by this. When the key to understanding has been found, however, what previously appeared bewildering now makes sense.

Any Grid style can be a back-up to any other. For example, even a 1,9-oriented manager, when sharply challenged, might turn stubborn and go 9,1. Again, a person who normally deals in a 9,9 way may meet continued resistance from a subordinate. Unable to find a way of getting on to an action basis with him or her, he or she may shift to a 5,5 approach, negotiating for some kind of compromise where both boss and subordinate will be partially satisfied.

There are no natural links between one particular Grid style and another in terms of dominant-to-back-up. It all depends on the individual and his or her situation. You may sometimes see a person who habitually comes on in a 9,1 way, pressing hard for a time, then breaking off, crestfallen. He or she has switched to a different set of assumptions and moved back to a 1,1 state of resignation, feeling a sense of powerlessness, feeling that he or she is a victim of hostile fate. Who knows, had he or she used a different style from the beginning, or another set of back-up assumptions, and continued talking with the subordinate, he or she might have gotten the reaction desired.

The 9,9 approach is acknowledged by managers as the soundest way to achieve excellence. This conclusion has been verified from studies throughout the U.S. and around the world. The 9,9 theory defines a model that people say with conviction they want, not only for a guide to their own conduct but also as a model of what they want their organization and agencies to become.

That's what the Grid is. The Grid can be used to investigate how a boss supervises in everyday work. There are many boss-subordinate issues that can be looked at in this way. How boss and subordinate communicate is one. Another is the manner in which the boss gives work directions. Others involve managing mistakes, dealing with complaints, and how the boss reacts to hostile feelings.

Successful Leadership: Managerial Achievement

Jay Hall and Susan M. Donnell

THE ACHIEVING MANAGER RESEARCH PROJECT

The Achieving Manager Research Project focused on five major areas of the management process: (1) managers' values and beliefs regarding the nature of those they manage; (2) managerial and subordinate motivational phenomena; (3) managers' use of participative practices and their related involvement effects as reported by their subordinates; (4) the issue of interpersonal competence, as reported by managers themselves and judged by their subordinates; and (5) managerial style, that cluster of behaviors resulting from all the former. These were taken as a basis for a social technology of management as it has been developed in the literature. Instrumentation involved the use of eight standardized and validated paper and pencil surveys, each based on a prominent behavioral science model of managerial and human functioning.

Pilot studies with over 5000 male managers were conducted and the present investigation involved 12,000 or more. All organizational levels, the full range of pertinent ages, and over 50 actual organizations—ranging from automotive, retail,

Excerpted and reprinted from Jay Hall and Susan M. Donnell, "Managerial Achievement: The Personal Side of Behavioral Theory," *Human Relations,* 1979, 32(1), 77-101. Copyright © 1979, Tavistock Institute of Human Relations. Adapted and used by permission of the authors and publisher, Plenum Publishing Corporation.

and drug firms to the federal government, non-profit social agencies, and research and development types—are represented. Blind sampling procedures were used, with most of the data collected and supplied by the organizations' own personnel, and statistical analyses were conducted by an independent third party[1]—steps designed to minimize the effects of researcher bias. In each research instance, managers were assigned to High, Average, or Low Managerial Achievement groups after assessment and on the basis of an objective and standardized grouping formula.

IDENTIFYING THE ACHIEVING MANAGER

Attempts at measuring managerial achievement evoke the perennial criterion problem. Whereas Ghiselli (1963) presented a good case for the use of subjective criteria, we desired a more objective index which incidentally incorporated those criteria subjectively used as reference points by managers themselves. A straightforward exemplary-case criterion, for example, was rejected because, although quite objective in a post facto sense, to study only those of high organizational rank would obscure potential for achievement while saying nothing to questions regarding the Low Achiever and his possible use of counterproductive behaviors. Purely subjective appraisals, on the other hand, often reflect cultural biases which might or might not relate to achievement in a generic sense. A broad yet rigorous and culture-free index of managerial achievement was needed.

A Formula for Measuring Achievement

For our measure of managerial achievement, we chose a variation of the formula developed by Dr. Benjamin Rhodes and used by Blake and Mouton (1964) in their study of managerial style as related to career accomplishment. The Rhodes *Managerial Achievement Quotient* (MAQ) affords an evaluation of an individual's career progress in light of his chronological age, taking into account the number of career moves necessary to reach the top of a typical organization and the age span most germane to career planning.

Whereas Blake and Mouton conducted their study in a single organization and were able to specify eight different levels of organizational rank, such precision seemed unfeasible in a study involving a wide range of organizations. Therefore, broadness of managerial representation and cultural range was purchased at the expense of precision by lowering the number of rank discriminations in the Rhodes index. As a generic index of managerial achievement, the following formula was used:

$$MAQ = \frac{5(6 - Rank)}{Age} \times 100$$

In the numerator, the number 5 is a constant progression factor representing the time in grade per number of career moves available if one were to spend his 40 year work life in an eight-level organization and reflecting potential mobility upward in the absence of any other forces such as politics, seniority, chance, etc. Also in the numerator, the quantity (6 − Rank) amounts to a rank index obtained by assigning numerical values of 1 to 5 to organizational levels ranging from top (L1) to nonmanagement (L5) and subtracting from the correction factor of 6. In the denominator, Age (20 to 50 years) represents a seniority index; the time, given a standard entry age of 20 and an upper cutoff of 50 beyond which age is not a factor, in which an individual might advance from lowest to highest organizational level if advancement were purely mechanical. Finally, the constant multiplier of 100 is used to eliminate decimals.

Normative Data Base for the MAQ

So that there might be confidence in both the selection mechanism and the cutoff points chosen to differentiate individuals of High, Average, and Low Managerial Achievement, demographic data necessary for computing the MAQ were collected on a base sample of 5451 male managers. All organizational levels, from nonmanagement supervisory personnel to Chief Executive Officer, ages from 19 to 64, and 26 different types of organizations were represented. MAQ raw scores ranged from 9 to 109.15. The average manager in this base sample had an MAQ of 39.4; he was approximately 38 years old and occupied a middle (L3) management position.

Raw scores were transformed to normalized standard scores with a mean of 50 and a standard deviation of 10 (Veldman, 1967), affording a control for bias and allowing us to categorize managers with standardized MAQs of 60 or above as High Achievers, 41 to 59 as Average Achievers, and those with 40 or below as Low Achievers. Finally, a number of pilot studies were conducted to determine the sensitivity and discriminant power of the index and their results confirmed the standardized MAQ as a robust and reliable indicator of managerial achievement.

MANAGERIAL ACHIEVEMENT AND PARTICIPATIVE MANAGEMENT

Employment of participative practices has long been con- sidered a point of departure among managers of differing persuasions as well as among management theorists. And whereas the efficacy of the participative approach vis-à-vis organizational effectiveness has been demonstrated (Coch & French, 1948; Marrow, 1972; Marrow, Bowers, & Seashore, 1967), no apparent attempt has been made to link reliance on such an approach to managerial achievement or career accomplishment. Theory lends itself to an implicit hypothesis that achievement and reliance on participative management might well covary significantly; to test this notion, a study was made of subordinate perceptions of and reactions to man- agers' participative or nonparticipative practices.

Subjects and Instrumentation

The assumption was made in this study that it is the subordi- nate who is best equipped to report on his manager's use of participative practices and his own resulting feelings. There- fore, the Personal Reaction Index (Hall, 1971) was adminis- tered to over 2000 subordinates of 731 managers in 18 types of organizations. The PRI assesses the degree to which the manager allows a subordinate to participate in making and encourages him to influence work-related decisions. It also gauges feelings flowing from such opportunities; affectual factors such as job satisfaction, sense of personal responsi- bility, commitment, pride in work, and frustration level which, when combined, reflect the kind of work climate the manager creates. The Spearman-Brown item-test estimate of reliability for this participation-involvement index has been found to be .68. In the present study, the mean subordinate score for each manager was used as a measure for that manager and the data were separated into three MAQ groups; 214 mean subordinate scores for Low Achievers, 417 for Average Achievers, and 100 for High Achievers.

Results and Discussion

A sophisticated form of analysis showed that the three achievement groups differed significantly with respect to their subordinates' self-reported feelings of participative involvement (p<.01). Breaking out the components of the involvement score, the greatest differences occurred with respect to feelings of participation, satisfaction with participation, commitment, and quality of decisions. On all of these, the higher the manager's achievement (MAQ) score, the more positive the subordinates' responses.

Figure 1 shows the mean subordinates' participation score for each of the three achievement groups into which the managers were divided. Subordinates perceive dramatic differences among managers of varying achievement with respect to their use of participative methods. Low Achievers,

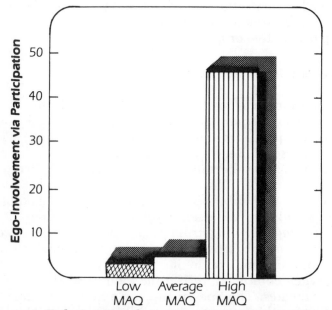

Figure 1. Relative Employment of Participative Practices by Managers of High, Average, and Low Achievement as Reported by Their Subordinates

according to their subordinates, offer very few opportunities to participate and Average Achievers offer only slightly more. However, High Achievers are reported to employ participative practices to such a greater extent that participative management may be said to be a major characteristic of the High Achieving Group.

The pattern of root correlations and discriminant weights indicates that the significant dimension compromises both participative opportunity and feeling data; it is best interpreted as an index of total ego involvement. In this light, only the subordinates of High Achievers may be found to enjoy the satisfaction and commitment that characterize a healthy organizational climate. Low Achievers, and to some extent Average Achievers, are reported by their subordinates to employ practices which repress and frustrate subordinate personnel. And so the manager's use of participative practices also emerges as a significant factor in managerial achievement with noteworthy implications for organizational well-being as well.

MANAGERIAL ACHIEVEMENT AND MANAGERIAL STYLE

Argyris (1962) has stressed interpersonal competence primarily as it relates to organizational effectiveness; questions regarding the possible link between competence and the effective management of production-centered, as well as interpersonal, facets of the organization naturally arise. Studies by Hall (1973) have confirmed a relationship between level of interpersonal competence and preferred manner for managing the people-production interface within the organization, and Blake and Mouton (1964) have reported that managerial style may also be linked to managerial achievement. In the Blake and Mouton study, however, no information was given regarding statistical procedures or levels of confidence and, since the study involved the ratings of co-members of seminar groups within a single organization, we have no assurance that the results are not merely cultural artifacts.

To achieve a more generic and realistic treatment, therefore, a multivariate study of managerial style as it relates to achievement was conducted with both managers and their subordinates in 23 types of organizations.

Subjects and Instrumentation

The Hall, Harvey, and Williams (1963) Styles of Management Inventory (SMI) was administered to 1878 managers. The SMI is based on the Blake-Mouton managerial grid model; it generates five scores—one per style—and measures the manager's strength of emphasis and responsiveness to task demands vis-à-vis social concerns. The median test-related coefficient of the SMI has been found to range from .69 to .74 over a 6 week period. The managerial SMI data were divided into three groups as follows: 445 Low Achievers, 1243 Average Achievers, and 190 High Achievers.

The Management Appraisal Survey (Hall, Harvey, & Williams, 1970), a companion instrument with reliability comparable to the SMI's wherein subordinates rate the style practices of their managers, was administered to 2024 subordinates. MAS scores were assigned to the appropriate manager for grouping by MAQ, yielding 505 subordinates of Low Achievers, 1197 of Average Achievers, and 322 of High Achievers.

Results and Discussion

Manager and subordinate data were analyzed separately. The SMI results showed a strong and significant ($p<.0002$) pattern differentiating managers according to their MAQ (achievement) scores. High achievers disliked a low-risk, bureaucratic, defensive management style, while the low achievers favored such a style. The high achievers showed a preference for an integrative pattern, with equally high concern for task and for social issues. The average achiever group did not have a clear preference of style, but seemed to dislike any style devoted primarily to maintaining the human system.

Further, the subordinate reports showed highly significant ($p<.0001$) differences in subordinate ratings of managerial style—again in terms of the manager's MAQ (achievement score). One major difference was in the manager's attention to task demands; the other was in terms of concern for quality of manager-subordinate relationships. These two factors conform closely to the task and the relationship dimensions of managerial behavior.

Because the study identified two dimensions, it is possible to plot the average scores for subordinates whose managers fit into each of the three achievement (MAQ) groups. Such a plot is shown in Figure 2, in which we define four general regions or styles of management: Low Task-Low Relationship, High Task-Low Relationship, Low Task-High Relationship, and High Task-High Relationship. Our labels are qualitative, capturing the general focus of a given cluster of practices; whether or not such a style corresponds to a Blake 9,9 or a Likert System 2, for example, is far less important than the significant differences found in the manner in which High, Average, and Low Achievers are perceived to approach management dynamics.

In essence, as the subordinate centroids graphically capture, subordinates and their managers tend to agree: a collaborative participative High Task-High Relationship managerial style typifies High Achievers who integrate maximum

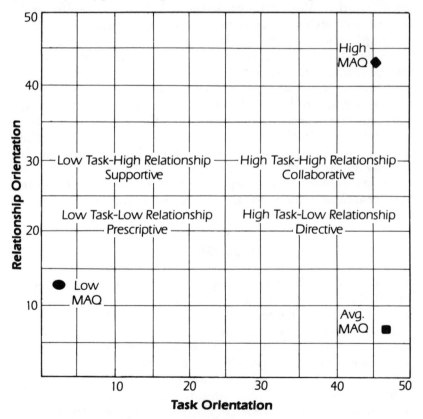

Figure 2. Managerial Styles of High, Average, and Low Achieving Managers as Reported by Their Subordinates

concern for task and relationship demands; Average Achievers, too preoccupied with production goals to adequately attend to people problems, appear to favor High Task-Low Relationship practices which are directive and self-authorizing; the Low Achievers' mechanical, prescriptive approach to the management process—evinced as Low Task-Low Relationship—makes sense in light of his motivational profile and social competencies.

These results tend to replicate those obtained by Blake and Mouton (1964) insofar as their overall implications are concerned; choice of management style does covary significantly with achievement status. The significance of specific styles, whether as dominant or back-up strategies, is less clear since the two-dimensional structure which emerged does not correspond to the Blake grid. Indeed, it is the multivariate interplay of styles which is captured in the present study and the implications of this are best appreciated against a backdrop of the managerial beliefs, motivational phenomena, interpersonal competencies, etc., portrayed in earlier sections. Style per se, it would appear, does not stand alone very well as a meaningful predictor of achievement any more than, say, participative practices. At issue is what the person does who is oriented to a High Task-High Relationship or some other posture and this question is best answered in reference to the posture. Style treatments, therefore, serve primarily as summary statements of a complex of sentiments, predilections, and practices which covary in determining one's level of managerial achievement.

DISCUSSION

The results of the studies reported support the normative implications of the models employed at a personal level. The intent here has not been the usual one of testing the applicability of social-industrial constructs to total systems. Our aim was to explore the relationship of those behavioral science values and practices typically aimed at organizational dynamics to the very personal and individual issue of managerial achievement. Our results suggest rather strongly that the teachings of Argyris (1957, 1962), Blake and Mouton (1964), Herzberg (1966), Likert (1961, 1967), Marrow (1967, 1972), Maslow (1954, 1965), and McGregor (1960) do apply at the individual level and are worthy of credibility among managers concerned with their own career progress. Although few of the theorists upon whose work our studies are based have ventured opinions about the personal significance of their theories for career growth, it would appear that those who achieve are in fact doing in their management essentially what applied behavioral thought would prescribe. Conversely, those who fail to achieve are found in the present studies to violate most of the same tenets. The major import of this series of studies, therefore, would seem to be neither one of alternative discovery nor theory validation so much as a refinement of applicability.

Note

[1]The authors are indebted to Dr. Hugh Poyner, now with Kirschner Associates in Washington, D.C., who conducted all statistical analyses for the present studies while at the University of Texas at Austin.

References

Argyris, C. *Personality and organization*. New York: Harper & Row, 1957.

Argyris, C. *Interpersonal competence and organizational effectiveness*. Homewood, IL: Dorsey Press, 1962.

Blake, R.R., & Mouton, J.S. *The managerial grid*. Houston: Gulf, 1964.

Coch, L., & French, J.R.P. Overcoming resistance to change. *Human Relations*, 1948, *1*(4), 512-532.

Ghiselli, E.E. Managerial talent. *American Psychologist*, 1963, *18*(10), 631-642.

Hall, J. *Personal reaction index*. Conroe, TX: Teleometrics International, 1971.

Hall, J. Communication revisited. *California Management Review*, 1973, *15*(3), 56-67.

Hall, J., Harvey, J.B., & Williams, M.S. *Styles of management inventory*. Conroe, TX: Teleometrics International, 1963.

Hall, J., Harvey, J.B., & Williams, M.S. *Management appraisal survey*. Conroe, TX: Teleometrics International, 1970.

Herzberg, F. *Work and the nature of man*. New York: John Wiley, 1966.

Likert, R. *New patterns of management*. New York: McGraw-Hill, 1961.

Likert, R. *The human organization*. New York: McGraw-Hill, 1967.

Marrow, A.J. (Ed.). *The failure of success*. New York: AMACOM, 1972.

Marrow, A.J., Bowers, D.G., & Seashore, S.E. *Management by participation*. New York: Harper & Row, 1967.

Maslow, A. *Personality and motivation*. New York: Harper & Row, 1954.

Maslow, A. *Eupsychian management*. Homewood, IL: Richard D. Irwin and Dorsey Press, 1965.

McGregor, D. *The human side of enterprise*. New York: McGraw-Hill, 1960.

An Introduction to Situational Leadership™

Paul Hersey and Kenneth H. Blanchard

The recognition of task and relationships as two important dimensions of leader behavior has pervaded the works of management theorists[1] over the years. These two dimensions have been variously labeled as "autocratic" and "democratic"; "authoritarian" and "equalitarian"; "employee-oriented" and "production-oriented"; "goal achievement" and "group maintenance"; "task-ability" and "likeability"; "instrumental and expressive"; "efficiency and effectiveness." The difference between these concepts and task and relationships seems to be more semantic than real.

For some time, it was believed that task and relationships were either/or styles of leader behavior and, therefore, should be depicted as a single dimension along a continuum, moving from very authoritarian (task) leader behavior at one end to very democratic (relationships) leader behavior at the other.[2]

OHIO STATE LEADERSHIP STUDIES

In more recent years, the feeling that task and relationships were either/or leadership styles has been dispelled. In particular, the leadership studies initiated in 1945 by the Bureau of Business Research at Ohio State University[3] questioned whether leader behavior could be depicted on a single continuum.

In attempting to describe *how* a leader carries out his activities, the Ohio State staff identified "Initiating Structure" (task) and "Consideration" (relationships) as the two most important dimensions of leadership. "Initiating Structure" refers to "the leader's behavior in delineating the relationship between himself and members of the work-group and in endeavoring to establish well-defined patterns of organization, channels of communication, and methods of procedure." On the other hand, "Consideration" refers to "behavior indicative of friendship, mutual trust, respect, and warmth in the relationship between the leader and the members of his staff."[4]

In the leadership studies that followed, the Ohio State staff found that leadership styles vary considerably from leader to leader. The behavior of some leaders is characterized by rigidly structuring activities of followers in terms of *task* accomplishments, while others concentrate on building and maintaining good personal *relationships* between themselves and their followers. Other leaders have styles characterized by both task and relationships behavior. There are even some individuals in leadership positions whose behavior tends to provide little structure or development of interpersonal relationships. No dominant style appears. Instead, various combinations are evident. Thus, task and relationships are not either/or leadership styles as an authoritarian-democratic continuum suggests. Instead, these patterns of leader behavior are separate and distinct dimensions which can be plotted on two separate axes, rather than a single continuum. Thus, the Ohio State studies resulted in the development of four quadrants to illustrate leadership styles in terms of Initiating Structure (task) and Consideration (relationships) as shown in Figure 1.

Concern for *production* is illustrated on the horizontal axis. Production becomes more important to the leader as his rating advances on the horizontal scale. A leader with a rating of 9 has a maximum concern for production.

Concern for people is illustrated on the vertical axis. People become more important to the leader as his rating progesses up the vertical axis. A leader with a rating of 9 on the vertical axis has a maximum concern for people.

The Managerial Grid, in essence has given popular terminology to five points within the four quadrants identified by the Ohio State studies.

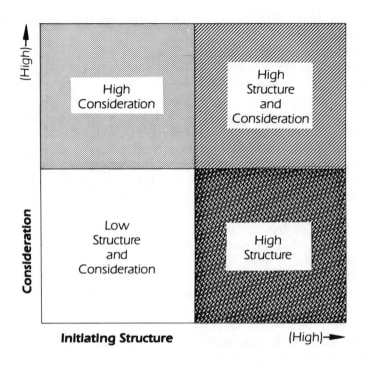

Figure 1. The Ohio State Leadership Quadrants

THE MANAGERIAL GRID®

Robert R. Blake and Jane S. Mouton[5] in their Managerial Grid® have popularized the task and relationships dimensions of leadership and have used them extensively in organization and management development programs.

In the Managerial Grid, five different types of leadership based on concern for production (task) and concern for people (relationships) are located in the four quadrants identified by the Ohio State studies.

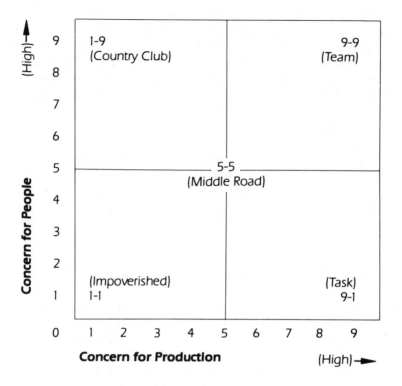

Figure 2. The Managerial Grid® Leadership Styles

SUGGESTING A "BEST" STYLE OF LEADERSHIP

After identifying task and relationships as two central dimensions of any leadership situation, some management writers have suggested a "best" style of leadership. Most of these writers have supported either an integrated leader behavior style (high task and high relationships) or a permissive, democratic, human relations approach (high relationships).

Andrew W. Halpin,[6] of the original Ohio State staff, in a study of school superintendents, pointed out that according to his findings "effective or desirable leadership behavior is characterized by high ratings on both Initiating Structure and Consideration. Conversely, ineffective or undesirable leadership behavior is marked by low ratings on both dimensions." Thus, Halpin seemed to conclude that the high Consideration and high Initiating Structure style is theoretically the ideal or "best" leader behavior, while the style low on both dimensions is theoretically the "worst."

Blake and Mouton in their Managerial Grid also imply that the most desirable leadership style is "team management" (maximum concern for production and people) and the least desirable is "impoverished management" (minimum concern for production and people). In fact, they have developed training programs designed to change the behavior of managers toward this "team" style.[7]

LEADERSHIP STYLE SHOULD VARY WITH THE SITUATION

While the Ohio State and the Managerial Grid people seem to suggest there is a "best" style of leadership,[8] recent evidence from empirical studies clearly shows that there is no single all purpose leadership style which is universally successful.

Some of the most convincing evidence which dispels the idea of a single "best" style of leader behavior was gathered and published by A.K. Korman[9] in 1966. Korman attempted to review all the studies which examined the relationship between the Ohio State behavior dimensions of Initiating Structure (task) and Consideration (relationships) and various measures of effectiveness, including group productivity, salary, performance under stress, administrative reputation, work group grievances, absenteeism, and turnover. Korman reviewed over twenty-five studies and concluded that:

> Despite the fact that "Consideration" and "Initiating Structure" have become almost bywords in American industrial psychology, it seems apparent that very little is now known as to how these variables may predict work group performance and the conditions which affect such predictions. At the current time, we cannot even say whether they have any predictive significance at all.

Thus, Korman found the use of Consideration and Initiating Structure had no significant predictive value in terms of effectiveness as situations changed. *This suggests that since situations differ, so must leader style.*

Fred E. Fiedler,[10] in testing his contingency model of leadership in over fifty studies covering a span of fifteen years (1951-1967), concluded that both directive, task-oriented leaders and non-directive, human relations-oriented leaders are successful under some conditions. Fiedler argues:

> While one can never say that something is impossible, and while someone may well discover the all-purpose leadership style or behavior at some future time, our own data and those which have come out of sound research by other investigators do not promise such miraculous cures.

A number of other investigators[11] besides Korman and Fiedler have also shown that different leadership situations require different leader styles.

In summary, empirical studies tend to show that there is no normative (best) style of leadership; that successful leaders are those who can adapt their leader behavior to meet the needs of their followers and the particular situation. Effectiveness is dependent upon the leader, the followers, and other situational elements. In managing for effectiveness a leader must be able to diagnose his own leader behavior in light of his environment. Some of the variables other than his followers which he should examine include the organization, superiors, associates, and job demands. This list is not all inclusive, but contains interacting components which tend to be important to a leader in many different organizational settings.

ADDING AN EFFECTIVENESS DIMENSION

To measure more accurately how well a leader operates within a given situation, an "effectiveness dimension" should be added to the two-dimensional Ohio State model. This is illustrated in Figure 3.

By adding an effectiveness dimension to the Ohio State model, a three-dimensional model is created.[12] This Leader Effectiveness Model attempts to integrate the concepts of leader style with situational demands of a specific environment. When the leader's style is appropriate to a given environment measured by results, it is termed *effective*; when his style is inappropriate to a given environment, it is termed *ineffective*.

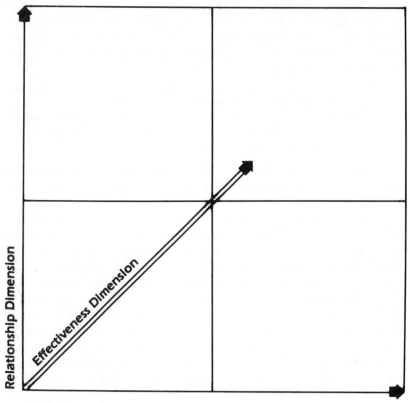

Figure 3. Adding an Effectiveness Dimension

If a leader's effectiveness is determined by the interaction of his style and environment (followers and other situational variables), it follows that any of the four styles depicted in the Ohio State model may be effective or ineffective depending on the environment.

Thus, there is *no* single ideal leader behavior style which is appropriate in all situations. For example, the high task and high relationships style is appropriate only in certain situations, but is inappropriate in others. In basically crisis-oriented organizations like the military or police, there is considerable evidence that the most appropriate style would be high task, since under combat or riot conditions success often depends upon immediate response to orders. Time demands do not permit talking things over or explaining decisions. For success, behavior must be automatic.

While a high task style might be effective for a combat officer, it might not be effective in other situations even within the military. This was pointed out when line officers trained at West Point were sent to command outposts in the Dew Line, which was part of an advanced warning system. The scientific personnel involved, living in close quarters in an Arctic region, did not respond favorably to the task-oriented behavior of these combat trained officers. The level of education and maturity of these people was such that they did not need a great deal of structure in their work. In fact, they tended to resent it.

Other studies of scientific and research-oriented personnel show also that many of these people desire, or need, only a limited amount of socio-emotional support. Therefore, there are situations in which the low task and relationships style, which has been assumed by some authors to be theoretically a poor leadership style, may be an appropriate style.

In summary, an effective leader must be able to *diagnose* the demands of the environment and then either *adapt* his leader style to fit these demands, or develop the means to *change* some or all of the other variables.

ATTITUDINAL VS. BEHAVIORAL MODELS

In examining the dimensions of the Managerial Grid (*concern* for production and *concern* for people), one can see that these are attitudinal dimensions. That is, concern is a feeling or emotion toward something. On the other hand, the dimensions of the Ohio State Model (Initiating Structure and Consideration) and Leader Effectiveness Models measure *how* people behave, while the Managerial Grid measures *predisposition* toward production and people. As discussed earlier, the Leader Effectiveness Model is an outgrowth of the Ohio State Model but is distinct from it in that it adds an effectiveness dimension to the two dimensions of behavior.

Although the Managerial Grid and the Leader Effectiveness Model measure different aspects of leadership, they are not incompatible. A conflict develops, however, because behavioral assumptions have often been drawn from analysis of the attitudinal dimensions of the Managerial Grid.[13] While high *concern* for both production and people is desirable in many organizations, managers having a high concern for both people and production do not always find it appropriate in all situations to initiate a high degree of structure and provide a high degree of socio-emotional support.

For example, if a manager's subordinates are emotionally mature and can take responsibility for themselves, his appropriate style of leadership may be low task and low relationships. In this case the manager permits these subordinates to participate in the planning, organizing and controlling of their own operation. He plays a background role, providing socio-emotional support only when necessary. Consequently, it is assumptions about behavior drawn from the Managerial Grid and not the Grid itself that are inconsistent with the Leader Effectiveness Model.

SITUATIONAL LEADERSHIP THEORY

Korman,[14] in his extensive review of studies examining the Ohio State concepts of Initiating Structure and Consideration, concluded that:

> What is needed. . . in future concurrent (and predictive) studies is not just recognition of this factor of "situational determinants" but, rather, a systematic conceptualization of situational variance as it might relate to leadership behavior (Initiating Structure and Consideration).

In discussing this conclusion, Korman suggests the possibility of a curvilinear relationship rather than a simple linear relationship between Structure and Consideration and other variables. The Life Cycle Theory of Leadership [later called Situational Leadership™] which we have developed is based on a curvilinear relationship between task and relationships and "maturity." This theory will attempt to provide a leader with some understanding of the relationship between an effective style of leadership and the level of maturity of one's followers.

The emphasis in Situational Leadership will be on the followers. As Fillmore H. Sanford has indicated, there is some justification for regarding the followers "as the most crucial factor in any leadership event."[15] Followers in any situation are vital, not only because individually they accept or reject the leader, but as a group they actually determine whatever personal power he may have.

According to Situational Leadership Theory, as the level of maturity of one's followers continues to increase, appropriate leader behavior not only requires less and less structure (task) but also less and less socio-emotional support (relationships). This cycle can be illustrated in the four quadrants of the basic styles portion of the Leader Effectiveness Model as shown in Figure 4.

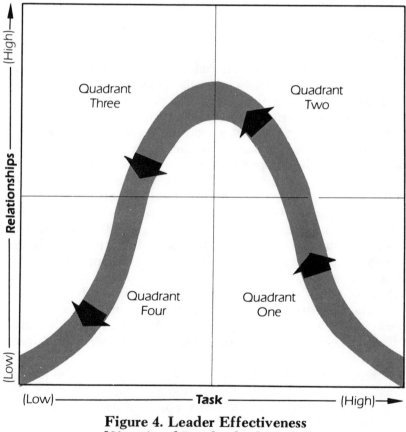

Figure 4. Leader Effectiveness [Situational Leadership] Model

Maturity is defined in Situational Leadership Theory by the relative independence,[16] ability to take responsibility, and achievement-motivation[17] of an individual or group. These components of maturity are often influenced by level of education and amount of experience. While age is a factor, it is not directly related to maturity as used in this Theory. Our concern is for psychological age, not chronological age. Beginning with structured task behavior which is appropriate for working with immature people, Situational Leadership Theory suggests that leader behavior should move from: (1) high task-low relationships behavior to (2) high task-high relationships and (3) high relationships-low task behavior to (4) low task-low relationships behavior, if one's followers progress from immaturity to maturity.

Parent-Child Example

An illustration of this Situational Leadership Theory familiar to everyone is the parent-child relationship. As a child begins to mature, it is appropriate for the parent to provide more socio-emotional support and less structure. Experience shows us that if the parent provides too much relationships before a child is somewhat mature, this behavior is often misinterpreted by the child as permissiveness. Thus it is appropriate to increase one's relationships behavior as the child is able to increase his maturity or capacity to take responsibility.

A child when first born is unable to control much of his own environment. Consequently, his parents must initiate almost all structure, i.e., dress the child, feed the child, bathe the child, turn the child over, etc. When it is appropriate for a parent to show love and affection toward a child, this is different than the mutual trust and respect which characterizes relationships behavior. Consequently, the most appropriate style for a parent to use with his children during the early preschool years may be high task-low relationships (quadrant 1).

Even when the child begins to attend school, the parent must provide a great deal of structure. The child is still not mature enough to accept much responsibility on his own. It may become appropriate at this state, as the child matures, for the parent to increase his relationships behavior by showing more trust and respect for his child. At this point, the parent's behavior could be characterized as high task-high relationships (quadrant 2).

Gradually as the child moves into high school and/or college, he begins to seek and accept more and more responsibility for his own behavior. It is during this time that a parent should begin to engage in less structured behavior and provide more socio-emotional support (quadrant 3). This does not mean that the child's life will have less structure, but it will now be internally imposed by the "young man" rather than externally by the parent. When this happens the cycle as depicted on the Model begins to become a backward bending curve. The child is not only able to structure many of the activities in which he engages, but is also able to provide self-control over his interpersonal and emotional needs.

As the child begins to make his own living, start his own family, and take full responsibility for his actions, a decrease in structure and socio-emotional support by the parents becomes appropriate. In reality, the umbilical cord has been severed and the child is now "on his own." At this stage of the parent-child relationship, a low task-low relationships style seems to be most appropriate (quadrant 4).

Although Situational Leadership suggests a basic style for different levels of maturity in meeting specific contingencies, it may be necessary to vary one's style anywhere within the four quadrants to deal appropriately with this event. For example, even when a young man is away at college and his parents are using a high relationships style with him, it might be appropriate for them to initiate some structure with their son if they discover that he is not behaving in as mature a way as expected (he has become a discipline problem). A change in parental behavior might even be necessary later in life after a son (or daughter) has had a family of his own for a number of years. If this son, for example, suddenly begins to experience marital difficulties and his family begins to disintegrate, it might be appropriate for his parents temporarily to increase their socio-emotional support.

Other Aspects of Situational Leadership

The parent-child relationship is only one example of Situational Leadership. This cycle is also discernible in other organizations in the interaction between superiors and subordinates. An interesting example is found in Research and Development work. In working with highly trained and educated Research and Development personnel, the most effective leader behavior style might be low task-low relationships. However, during the early stages of a particular project, the director must impose a certain amount of structure as the requirements and limitations of the project are established. Once these limitations are understood, the R & D director moves rapidly through the *"project cycle"* back to the mature low task-low relationships style.

In a college setting, Situational Leadership Theory has been validated in studying the teacher-student relationship. Effective teaching of lower division students (freshmen and sophomores) has been characterized by structured behavior on the part of the teacher as he reinforces appropriate patterns in attendance and study habits, while more relationships behavior seems to be appropriate for working with upper division undergraduates and Master's students. And finally the cycle seems to be completed as a teacher begins to work with mature Ph.D. candidates, who need very little guidance or socio-emotional support.

We realize that most groups in our society do not reach the backward bending aspect of the cycle. But there is some evidence that as the level of education and experience of a group increases, appropriate movement in this direction will take place. However, the demands of the job may often be a limiting factor on the development of maturity in workers. For example, an assembly line operation in an automobile plant is so highly structured that it offers little opportunity for the maturing process to occur. With such monotonous tasks, workers are given minimal control over their environment and are often encouraged to be passive, dependent, and subordinate.

Situational Leadership™ and Span of Control

For years it has been argued by many management writers that one man can *supervise* only a relatively few people; therefore, all managers should have a limited span of control. For example, Harold Koontz and Cyril O'Donnell[18] state that:

> In every organization it must be decided how many subordinates a superior can manage. Students of management have found that this number is usually four to eight subordinates at the upper levels of organization and eight to fifteen or more at the lower levels.

While the suggested number of subordinates which one can supervise varies anywhere from three to thirty, the principle usually states that the number should decrease as one moves higher in the organization. Top management should have fewer subordinates to supervise than lower level managers. Yet Situational Leadership suggests that span of control may not depend on the level of the management hierarchy but should be a function of the maturity of the individuals being supervised. The more independent, able to take responsibility, and achievement-motivated one's subordinates are, the more people a manager can supervise. It is theoretically possible to supervise an infinite number of subordinates if every one is completely mature and able to be responsible for his own job. This does not mean there is less control, but these subordinates are self-controlled rather than externally controlled by their superior. Since people occupying higher level jobs in an organization tend to be more "mature" and therefore need less close supervision than people occupying lower level jobs, it seems reasonable to assume that top managers should be able to supervise more subordinates than their counterparts at lower levels.[19]

CONCLUSIONS

Rensis Likert[20] found in his research that supervisors with the best records of performance were employee-centered (high relationships), while job-centered (high task) supervisors were found more often to have low-producing sections. While this relationship seemed to exist, Likert raised the question of which variable was the causal factor. Is the style of the supervisor causing the level of production or is the level of production encouraging the style of the managers? As Likert suggests, it may very well be that high-producing sections allow for general supervision rather than close supervision and relationship behavior rather than task behavior. The supervisor soon learns that his subordinates are mature enough to structure their own environment, thus leaving him time for other kinds of activities. At the same time a low-producing section may leave the supervisor with no choice but to be job-centered. If he attempted to use a relationships style this may be misunderstood and interpreted as reinforcement for their low level of performance. The point is, the supervisor must change appropriately.

Changing Style

The problem with the conclusions of Likert and other behavioral scientists comes in implementation. Practitioners read that employee-centered supervisors tend to have higher-producing sections than job-centered supervisors. Wanting to implement these findings overnight, they encourage all supervisors to become more employee-oriented. Consequently, a foreman who has been operating as a task-oriented, authoritarian leader for many years may be encouraged to change his style—"get in step with the times." Upon returning from a "human relations" training program, the foreman will probably try to utilize some of the new relationships techniques he has recently been taught. The problem is that his personality is not compatible with the new concepts, but he tries to use them anyway. As long as things are running smoothly, there is no difficulty. However, the minute an important issue or crisis develops he tends to revert to his old basic style and becomes inconsistent, vacillating between the new relationships style he has been taught, and his old task style which has the force of habit behind it.

This idea was supported in a study conducted by the General Electric Company at one of its turbine and generator plants. In this study, the leadership styles of about 90 foremen were analyzed and rated as "democratic," "authoritarian" or "mixed." In discussing the findings, Saul W. Gellerman[21] reported that:

> The lowest morale in the plant was found among those men whose foremen were rated *between* the democratic and authoritarian extremes. The GE research team felt that these foremen might have varied inconsistently in their tactics, permissive at one moment and hardfisted the next, in a way that left their men frustrated and unable to anticipate how they would be treated. The naturally autocratic supervisor who is exposed to human relations training may behave in exactly such a manner...a pattern which will probably make him even harder to work for than he was before being "enlightened."

Thus, changing the style of managers is a difficult process, and one that takes considerable time to accomplish. Expecting miracles overnight will only lead to frustration and uneasiness for both managers and subordinates. Yet industry invests many millions of dollars annually for training and development programs which concentrate on effecting change in the style of managers. As Fiedler[22] suggests:

> A person's leadership style...reflects the individual's basic motivational and need structure. At best it takes one, two, or three years of intensive psychotherapy to effect changes in personality structure. It is difficult to see how we can change in more than a few cases an equally important set of core values in a few hours of lectures and role playing or even in the course of a more intensive training program of one or two weeks.

Fiedler's point is well-taken. It is indeed difficult to effect changes in the styles of managers overnight. However, it is not completely hopeless. But, at best, it is a low and expensive process which requires creative planning and patience. In fact, Likert[23] found that it takes from three to seven years, depending on the size and complexity of the organization, to effectively implement a new management theory.

> Haste is self-defeating because of the anxieties and stresses it creates. There is no substitute for ample time to enable the members of an organization to reach the level of skillful and easy, habitual use of the new leadership... .

Changing Performance

Not only is it difficult to effect changes in the styles of managers overnight, but the question that we raise is whether it is even appropriate. It is questionable whether a work group whose performance has been continuously low would suddenly leap to high productivity with the introduction of an employee-centered supervisor. In fact, they might take advantage of him and view him as a "soft-touch." These workers lack maturity and are not ready for more responsibility. Thus the supervisor must bring them along slowly, becoming more employee-centered and less job-centered as they mature. When an individual's performance is low, one cannot expect drastic changes overnight, regardless of changes in expectations or incentives. The key is often reinforcing positively "*successive approximations.*" By successive approximations we mean behavior which comes closer and closer to the supervisor's expectations of good performance. Similar to the child learning some new behavior, a manager should not expect high levels of performance at the outset. As a parent or teacher, we would use positive reinforcement as the child's behavior approaches the desired level of performance. Therefore, the manager must be aware of any progress of his subordinates so that he is in a position to reinforce appropriately improved performance.

Change through the cycle from quadrant 1 to quadrant 2, 3 and then 4 must be gradual. This process by its very nature cannot be revolutionary but must be evolutionary—gradual developmental changes, a result of planned growth and the creation of mutual trust and respect.

Notes

[1] As examples see the following: Robert F. Bales, "Task Roles and Social Roles in Problem-Solving Groups," in *Readings in Social Psychology*, E.E. Maccoby, T.M. Newcomb, and E.L. Hartley (Eds.), Holt, Rinehart and Winston, 1958; Chester I. Barnard, *The Functions of the Executive*, Harvard University Press, 1938; Dorwin Cartwright and Alvin Zander (Eds.), *Group Dynamics: Research and Theory* (2nd ed.), Row, Peterson, 1960; D. Katz, N. Maccoby, and Nancy C. Morse, *Productivity Supervision, and Morale in an Office Situation*, The Darel Press, 1950; Talcott Parsons, *The Social System*, The Free Press, 1951.

[2] Robert Tannenbaum and Warren H. Schmidt, "How to Choose a Leadership Pattern," *Harvard Business Review*, March-April 1957, pp. 95-101.

[3] Roger M. Stogdill and Alvin E. Coons (Eds.), *Leader Behavior: Its Description and Measurement*, Research Monograph No. 88, Bureau of Business Research, The Ohio State University, 1957.

[4] *Ibid*. See also Andrew W. Halpin, *The Leadership Behavior of School Superintendents*, Midwest Administration Center, The University of Chicago, 1959.

[5] Robert R. Blake and Jane S. Mouton, *The Managerial Grid*, Gulf Publishing, 1964.

[6] Halpin, *The Leadership Behavior of School Superintendents*.

[7] Robert R. Blake *et al*., "Breakthrough in Organization Development." *Harvard Business Review*, November-December 1964.

[8] See also Rensis Likert, *New Patterns of Management*, McGraw-Hill, 1961.

[9] A.K. Korman, " 'Consideration,' 'Initiating Structure,' and Organizational Criteria—A Review," *Personnel Psychology: A Journal of Applied Research, 19*(4), (Winter, 1966), pp. 349-361.

[10] Fred E. Fiedler, *A Theory of Leadership Effectiveness*, McGraw-Hill, 1967.

[11] See C.A. Gibb, "Leadership"; A.P. Hare, *Handbook of Small Group Research*, John Wiley, 1965; and D.C. Pelz, "Leadership Within a Hierarchical Organization," *Journal of Social Issues*, 1961, 7, pp. 49-55.

[12] Paul Hersey and Kenneth H. Blanchard. *Leader Behavior*, Management Education & Development, 1967; see also Hersey and Blanchard, *Management of Organizational Behavior: Utilizing Human Resources*, Prentice-Hall, 1969; and William J. Reddin, "The 3-D Management Style Theory," *Training and Development Journal*, April 1967.

[13] Fred E. Fiedler in his Contingency Model of Leadership Effectiveness (Fiedler, *A Theory of Leadership Effectiveness*) tends to make behavioral assumptions from data gathered from an attitudinal measure of leadership style. A leader is asked to evaluate his least preferred co-worker (LPC) on a series of Semantic Differential type scales. Leaders are classified as high or low LPC depending on the favorableness with which they rate their LPC.

[14] Korman, " 'Consideration,' 'Initiating Structure,' and Organizational Criteria—A Review."

[15] Fillmore H. Sanford, *Authoritarianism and Leadership*, Institute for Research in Human Relations, 1950.

[16]Chris Argyris, *Personality and Organization*, Harper & Row, 1957; *Interpersonal Competence and Organizational Effectiveness*, Dorsey Press, 1962; and *Integrating the Individual and the Organization*, John Wiley, 1964.

[17]David C. McClelland, J.W. Atkinson, R.A. Clark, and E.L. Lowell, *The Achievement Motive*, Appleton-Century-Crofts, 1953, and *The Achieving Society*, Van Nostrand Reinhold, 1961.

[18]Harold Koontz and Cyril O'Donnell, *Principles of Management* (4th ed.), McGraw-Hill, 1968.

[19]Support for this discussion is provided by Peter F. Drucker, *The Practice of Management*, Harper & Row, 1954, pp. 139-140.

[20]Rensis Likert, *New Patterns of Management*, McGraw-Hill, 1961.

[21]Saul Gellerman, *Motivation and Productivity*, American Management Association, 1963.

[22]Fiedler, *A Theory of Leadership Effectiveness*.

[23]Likert, *New Patterns of Management*.

The Contingency Model— New Directions for Leadership Utilization

Fred E. Fiedler[1]

Leadership research has come a long way from the simple concepts of earlier years which centered on the search for the magic leadership trait. We have had to replace the old cherished notion that "leaders are born and not made." These increasingly complex formulations postulate that some types of leaders will behave and perform differently in a given situation than other types. The Contingency Model is one of the earliest and most articulated of these theories;[2] taking into account the personality of the leader as well as aspects of the situation which affect the leader's behavior and performance. This model has given rise to well over one-hundred empirical studies. This article briefly reviews the current status of the Contingency Model and then discusses several new developments which promise to have considerable impact on our thinking about leadership as well as on the management of executive manpower.

THE CONTINGENCY MODEL

The theory holds that the effectiveness of a task group or of an organization depends on two main factors: the personality of

Reprinted from the *Journal of Contemporary Business*, 1974, 3(4), 65-79. Copyright © 1974, Graduate School of Business Administration, University of Washington. Used by permission of the author and publisher.

the leader and the degree to which the situation gives the leader power, control and influence over the situation or, conversely, the degree to which the situation confronts the leader with uncertainty.[3]

Leader Personality

The first of these factors distinguishes leader personality in terms of two different motivational systems, i.e., the basic or primary goals as well as the secondary goals which people pursue once their more pressing needs are satisfied. One type of person, whom we shall call "relationship-motivated," primarily seeks to maintain good interpersonal relationships with coworkers. These basic goals become very apparent in uncertain and anxiety provoking situations in which we try to make sure that the important needs are secured. Under these conditions the relationship-motivated individual will seek out others and solicit their support; however, under certain conditions in which he or she feels quite secure and relaxed—because this individual has achieved the major goals of having close relations with subordinates—he or she will seek the esteem and admiration of others. In a leadership situation where task performance results in esteem and admiration from superiors, this leader will tend to concentrate on behaving in a task-relevant manner, sometimes to the detriment of relations with immediate subordinates.

The relationship-motivated leader's counterpart has as a major goal the accomplishment of some tangible evidence of his or her worth. This person gets satisfaction from the task itself and from knowing that he or she has done well. In a leadership situation which is uncertain and anxiety provoking, this person will, therefore, put primary emphasis on completing the task. However, when this individual has considerable control and influence and knows, therefore, the task will get done, he or she will relax and be concerned with subordinates' feelings and satisfactions. In other words, business before pleasure, but business with pleasure whenever possible.

Of course, these two thumbnail sketches are oversimplified, but they do give a picture which tells us, first, that we are dealing with different types of people and, second, that they differ in their primary and secondary goals and, consequently, in the way they behave under various conditions. Both the relationship-motivated and the task-motivated persons may be pleasant and considerate toward their members. However, the task-motivated leader will be considerate in situations in which he or she is secure, i.e., in which the individual's power and influence are high; the relationship-motivated leader will be considerate when his or her control and influence are less assured, when some uncertainty is present.

These motivational systems are measured by the Least Preferred Coworker score (LPC) which is obtained by first asking an individual to think of all people with whom he or she has ever worked, and then to describe the one person with whom this individual has been able to work least well. The description of the least preferred coworker is made on a short, bipolar, eight-point scale, from 16 to 22 item-scale of the semantic differential format. The LPC score is the sum of the item scores, e.g.:

Friendly ⊢——⊥——⊥——⊥——⊥——⊥——⊥——⊥——⊣ Unfriendly
            1   2   3   4   5   6   7   8

Cooperative ⊢——⊥——⊥——⊥——⊥——⊥——⊥——⊥——⊣ Uncooperative
            1   2   3   4   5   6   7   8

High-LPC persons, i.e., individuals who describe their LPC in relatively positive terms, seem primarily relationship-motivated. Low-LPC persons, those who describe their least preferred coworker in very unfavorable terms, are basically task-motivated. Therefore, as can be seen, the LPC score is not a description of leader behavior because the behavior of high- and low-LPC people changes with different situations.

Relationship-motivated people seem more open, more approachable and more like McGregor's "Theory Y" managers, while the task-motivated leaders tend to be more controlled and more controlling persons, even though they may be as likeable and pleasant as their relationship-motivated colleagues.[4]

Current evidence suggests that the LPC scores and the personality attributes they reflect are almost as stable as most other personality measures. (For example, test-retest reliabilities for military leaders have been .72 over an 8-month period[5] and .67 over a 2-year period for faculty members.)[6] Changes do occur, but in the absence of major upsets in the individual's life, they tend to be gradual and relatively small.

The Leadership Situation

The second variable, "situational favorableness,"[7] indicates the degree to which the situation gives the leader control and influence and the ability to predict the consequences of his or her behavior.[8] A situation in which the leader cannot predict the consequences of the decision tends to be stressful and anxiety arousing.

One rough but useful method for defining situational favorableness is based on three subscales. These are the degree to which (a) the leader is, or feels, accepted and supported by his or her members (leader-member relations); (b) the task is clear-cut, programmed and structured as to goals, procedures and measurable progress and success (task structure); and (c) the leader's position provides power to reward and punish and, thus, to obtain compliance from subordinates (position power).

Groups then can be categorized as being high or low on each of these three dimensions by dividing them at the median or, on the basis of normative scores, into those with good and poor leader-member relations, task structure and position power. This leads to an eight-celled classification shown on the horizontal axis of Figure 1. The eight cells or "octants" are scaled from "most favorable" (octant I) to the left of the graph to "least favorable" (octant VIII) to the right. A leader obviously will have the most control and influence in groups that fall into octant I; i.e., in which this leader is accepted, has high position power and structured task. The leader will have somewhat less control and influence in octant II, where he or she is accepted and has a structured task, but little position power, and so on to groups in octant VIII, where control and influence will be relatively small because the leader is not accepted by his or her group, has a vague, unstructured task and little position power. Situational favorableness and LPC are, of course, neither empirically nor logically related to each other.

The Personality-Situation Interaction

The basic findings of the Contingency Model are that task-motivated leaders perform generally best in very "favorable" situations, i.e., either under conditions in which their power, control and influence are very high (or, conversely, where uncertainty is very low) or where the situation is unfavorable, where they have low power, control and influence. Relationship-motivated leaders tend to perform best in situations in which they have moderate power, control and influence. The findings are summarized in Figure 1. The horizontal axis indicates the eight cells of the situational favorableness dimension, with the most favorable end on the left side of the graph's axis. The vertical axis indicates the *correlation coefficients* between the leader's LPC score and the group's

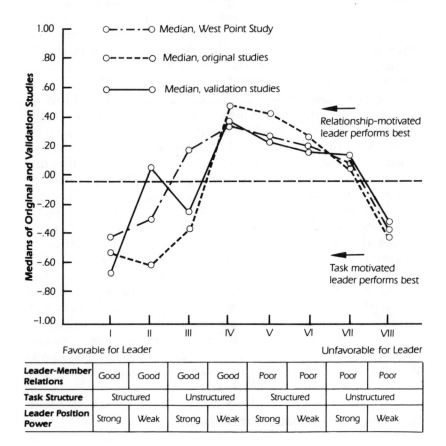

Figure 1. Studies of Leader Motivation and Situational Variables

performance. A high correlation in the positive direction, indicated by a point above the midline of the graph, shows that the relationship-motivated leaders performed better than the task-motivated leaders. A negative correlation, shown by a point which falls below the midline of the graph, indicates that the task-motivated leaders performed better than relationship-motivated leaders, i.e., the higher the LPC score, the lower the group's performance.

The solid curve connects the median correlations within each of the octants obtained in the original studies (before 1963) on which the model was based. The broken line connects the median correlations obtained in various validation studies from 1964-1971.[9] As can be seen, the two curves are very similar, and the points on the curves correlate .76 (p <.01). Only in octant II is there a major discrepancy. However, it should be pointed out that there are very few groups in real life which have a highly structured task while the leader has low position power, e.g., in high school basketball teams and student surveying parties. Most of the validation evidence for octant II comes from laboratory studies in which this type of situation may be difficult to reproduce. However, the field study results for this octant are in the negative direction, just as the model predicts.

The most convincing validation evidence comes from a well-controlled experiment conducted by Chemers and Skrzypek at the U.S. Military Academy at West Point.[10] LPC scores as well as sociometric performance ratings to predict leader-member relations were obtained several weeks *prior* to the study, and groups then were assembled in advance, based on having the leader's LPC score and the expressed positive or negative feelings of group members about one another. The results of the Chemers and Skrzypek study are shown in the figure as a dotted line and give nearly a point-for-point replication of the original model with a correlation of .86 (p<.01). A subsequent reanalysis of the Chemers and Skrzypek data by Shiflett showed that the Contingency Model accounted for no less than 28 percent of the variance in group performance.[11] This is a very high degree of prediction, especially in a study in which variables such as the group members' intelligence, the leader's ability, the motivational factors of participants and similar effects were uncontrolled. Of course, it is inconceivable that data of this nature could be obtained by pure chance.

A different and somewhat clearer description of the Contingency Model is presented schematically in Figure 2. As before, the situational favorableness dimension is indicated on the horizontal axis, extending from the most favorable situation on the left to the relatively least favorable situation on the right. However, here the vertical axis indicates the group or organizational performance; the solid line on the graph is the schematic performance curve of relationship-motivated (high-LPC) leaders, while the dashed line indicates the performance of task-motivated (low-LPC) leaders.

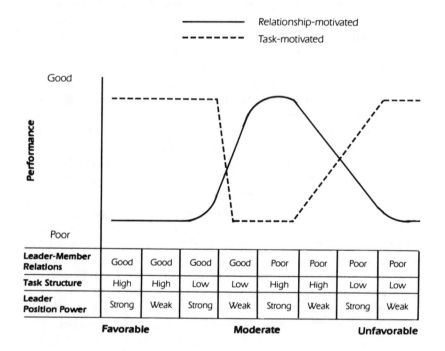

Leader-Member Relations	Good	Good	Good	Good	Poor	Poor	Poor	Poor
Task Structure	High	High	Low	Low	High	High	Low	Low
Leader Position Power	Strong	Weak	Strong	Weak	Strong	Weak	Strong	Weak

Favorable   Moderate   Unfavorable

Figure 2. The Performance of Relationship- and Task-Motivated Leaders in Different Situational-Favorableness Conditions

These curves show, first of all, that both the relationship- and the task-motivated leaders perform well under some situations but not under others. Therefore, it is not accurate to speak of a "good" or a "poor" leader, rather, a leader may perform well in one type of situation but not in another. Outstanding directors of research teams do not necessarily make good production foremen or military leaders, and outstanding battle field commanders, like General Patton, do not necessarily make good chiefs of staff or good chairmen of volunteer school picnic committees.

The second major implication of Figure 2 is that leader performance depends as much on the situation to which the organization assigns him (her) as on his or her own personality. Hence, organizational improvement can be achieved either by changing the leader's personality and motivational system—which is at best a very difficult and uncertain process— or by modifying the degree to which the situation provides the leader with power and influence. It should be obvious from the graph that certain leaders perform better with less rather than more power, i.e., some leaders let the power "go to their heads," they become cocky and arrogant, while others need security to function well.

EXTENSIONS OF THE CONTINGENCY MODEL

Two important tests of any theory are the degree to which it allows us to understand phenomena which do not follow common-sense expectations and, second, the extent to which it predicts nonobvious findings. In both of these respects, the Contingency Model has demonstrated its usefulness. We present here several important findings from recent studies, and then discuss some implications for management.

Effects of Experience and Training

One of the major research efforts in the area of leadership and management has been the attempt to develop training methods which will improve organizational performance. However, until now the various training programs have failed to live up to their expectations. Stogdill concluded that:

> the research on leadership training is generally inadequate in both design and execution. It has failed to address itself to the most crucial problem of leadership...[the] effects of leadership on group performance and member satisfaction.[12]

The Contingency Model would predict that training should increase the performance of some leaders and also decrease the performance of others. However, it raises the question of whether any current method of training logically can result in an across-the-board increase in organizational leadership performance.[13]

As pointed out before, a group's performance depends on the leader's personality as well as the degree to which the situation provides him or her with control, power and influence. If the leader's power and influence are increased by experience and training, the "match" between leader personality and situational favorableness would change. However, increasing the leader's power and influence is exactly the goal of most leadership training. For example, technical training increases the leader's expert power; coaching and orthodox training programs which use the case study and lecture method are designed to increase the structure of the task by providing the leader with methods for dealing with problems which, otherwise, would require him or her to think of new solutions. Human relations training is designed to develop better relations with group members, thus enabling the leader to exert more personal influence or "referent power."

For example, let us take a newly promoted supervisor of a production department in which he has not worked before. As he begins his new job, some of the tasks may seem unfamiliar and he will be unsure of his exact duties and responsibilities. He also may be uncertain of the power his position provides—how, for example, will the group react if he tries to dock an old, experienced worker who had come in late? Is this type of disciplinary measure acceptable to the group even though it may be allowed by the union contract? He may wonder how he should handle a problem with a fellow supervisor in the plant on whom he has to depend for parts and supplies. Should he file a formal complaint or should he talk to him personally?

After several years on the job, our supervisor will have learned the ropes; he will know how far he can go in disciplining his workers, how to troubleshoot various machines and how to deal with other managers in the organization. Thus, for the experienced supervisor the job is structured, his position power is high and his relations with his group are probably good. In other words, his leadership situation is very favorable.

When he first started on the job, his leadership situation probably was ony moderately favorable. If you will recall, relationship-motivated leaders tend to perform best in moderately favorable situations, while task-motivated leaders perform better in very favorable situations. Therefore, a relationship-motivated leader will perform well at first before gaining experience (e.g., by using the resources of group members and inviting their participation); a task-motivated leader will perform well after becoming experienced. In other words, the relationship-motivated leader actually should perform less well after gaining experience, while the task-motivated leader's performance should increase with greater experience.

A substantial number of studies now support this prediction.[14] A good example comes from a longitudinal study of infantry squad leaders who were assigned to newly organized units.[15] Their performance was evaluated by the same judges shortly after they joined their squads and, again, approximately 5 months later after their squads had passed the combat readiness test. As Figure 3 shows, the data are exactly as predicted by the Contingency Model. Similar results have been obtained in studies on the effects of training and experience of post office managers, managers of consumer cooperatives, police patrol supervisors and leaders of various military units.

The effect of leadership training on performance also was demonstrated by a very ingenious experiment conducted at the University of Utah.[16] ROTC cadets and students were assembled a priori into four-man teams with high- and low-LPC leaders. One-half of the team leaders were given training in decoding cryptographic messages, i.e., they were shown how to decode simple messages easily by first counting all the letters in the message and considering the most frequent letter an "e." A three-letter word, ending with the supposed "e" is then likely to be a "the," etc. The other half of the leaders were given no training of this type.

All teams operated under a fairly high degree of tension, as indicated by subsequent ratings of the group atmosphere. Because the task is by definition unstructured, the situation was moderately favorable for the trained leaders but unfavorable for the untrained leaders. Therefore, we would expect that the relationship-motivated leaders would perform better with training, while the task-motivated leaders would perform more effectively in the unfavorable situation, i.e., without the benefit of training. As can be seen in Figure 4, the findings support the predictions of the model.

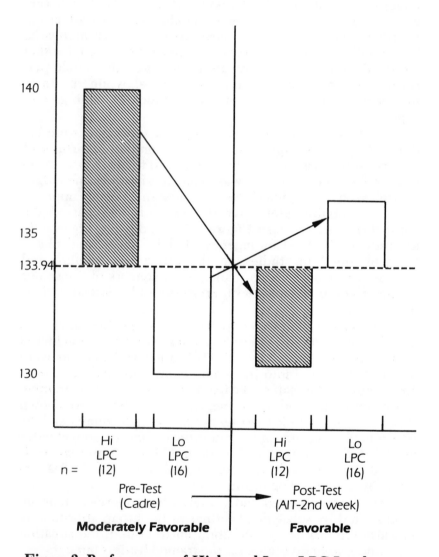

Figure 3. Performance of High- and Low-LPC Leaders as a Function of Increased Experience and More Structured Task Assignment over Five Months

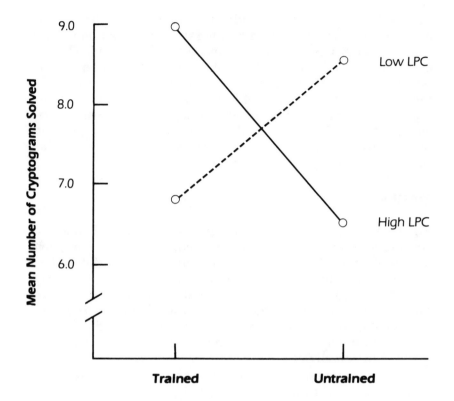

**Figure 4. Interaction of Training and LPC
on Group Productivity**

FURTHER IMPLICATIONS

Selection

It seems highly likely from these and similar findings that we
need to reconsider our management selection strategies.
Obviously, the old adage calling for "the right man for the
right job" is not as simple as it once appeared. The right
person for a particular job today may be the wrong person in
6 months or in 1 or 2 years. As we have seen, the job which

presents a very favorable leadership situation for the experienced leader presents a moderately favorable situation for the leader who is new and inexperienced or untrained. Hence, under these conditions a relationship-motivated leader should be chosen for the long run. The job which is moderately favorable for the experienced and trained leader is likely to represent an unfavorable leadership situation for the inexperienced leader. Hence, a task-motivated leader should be selected for the short run, and a relationship-motivated leader should be selected for the long run.

Rotation

Figure 4 suggests that certain types of leaders will reach a "burn-out point" after they have stayed on the job for a given length of time. They will become bored, stale, disinterested and no longer challenged. A rational rotation policy obviously must be designed to rotate these leaders at the appropriate time to new and more challenging jobs. The other types of leaders, e.g., the task-motivated leaders represented in Figure 4, should be permitted to remain on the job so that they can become maximally efficient.

Most organizations and, in particular, the military services, have a rotation system which (at least in theory) moves all officers to new jobs after a specified period of time. Such a rigid system is likely to be dysfunctional because it does not properly allow for individual differences which determine the time required by different types of people to reach their best performance. Recent research by Bons also has shown that the behavior and performance of leaders is influenced by such other organizational changes as the transfer of a leader from one unit to a similar unit and by a reorganization which involves the reassignment of the leader's superiors.[17]

The Contingency Model clearly is a very complex formulation of the leadership problem. Whether it is more complex than is necessary, as some of its critics have claimed, or whether it is still not sufficiently complex, as others have averred, remains an open question. It is clear at this point that the theory not only predicts leadership performance in field studies and laboratory experiments, but also that it serves as a very important and fruitful source of new hypotheses in the area of leadership.

Notes

[1]This paper is based on research performed under ARPA Order 454, Contract N00014-67-A-0103-0013 with the Advanced Research Projects Agency, United States Navy (Fred E. Fiedler, Principal Investigator) and Contract NR 177-472, N00014-67-A0103-0012 with the Office of Naval Research, Department of the Navy (Fred E. Fiedler, Principal Investigator).

[2]Fiedler, F.E. A contingency model of leadership effectiveness. In L. Berkowitz (Ed.), *Advances in experimental social psychology.* New York: Academic Press, 1964; Fiedler, F.E. *A theory of leadership effectiveness.* New York: McGraw-Hill, 1967; and Fiedler, F.E., & Chemers, M.M. *Leadership and effective management.* Glenview, IL: Scott, Foresman, 1974.

[3]Nebeker, D. Situational favorability and perceived environmental uncertainty: An integrative approach. *Administrative Science Quarterly,* 1975, *20,* pp. 281-294.

[4]Michaelsen, L.K. Leader orientation, leader behavior, group effectiveness and situational favorability: An empirical extension of the contingency model. *Organizational Behavior and Human Performance,* 1973, *9,* pp. 226-245.

[5]Bons, P.M. The effect of changes in leadership environment on the behavior of relationship- and task-motivated leaders (Ph.D. dissertation, University of Washington, 1974).

[6]Prothero, J. Personality and situational effects on the job-related behavior of faculty members (Honors thesis, University of Washington, 1974).

[7]Fiedler, F.E. *A theory of leadership effectiveness.*

[8]Nebeker, D. *op. cit.*

[9]Fiedler, F.E. Validation and extension of the contingency model of leadership effectiveness: A review of empirical findings. *Psychological Bulletin,* 1971, *76,* pp. 128-148.

[10]Chemers, M.M., & Skrzypek, G.J. Experimental test of the contingency model of leadership effectiveness. *Journal of Personality and Social Psychology,* 1972, *24,* pp. 172-177.

[11]Shiflett, S.C. The contingency model of leadership effectiveness: Some implications of its statistical and methodological properties. *Behavioral Science,* 1973, *18,* pp. 429-441.

[12]Stogdill, R.M. *Handbook of leadership: A survey of theory and research.* New York: Free Press, 1974.

[13]Fiedler, F.E. The effects of leadership training and experience: A contingency model interpretation. *Administrative Science Quarterly,* 1972, *17,* pp. 453-470.

[14]*Ibid.*

[15]Fiedler, F.E., Bons, P.M., & Hastings, L.L. The utilization of leadership resources. In W.T. Singleton & P. Spurgeon (Eds.), *Measurement of human resources.* London: Taylor and Francis, 1975.

[16]Chemers, M.M., Rice, R.W., Sundstrom, E., & Butler, W.M. Leader esteem for the least preferred co-worker score, training, and effectiveness: An experimental examination. *Journal of Personality and Social Psychology,* 1975, *31,* pp. 401-409.

[17]Bons, P.M. *op. cit.*

Collaborative Leadership in Work Settings

Frederic E. Finch

If the quality of life in work settings is to be improved so that outcomes of human growth, satisfaction, and productivity are increased, one key organizational process that must be altered is the leadership process. Traditional authority-based leadership diminishes the full utilization of human resources in organizations, largely by centralizing problem solving and decision making and control over work in the leader rather than in the people doing the work. This has serious negative consequences, not only for the effective functioning of organizations but also for the mental and physical well being of the workers involved (see Argyris, 1957, 1964; McGregor, 1960; Presthus, 1962; Blauner, 1964; Kornhauser, 1965; Jenkins, 1973; *Work in America,* 1973; Quinn, Staines, & McCullough, 1974).

Leadership and hierarchical organizational position are equated in the minds of the general public, greatly reducing the range of leadership potential by ignoring leadership functioning by many people in many work settings other than formal organizational office. Similarly, leadership theory and research are solidly based on traditional conceptions of organizational functioning. The conceptual frameworks that guide leadership research take current modes of organizational

Reproduced by special permission from *The Journal of Applied Behavioral Science,* "Collaborative Leadership in Work Settings," by Frederic E. Finch, Volume 13, Number 3, pp. 292-302, copyright © 1977, NTL Institute. Excerpted and used by permission of the author and publisher.

functioning as a given, and most of the research on leadership has been conducted on managers who work in traditional hierarchical organizations. It is difficult to find any leadership literature in which terms such as superior, subordinate, superior-subordinate relations, positions power, leader-group relations, and the like are not pervasive. Such theory and research tend to confirm and reinforce what is—it is descriptive—or at best identify the least painful ways of adapting to what is, rather than exploring alternatives.

Thus both common perceptions of what a leader is and does, and research conducted in the area of organizational leadership, tend to reinforce traditional, hierarchical, authoritarian leadership.

The notion that a workgroup can provide its own leadership functions is seldom explored in theory or research, although some research currently taking place in the areas of improving of work life, or industrial democracy, is demonstrating viable alternatives to hierarchical leadership (Davis, Cherns, & Associates, 1975a, b; Thorsrud, Sorensen, & Gustavsen, 1976).

COLLABORATIVE LEADERSHIP FOR THE WORKER AND THE MANAGER

In a general sense collaborative leadership is a situation in which the workgroup provides its own leadership behaviors (task, relationships, and decision making) and functions according to individual and group capacities and task requirements. The traditional functions of the manager, such as planning, organizing, directing, and control of work, is vested in the workgroup. The focus of these behaviors and functions is centered around how work is accomplished. In a fully collaborative organization these activities can be expanded to include such functions as hiring and retention of team members, training, design of pay systems, quality control, maintenance, etc., up to having a voice in the establishment of organizational policy.

The actual processes of collaborative group functioning will not be dealt with here, as there is a considerable body of literature in this area (Gulowsen, 1972; Davis & Taylor, 1972; *Work in America*, 1973; Davis, Cherns, & Associates, 1975b; Thorsrud, Sorensen, & Gustavsen, 1976). We will consider a more critical question: "How must our traditional notions of the manager/leader role change if the functioning of workgroups is going to move in collaborative directions?"

Under conditions where the workgroup undertakes its own task, relationships, and decision-making functions, it is obvious that the role of the manager, as he or she currently functions, atrophies. There is evidence that when this happens (i.e., when decision making normally vested in the managerial role is vested in the workgroup) and the manager's role is not redefined, the manager's job becomes boring and satisfaction with his or her work decreases markedly. Thus managerial resistance to a movement toward collaborative leadership is often high (Archer, 1975; Jacobs, 1975; Thorsrud, Sorensen, & Gustavsen, 1976). The challenge, power, control, status, privilege—those characteristics of being a manager in the traditional sense—are removed from the manager's role with such a change.

The implications of increased workgroup autonomy can have ramifications far beyond the immediate workgroup manager. For example, in one case, relatively minor changes in job design produced a 20-25 per cent increase in productivity, workgroup members preferred the new system, indicated greater job interest, more variety, and greater group involvement. Nevertheless, the experiment was halted because:

> For management, conditions were rather good as they were, at least in most other departments, and no one could guarantee that the new system would not bring new problems along with the rather striking benefits that had been demonstrated. The exposure of an illogical piece rate system and a gross suboptimization of the previous man-machine system was a threat to the prevailing management philosophy. An even greater threat (or embarrassment) was the fact that workers could organize and control their work better than the engineers had been able to do. (Thorsrud, Sorensen, & Gustavsen, 1976, p. 431)

Changing the Role of the Manager—Boundary Maintenance

Given that the traditional leader role is so firmly entrenched as a set of expectations and patterns of behaviors and that the pressures for maintaining such a role are intense, change to a new role must be highly rewarding. Some insights into what such a role might look like are emerging in the literature in the areas of 1) sociotechnical systems (Emery & Trist, 1960; Miller

& Rice, 1967; Emery, 1969; Herbst, 1974); 2) the relationship between technological change and the increased potential for workgroup involvement in problem solving and decision making (Davis & Taylor, 1975; Susman, 1975b; Davis & Taylor, 1976); and 3) experiments in enhancing quality of work life (Davis, Cherns, & Associates, 1975b; Thorsrud, Sorensen, & Gustavsen, 1976).

The focus of this new role is on the management of organizational boundaries. The basic observation underlying this perspective is that as technologies and organizations become more complex it becomes increasingly necessary to manage the interdependencies between the parts of the system. It is particularly important that top management focus their attention on the relationships between [the] organization and its environment, for such a focus enables the rest of the organization to reorient its focus:

> ...if top management develops an inward-directed orientation, they will usually force the rest of the managerial hierarchy to do the same, resulting in decreasing possibilities for autonomy as one approaches the shop floor. (Thorsrud, Sorensen, & Gustavsen, 1976, pp. 457-458)

Other clues as to the importance of this boundary role comes from research on how managers spend their time, with respect to their interactions with others. For example, Mintzberg (1973) indicates that managers spend a considerable amount of time in "lateral" relationships—with peers or others outside the hierarchical relationship. Another study indicates that the effective manager spends 70-75 per cent of his or her total time interacting with others in such lateral relationships, 20-25 per cent with workgroup members, and 3-5 per cent with superiors (Sayles, 1964).

Some of the central functions of a role that focuses on the management of boundaries are already inherent in the traditional hierarchical managerial role. Such boundary functions include:

1. *Planning:* Both short- and long-term planning where the boundary maintainer is involved with other parts of the organization acting as a representative of his or her group. Equally important, he or she must be involved with the workgroup in the planning process, acting, in part, as a representative of the larger organization.

2. *Goal Setting:* Involved with relevant parts of the larger organization and with the workgroup, acting, as above, in the dual representative role.
3. *Coordination:* Coordinating work flows with other departments with which the workgroup is interdependent and facilitation to ensure that support and resources are available to the group.
4. *Workgroup Representative:* Interacting with other parts of the organization to communicate and represent the workgroup's position on issues affecting the members and ensuring support and resources necessary for effective workgroup functioning.
5. *Organizational Representative:* Equally important is the necessity for the larger issues of the organization to be communicated, translated, and represented to the workgroup.
6. *Consultant:* Another key activity is "consulting" to the workgroup with respect to its functioning. Since the boundary role does not include authority and control over central aspects of workgroup functioning it would be possible for the role to be freed from the dysfunctional hierarchical dynamics of the managerial role. It would be possible for such a person to be helpful as an advisor/consultant with respect to the group's functioning.

It may seem that such a drastic change in the traditional role of the manager is not feasible. However, parts—including significant parts—of such a change have been experimented with and implemented (Agervold, 1975; Iman, 1975; Janson, 1975; McCullough, 1975; Thorsrud, Sorensen, & Gustavsen, 1976). There is increasing evidence that not only is such a role viable but that if such changes do not take place, the outcomes of increased workgroup member satisfaction, growth, and productivity are unlikely. It should also be noted that the potential for growth and development, for excitement and challenge, for the development of new and very different skills, attitudes, values, and abilities are highly possible for the individual filling the boundary maintenance role.

SUMMARY

The emphasis of this paper is on the role of the leader in work organizations. Our traditional conception of leadership as being vested in the formal leader must change if human growth, satisfaction, and increased organizational effectiveness are valued outcomes associated with work in our society. Both the design of work and the locus of decision making must be altered so that the work group becomes responsible for the planning, organization, direction, and control of work.

The change of the focus of the managerial role to the management of the interdependencies in organizations is an enabling change. It enables workgroups to work collaboratively because they have the power to make decisions with respect to how work gets done. Similarly, the role of the manager changes from a hierarchical to a collaborative role. The role requires dual representation—representing the workgroup to the organization and the larger organization to the workgroup. It becomes more of a facilitative, advising and negotiating role, a role that will offer new challenges and require very different values and skills.

References

Agervold, M. Swedish experiments in industrial democracy. In L.E. Davis, A.B. Cherns, and Associates (Eds.), *The quality of working life: Cases and commentary* (Vol. 2). New York: Free Press, 1975.

Archer, J.T. Achieving joint organizational, technical, and personal needs: The case of the sheltered experiments of Aluminum Casting Team. In L.E. Davis, A.B. Cherns, and Associates (Eds.), *The quality of working life: Cases and commentary* (Vol. 2). New York: Free Press, 1975.

Argyris, C. *Personality and organization.* New York: Harper & Row, 1957.

Argyris, C. *Integrating the individual and the organization.* New York: John Wiley, 1964.

Blauner, R. *Alienation and freedom.* Chicago: University of Chicago Press, 1964.

Davis, L.E., & Taylor, J.C. (Eds.). *The design of jobs.* Baltimore, MD: Penguin, 1972.

Davis, L.E., & Taylor, J.C. Technology effects on job, work and organizational structure: A contingency view. In L.E. Davis, A.B. Cherns, & Associates (Eds.), *The quality of working life: Problems, prospects, and the state of the art* (Vol. 1). New York: Free Press, 1975.

Davis, L.E., & Taylor, J.C. Technology, organization and job structure. In R. Dubin (Ed.), *Handbook of work, organization, and society.* Chicago: Rand McNally, 1976.

Davis, L.E., Cherns, A.B., and Associates (Eds.). *The quality of working life: Problems, prospects, and the state of the art* (Vol. 1). New York: Free Press, 1975a.

Davis, L.E., Cherns, A.B., and Associates (Eds.). *The quality of working life: Cases and commentary* (Vol. 2). New York: Free Press, 1975b.

Emery, F.E. (Ed.). *Systems thinking.* Baltimore, MD: Penguin, 1969.

Emery, F.E., & Trist, E.L. Socio-technical systems. In C.W. Churchman and M. Verhulst (Eds.), *Management science* (Vol. 2). Oxford: Pergamon Press, 1960.

Gulowsen, J. A measure of work group autonomy. In L.E. Davis and J.C. Taylor (Eds.), *The design of jobs.* Baltimore, MD: Penguin, 1972.

Herbst, P.G. *Socio-technical design*. London: Tavistock, 1974.

Iman, S.C. The development of participation by semiautonomous work teams: The case of Donnelly Mirrors. In L.E. Davis, A.B. Cherns, and Associates (Eds.), *op. cit.*, 1975.

Jacobs, C.D. Job enrichment of field technical representatives—Xerox Corporation. In L.E. Davis, A.B. Cherns, and Associates (Eds.), *op. cit.*, 1975.

Janson, R. A job enrichment trail in data processing. In L.E. Davis, A.B. Cherns, and Associates (Eds.), *op. cit.*, 1975.

Jenkins, D. *Job power: Blue and white collar democracy*. New York: Penguin, 1973.

Kornhauser, A. *Mental health of the industrial worker*. New York: John Wiley, 1965.

McCullough, G.E. The effects of changes in organizational structure: Demonstration projects in an oil refinery. In L.E. Davis, A.B. Cherns, and Associates (Eds.), *op. cit.*, 1975.

McGregor, D. *The human side of enterprise*. New York: McGraw-Hill, 1960.

Miller, E.J., & Rice, A.K. *Systems of organization*. London: Tavistock, 1967.

Mintzberg, H. *The nature of managerial work*. New York: Harper & Row, 1973.

Presthus, R. *The organizational society*. New York: Vintage, 1962.

Quinn, R.P., Staines, G.L., & McCullough, M.R. *Job Satisfaction: Is there a trend?* U.S. Department of Labor, Manpower Research Monograph No. 30. Washington, DC: Government Printing Office, 1974.

Sayles, L.R. *Managerial behavior: Administration in complex enterprises*. New York: McGraw-Hill, 1964.

Susman, G.I. Technological prerequisites for delegation of decision making to work groups. In L.E. Davis, A.B. Cherns, and Associates (Eds.), *op. cit.*, 1975.

Thorsrud, E., Sorensen, B.A., & Gustavsen, B. Sociotechnical approach to industrial democracy in Norway. In R. Dubin (Ed.), *Handbook of work, organization, and society*. Chicago: Rand McNally, 1976.

Work in America. Report prepared by the Special Task Force for the Secretary of HEW. Cambridge, MA: M.I.T. Press, 1973.

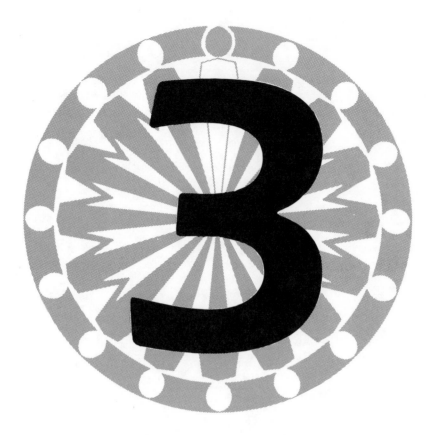

Leadership in
Educational Settings

Introduction to Part 3: Leadership in Educational Settings

Leaders in educational institutions have been widely criticized for ineffectiveness in adjusting to changing times. The turn-over rate among educational administrators is relatively high throughout all levels of education, but particularly at the college and university levels. This may occur in part because of advancement to better positions, but departure to less responsible positions does occur, often by choice (although it may be the only choice) for those who are judged to have failed. Such failure may occur for a variety of reasons, but inadequate preparation for leadership, failure to understand the uniqueness of leadership in education, and unrealistic expectations among constituents are surely among the most common causes.

Gibb offers an eloquent treatment of the basis for failure in educational leadership. He also identifies principles that could increase both realism and effectiveness. Two polar views are outlined as an explanation of what educational leaders ought to be. The first is much like the authoritarian, Theory X, leadership approach defined by McGregor. Gibb calls this "defensive" leadership; it arises from insecurity about position and external criticism. Defensive leadership is based on fear and distrust; defensiveness generates more fear and greater distrust, which tend to expand in educational systems. Eventually, such an approach can become a self-fulfilling prophecy, much as McGregor attributed Theory X to be.

Gibb suggests that educational-leader authoritarianism increases dissonance among subordinates as well as in society at large. Defensive leadership results in a cycle of fear, hostility, and inappropriate controls, all of which run counter to the more desirable cycle of esteem, trust, and mutual confidence.

Participative leadership is recommended as the more effective alternative. Self-determination and self-assessment are encouraged. Joint and interdependent planning among administrators, faculty, staff, and students is a central concept. Valid, direct, authentic, and open communication is essential to a more healthy environment for learning and growth.

In concluding his argument, Gibb notes that effective participative leadership seems to be more common in industrial, and even in military, organizations than it is in educational institutions. He suggests that internal conflicts and external attacks on university systems make them susceptible to defensive leadership. Furthermore, the traditional "ivory tower" isolation of the university from society supports continuation of authoritarianism.

Cohen and March also attempt to explain why institutions of higher education may be prone to defensive leadership. There is an inherently high degree of ambiguity in these "loosely-coupled systems." At least four major sources of such ambiguity are evident: ambiguous goals, ambiguous power relationships, ambiguous experiential information, and ambiguous success. These ambiguities lead to the characterization of higher educational institutions as "organized anarchies." Organizational leadership is exceptionally difficult to exercise in such situations. Under conditions of high ambiguity, most people try to increase their security and certainty. A typical reaction, in the case of presidents and other college administrators, is defensive leadership as defined by Gibb.

To overcome the negative effects of ambiguity, without resort to defensive leadership, Cohen and March offer eight specific behavioral tactics. These tactics can be used by anyone who wants to influence decision making in institutions of higher education. In a sense, Cohen and March see the educational institution as though it were made of many large chunks of gelatin. One cannot simply tie ropes around them, pull, and expect them all to move in the same direction. Rather, one develops smooth surfaces in front and pushes very gently and from several directions. The college president has the advantage of being more interested in doing this— affecting the overall direction of the organization—and having more time to do it than most of the other members of the organization.

The tactics offered by Cohen and March for leading educational institutions do not directly address the issue raised by Gibb. Use of "tactics" may help the educational administrator implement desirable policies and decisions or direct the organization toward desirable goals, but the system will not be any less ambiguous. Thus, defensive leadership may still occur. Cohen and March offer suggestions for leading effectively in a situation of high fear and high defensiveness. Gibb would rather try to change the situation by altering the fear-reinforcing, defensive leadership behavior.

Stogdill offers an alternative viewpoint. He argues that effective educational administrators are demonstrably high on "consideration" and "initiation of structure." In this respect, Stogdill echos the prescription of Blake and Mouton, in Part II, but applies it to institutions of higher education. However, very few of the studies he cites, such as Hemphill and Halpin's Ohio State research of the 1950's, actually linked effectiveness to high ratings of consideration and initiation of structure in higher education. More recent work, by Andrews and his colleagues, provides evidence that principals high on both dimensions have subordinates (teachers) who *are* more effective; their students learn more. The most positive impact on student performance seems to occur when teachers rank high on both dimensions.

At the larger system level, Stogdill argues that higher educational institutions "drift" because of a widespread "laissez-faire" leadership philosophy. This philosophy emphasizes "consideration" but rejects sustained initiation of structure as too autocratic. This leads to educational organizations that are characterized by a lack of clear purpose and with no strongly felt commitment by members. Greater democracy is needed to produce high morale and strong feelings of attachment to the organization; this can be achieved by "consideration" behaviors from leaders *and* can provide clear direction or purpose through the leader's initiation of democratic rather than authoritarian structure.

Teacher-leadership in the classroom clearly varies from the usual leadership setting. The "subordinates" are not employees. They often have no choice about staying or leaving. Nor do they work to produce a group product; the output is their own learning and individual development.

Stogdill notes that classroom studies by Anderson showed that high degrees of both "consideration" and "initiation of structure" behaviors were positively related to students' achievement, but that neither democratic nor autocratic patterns seemed effective. This apparent contradiction is addressed by Hersey and his colleagues.

Situational Leadership™ theory has been used for over a decade in management training throughout the world. Controlled experiments with executives in classroom training situations were used by Hersey, Angelini, and Carakushansky to test the effects of Situational Leadership™ theory as compared with more conventional classroom teaching methods. The experimental groups were generally low in "task maturity" at the outset; that is, they were unwilling and unable to take responsibility for learning the assigned materials. The leader therefore provided high structure and specific instructions, with only a minimum of emotional support. As the class increased in maturity and responsibility, the instructor altered the leadership style to increase the participants' responsibility while increasing emotional support and encouragement from the leader. This corresponds roughly to a pattern of leader behavior that is high on both the consideration and structure dimensions.

As the participants' task maturity increased (with trainees who were now "able" but not "willing" to take responsibility for their own learning), the instructor moved to a style of full participation, providing support (consideration) and guidance, but allowing the trainees to plan and carry out their own learning activities. When the trainees were both willing and able, the instructor delegated the learning activities to them, reducing the consideration (support) to its original minimum and eliminating directive behavior almost entirely.

Hersey and his colleagues argue that while a leader in educational settings should always exhibit a high concern for both dimensions of leader behavior, no single behavior pattern, autocratic or democratic, can be effective all the time. This fits with Stogdill's conclusions. The leader's behavior must be "tuned" to match the needs of subordinates.

Educational institutions deserve special analysis because of their uniquely loosely coupled nature, because of the ambiguity in which the leaders must operate, and because of the uncertain quasi-leadership role of instructors. Educational institutions are nonetheless prone to many of the same conditions that affect other complex organizations. Many of the same approaches of leadership development can therefore be effective. Gibb emphasizes the significance of participative leadership; Cohen and March designed their tactics to subtly draw leaders in higher education into participation. The participative model appears likely to yield the best outcome.

Dynamics of Educational Leadership

Jack R. Gibb

People must be led. People perform best under leaders who are creative, imaginative and aggressive—under leaders who lead. It is the responsibility of the leader to marshal the forces of the organization, to stimulate effort, to capture the imagination, to inspire people, to coordinate efforts, and to serve as a model of sustained effort.

The leader should keep an appropriate social distance, show no favorites, control his emotions, command respect, and be objective and fair. He must know what he is doing and where he wants to go. He must set clear goals for himself and for the group or institution, and then communicate these goals well to all members of the organization. He must listen for advice and counsel before making decisions. But it is his responsibility to make decisions and to set up mechanisms for seeing that the decisions are implemented. After weighing the facts and seeking expert counsel, he must make policy and rules, set reasonable boundaries, and see that these are administered with justice and wisdom, even compassion.

The leader should reward good performance and learn effective ways of showing appreciation. He must be equally ready to give negative criticism where warranted and to appraise performance frequently, fairly, and unequivocally. He must command strong discipline, not only because people respect a strong leader, but because strength and firmness communicate care and concern. Good leadership requires good followship. People tend to follow good leaders. Leaders are born. Methods of election and selection are thus very important. Finding the right chairman or president is the critical variable in the success of a program or an institution. The quality of an organization is often judged by the perceived quality of the leadership.

The above is an oversimplified statement of one view of leadership theory and practice. A similarly oversimplified statement of an alternative viewpoint follows.

People grow, produce, and learn best when they set their own goals, choose activities that they see as related to these goals, and have a wide range of freedom of choice in all parts of their lives. Under most conditions persons are highly motivated, like to take responsibilities, can be trusted to put out a great deal of effort toward organizational goals, are creative and imaginative, and tend to want to cooperate with others.

Leadership is only one of several significant variables in the life of the group or the institution. Leaders can be helpful and often are. The most effective leader is one who acts as a catalyst, a consultant, and a resource to the group. His job is to help the group to grow, to emerge, and to become more free. He serves the group best when he is a whole person, is direct, real, open, spontaneous, permissive, emotional, and highly personal. The leader at his best is an effective member. He acts in such a way as to facilitate group strength, individual responsibility, diversity, nonconformity, and aggressiveness. The leader is thus not necessary to the group and quickly becomes replaceable, dispensable, and independent. The good leader tends not to lead. He permits, feels, acts, relates, fights, talks—acts human as do other members of the group and the institution. The leader is present, available, and with the group as a person, not as a role.

We find many shades and variations of each of these two over-simplified statements of the theory and practice of leadership in our society. Several years of consulting and research in representative organizations make it very clear to me that attitudes toward leadership tend to cluster around these two poles. This bifurcation has analogues in current educational theory, politics, religion, philosophy, and administration.

DEFENSIVE LEADERSHIP

The first view, described variously as authoritarian, paternalistic, or conservative, I classify as defensive because dynamically the view defends the administrator against his own fears and distrusts and against perceived or anticipated attack from the outside.

This authoritarian or defensive view is particularly appropriate to some viable aspects of the culture we live in: to organizational norms inherited from the medieval church and military; to a life of vertical hierarchy, prescribed role responsibilities, and delegated authority; to a highly competitive economic and educational system; to the current dominant values of efficiency, excellence, productivity, task performance, and perfectionism; to the impersonality, alienation, loneliness, impotence, and indifference in our people; to a world of automation, programming, data processing, and engineering; to a forensic, persuasive, public relations, and marketing mode of interpersonal commerce; to a world continually at war, threatened by war, or preparing for war; in short, to a world of machines. It is not accidental that all around the country when administrators administer the ultimate forensic weapon in arguing against participative forms of leadership they say, "but it would never work in the military or on the production line." Actually, research indicates that this point is probably not true, but in any event the image of the leaders of our educational and governmental institutions using as a reference point for administrative theory the demands of the military organization and the production line is at least disconcerting.

It seems to me equally clear that defensive leadership is highly inappropriate and perhaps even fundamentally dissonant with another viable side of the world we live in: with education for growth, intimacy, authenticity, humanness, and creativity; with the Judeo-Christian ethics of love, honesty, intimacy, faith, cheek-turning, and brotherhood; with a climate for research, inquiry, scholarship, contemplation, and learning; with cooperation, group planning, team building, and various successful forms of group effort; with the new emerging models of industrial organization and manufacturing productivity; with what might be thought of as the behavioral science approach to organizational change; with the world of ambiguity, feeling, conflict, sorrow, creativity, and diversity; with many new and exciting developments in education, architecture, the creative arts, economics, management, and all phases of modern life; in short, with the world of human beings, with people.

I have deliberately drawn sharp and oversimplified distinctions in a problem area which is very complex and legitimately polemic. It is essential today that those who are administratively responsible for the colleges and universities of America see clearly this conflict and its implications for all facets of American Life. It is my observation that much of the dysfunctional disturbance that the papers report daily from the college campuses is created as unintended but inevitable effects of defensive leadership practices among administrators of American colleges.

Let us look at the dynamics of defensive leadership. The major dynamic of the defensive model is fear and distrust. Observations indicate that people who have mild or more serious fears tend to do several things: distrust the people being led; filter the data that are given to the followers and develop strategies for such filtering and programming of data dissemination; attempt to control and manipulate the motivations of the followers; and attempt to control their behavior. The incidence and degree of low trust, strategic, persuasional, and controlling behavior varies directly with the amount of fear. Most of us who are leaders or are placed in leadership roles have varying degrees of fear about our own adequacy, how we are seen by others, the effectiveness of our leadership strategies, the effects of rebellion, the anxieties about insubordination and other unfollowerlike behavior. I guess that our major fear has to do with anxiety about being followed!

The behavior of leaders tends to camouflage, perhaps even to themselves, the underlying fears which support the strategic, manipulative, and controlling behavior. For images of fear on assuming leadership roles one has but to think of the new teachers in the schoolroom, the new mother bringing back her first baby from the hospital, the new lieutenant guiding a patrol into action, or the newly appointed administrative official handling a student riot. The fears that we all have are quelled and softened by various adaptive, self-deceptive, and facade-building mechanisms for presenting ourselves to ourselves and to others.

Some educational leaders are today more fearful than ever. In reaction to student strikes, riots, demonstrations, and protests, as well as to the more normal vicissitudes of campus life, college and university leaders utilize defensive practices that generate unintended byproducts of fear, distrust, hostility, and counter-defensive behavior. The classical models of leadership are time and again proved to be ineffective. Why does defensive leadership arise and persist among educational leaders?

A reciprocal or circular process seems to be operating. Normal fears of life are exacerbated by the ambiguity, high control, and threat of the group or organization. However necessary this ambiguity and control is thought to be, it serves to create fears and hostilities which in turn call forth still more restrictive ambiguity and controlling behavior. This reciprocal fear-distrust cycle sustains the defensive behavior of leadership. The fears accompany and reinforce feelings of inadequacy and self-rejection in leaders and other members of the group or organization.

But the fears, hostilities, and distrusts are so successfully camouflaged in the social defenses that the casual observer might well think the above description of educational life to be strangely out of touch with reality as he sees it. Certainly it is not the conscious intent of educational leaders to create such a state of affairs.

Why is it then that we get in the university so many unintended effects? These unintended effects seem to result from a kind of self-fulfilling prophecy: low-trust, high-fear theories, when put into practice, actually generate distrust and fears that not only confirm the assumptions underlying the theories, but also provide emotional support and strong motivation to continue the low-trust, high-fear behavior. An interactive and self-preserving cycle is thus set in motion, supported in depth by latent fear-distrust and by rationalized theories which appear to be confirmed. Leadership behavior, thus supported, is exceedingly difficult to change.

Behind the facade of paternalism, politeness, one-big-happy-family-living, heartiness, and the accompanying soft-sell influence and velvet-glove control lie defensive relationships that pervade the colleges. Defensive leadership is characterized by low trust, data distortion, persuasion, and high control. These four aspects of defensive leadership are parallel to four basic dimensions of all group or social behavior: the feeling climate, the flow of data within the system, the formation of goals, and the emergence of control.

The key to defensive leadership is a state of low trust. The defensive leader assumes that the average person cannot be trusted, he is essentially lazy and irresponsible, action must be taken to inspire and motivate him, and he requires supervision and control. The defensive leader can counteract his feelings of inferiority by assuming that his subordinates are less than they actually are; and he can service his hostile feelings by keeping the subordinate in demeaning, dependent, and inferior roles in relation to himself and to leadership as a class.

The defensive leader or administrator rationalizes the service of his needs by developing formal or informal leader theories which both justify and camouflage his fears and hostilities. An essential step in theory and practice is to manipulate the flow of information and communication within the organization. Information sent down from the top is often deliberately "corrected" to increase morale, to allay fears, to put the best administrative foot forward and to justify administrative action. "Correction" is achieved by consciously or unconsciously filtering and distorting information to present a good image, to encourage positive thinking, or to build loyalty.

Strategies are devised to improve the administrative image: a worker's name is remembered to make him feel good; a birthday file is kept to demonstrate that the administrator feels the subordinate is important enough to warrant a birthday card. The "good" administrator is especially careful to smile acceptingly at those members of the "family" team towards whom he has temporary or sustained feelings of animosity. Interpersonal cues are thus manipulated and distorted to present a facade of warmth, friendliness, or cohesiveness.

The defensive leader is continually challenged to create new prods, rewards, and gimmicks as the old ones become ineffective. Thus the responsibility for sustaining motivations is thrust upon the administrator or teacher rather than upon the student. The inherent impetus to derive self-satisfaction and self-respect through accomplishment for its own sake becomes atrophied and lost. Self-satisfaction becomes dysfunctional as an incentive system.

The Reward System

The person who is being motivated by others through extrinsic rewards tends either to resist being influenced or to come under the control of the rewarder. He is motivated, not to achieve something, but to gain the approval of the teacher or administrator, to hunt for his satisfactions in status, grade, and social approval rather than to look for his satisfactions within, in terms of self-respect, self-approval, and the achievement of personal goals.

Thus the roots of dependence and apathy lie in the reward system, for the person who learns to find his values from without is always at the mercy of other persuaders—teachers, companions, demogogues, groups, or other sources of approval and authority. He becomes dependent, passive, and susceptible to all sorts of external controls.

The reward system may in others foster resistance and rebellion, resentment, cynicism, and a variety of negative and competitive feelings. People who work under competition learn to be competitive, and the extrinsic rewards do not satisfy the deep needs for self-satisfaction and self-respect which are gained by achieving our personal goals as unique individuals.

Both dependency and resistance require controls, and the defensive leader expends a considerable amount of energy devising a variety of controls both for the people and for the processes of the enterprise. The more fearful and anxious he is, the more he feels caught in recurring emergencies and the greater is his need to control. Regulations are put on car-parking, coffee break duration, channels of reporting, library schedules, methods of work, habits of dress, use of safety devices, more and more complex filing systems, rigid report systems—until all aspects of living in the organization are controlled.

The conscious and official reasons given for the controls usually relate to organization and productive efficiency, but the underlying impulses often spring from, or are reinforced by, the leader's personal needs for rigid order or needs to demonstrate his superiority and strength, express hostility, exercise power, justify his position ("What else would I do if I didn't plan these controls?"), reinforce hierarchy, force people to be orderly or confirming, and keep them in line.

Control systems become functionally autonomous—traditional and conventional elements of the organizational system—and often outlive any practical utility. Indeed, people seem to sense that many regulations actually serve personal needs for punishment or power and bear little relation to the actual needs of the organization itself. In looking at organizations we have often found that many controls are universally violated in the system by common consent. In fact, there is clear indication—and often conscious awareness—that some controls are so dysfunctional that if everyone obeyed them the system would come to a grinding halt.

These defensive techniques of leadership produce certain predictable results. Fear and distrust beget fear and distrust. People who are distrustful tend to see untrustworthy behavior in others. If the relationship between an administrator and his subordinate is basically one of distrust, almost any action on either's part is perceived by the other as untrustworthy. Thus a cycle is created which nurtures self-corroborating leadership hypotheses.

This cycle is well illustrated in connection with communications. Any restriction of the flow of information and any closed strategy arouses energy devoted to circumventing the strategy and fosters counter-strategies that are at least as imaginative and often more effective than the original inducing strategy. A familiar example is the strategy of countering the top brass by distorting the upward-flowing data: feelings of hostility are camouflaged by deferential politeness; reports are "fixed up," records are doctored or "cooked" to fit administrative goals and directives. Such attempts are augmented by emergency and threat; the greater the fear and distrust, the greater the circumvention, counter-strategy, and counter-distortion.

Defensive leaders use various forms of persuasion to motivate subordinates toward the organization's goals, but often the results are either apathy and passivity or frenetic conformity. Persuasion is a form of control and begets resistance, which may take many subtle forms. Open and aggressive cold war between teachers and administrators, for instance, is an obvious form. More common—and less easy to deal with—is passive, often unconscious resistance such as apathy, apparent obtuseness, dependent demands for further and more minute instructions, bumbling, wheel-spinning, and a whole variety of inefficiencies that reduce creative work.

As we have seen, tight control leads to some form of dependency and its accompanying hostility; it may vary from the yes-man's deference and conformity to the no-man's rebellion against even the most reasonable and normal requests and rules. Deference and rebellion are cut from the same cloth. When unnecessary and arbitrary controls are imposed, or when normal controls are seen as unnecessary or arbitrary, as is the case when there is fear and distrust, then almost all members of the hierarchy become concerned with their feelings about authority. Most of us are ambivalent toward authority figures, and these mixed feelings are augmented in periods of stress and fear. In tightly controlled, disciplining, and disciplined organizations members demand clarity in rules and in boundary demarcations. But rules can never be made completely clear in practical work situations; boundaries are always permeable and inadequately defined. Thus the demands for further clarification are endless, and controls lead to further controls.

We see how the cycle is set up: hostility and its inevitable counterpart, fear, are increased by the distrust, distortion, persuasion-reward, and control systems of defensive leadership; and the continuing cycle is reinforced at all stages, for as fear breeds distrust, distrust is rationalized and structured into theories which sanction distrustful leadership practices. The practices reinforce distrust; now the theorist is justified, and latent motivation to continue the cycle is itself reinforced.

Defensive leadership theories and practices permeate our society. We find them in the home, in school, and in the church, as well as in business organizations. Let us see, for instance, how the child-rearing patterns of our culture fit the picture described above. There are so many frightening things in the world that can harm helpless children. The fearful person can, with little effort, find a variety of frightening aspects in the environment of the child—anything from matches and electric outlets to busy roads and unacceptable playmates. Anxiety makes it easy to exaggerate the number of people ready to kidnap and even rape one's child; the fears of the parent embellish natural dangers and provide nourishment and comforting rationalization for defensive practices.

Communications must be managed for the good of the child. Because he might be worried or upset, emotional and financial discord must be camouflaged and a facade of security and serenity maintained. Children are inexperienced and immature, therefore they cannot be trusted to do things on their own. Moreover, since the natural interests of the child are likely to be frivolous, demeaning, or harmful, he should be carefully guided and persuaded to do what is right—to select appropriate playmates, read good books, and generally adopt goals set by the parental culture or aspirations. To protect the child from ubiquitous dangers and to set his feet on the proper path, parents readily learn to use bribes, praise, and deprivation as tools of coercion. And because children are initially dependent and helpless, it is easy for the fearful parent to prolong the period of dependency.

Schools reinforce these patterns. They receive children whose dependency has been created by defensive parental techniques, and they maintain the dependency by continuing these practices. Having been distrusted, children continue to be untrustworthy. The insecure teacher finds it necessary to maintain a protective facade; she rationalizes her behavior by making a number of low-trust, tight-control assumptions about the children under her tutelage. She builds a changing repertoire of tricks to keep them busy, orderly, neat, attentive, and—she hopes—motivated. Impressed by the awesome culture heritage she is charged to transmit, she feels it imperative that she instill in her pupils the goals, ideals, and rules of the culture. As bodies of knowledge become increasingly standardized, pressures towards indoctrination increase. By codifying rules, regulations, and standards, the teachers build internal control systems—in the classroom, and hopefully, in the children themselves. As part of the informal curriculum, children are taught facade-building; they are encouraged to put the best foot forward, to be polite, to be decorous, and to adopt the essentially hypocritical social graces of the dominant middle class.

AN ALTERNATIVE—PARTICIPATIVE LEADERSHIP

What is the alternative to defensive leadership? This is not as easy to specify. The key to emergent leadership centers in a high degree of trust and confidence in people. Leaders who trust their colleagues and subordinates and have confidence in them tend to be open and frank, to be permissive in goal setting, and to be noncontrolling in personal style and leadership policy. People with a great deal of self-acceptance and personal security do trust others, do make trust assumptions about their motives and behavior. The self-adequate person tends to assume that others are also adequate and, other things being equal, that they will be responsible, loyal, appropriately work-oriented when work is to be performed, and adequate to carry out jobs that are commensurate with their levels of experience and growth.

Just as we saw that distrust arises from fear and hostility, so we can see that people with little fear and minimal needs to be hostile are ready to trust others. Of course, there is some risk in trusting others, in being open and freedom-giving.

People naturally tend to share their feelings and concerns with those whom they trust, and this is true at the simplest and most direct level of inter-personal relationships as well as at more complex levels of organizational communication. Thus a high-trust system may institute open planning meetings and evaluation meetings; public criteria for promotion; easily available information on salaries, cost figures, and budgets; and easy access to material in the files. There is comparatively little concern with public relations, with the corporate or family image, or with communications programs. Communication in such a system is a process rather than a program.

The participative leader is permissive in his relations with subordinates, for he assumes that as people grow they learn to assess their own aptitudes, discover their deep-lying interests, and develop their basic potentials. Therefore he gives his subordinates every opportunity to maximize self-determination and self-assessment, to verbalize their goals, to try new jobs or enlarge the scope of the work they are doing, and he trusts them to make mature judgments about job assignments. Where he is dealing with a work-team or a group, he lets the group make decisions about job allotments and work assignments.

This process of allowing people to be responsible for their own destinies, for setting their own targets, assessing their own development needs, searching out resources to aid in job accomplishment, and participating in setting organizational objectives is basic to high-trust leadership. Instead of using conventional defensive-leadership techniques of skilled persuasion to induce acceptance of leadership goals, the high-trust administration participates in cooperative determination of goals and in cooperative definition of production and staff problems. He [sic]knows that goal-information is a significant skill that must be learned, and that to develop such skill students and adults must exercise a variety of opportunities to make decisions, explore goals, and experiment with many kinds of activities.

The participative administrator joins in creating a climate in which he has no need to impose controls. He knows that in a healthy group controls emerge from group processes as the need is perceived. Then controls are mediated by group or organization objectives and by such relevant data as deadlines and target dates. People or groups who have set their own objectives and have clearly stated their own goals build internal tension-systems which maintain goal orientation and create appropriate boundaries.

Formal and written rules about such things as work space, library use, and stockroom neatness are less and less necessary when people are engaged in a common task with others whose feelings and perceptions they freely share; when there is trust and mutuality, people are inclined to respect the rights and concerns of fellow members. This principle applies to large and small systems alike—in either, the participative administrator reduces as far as practicable all formal controls evidenced by rules, regulations, written memoranda, signs, formal job specification sheets, rigid lines of responsibility and authority, and the like.

The effects of participative leading are diametrically contrary to those of defensive leading. Love begets love. Respect begets respect. Trust produces trust. People who are trusted tend to trust themselves and to trust those in positions of responsibility. Moreover, the feeling that one is trusted encourages exploration, diversity, and innovation, for the person spends little time and energy trying to prove himself. His time and energy are freed to define and solve problems, accomplish work, and create new dimensions of his job. A fearful person uses a great deal of energy in defending himself against present or anticipated threat or attack; a confident and self-assured person can direct his energy towards goals that are significant to him as a person.

Again, openness begets openness. In the long run, at least, one who freely shares data, whether of feelings or of figures, reduces fear and distrust in himself and in others. Defensive administrators build massive communication programs, not to disseminate objective information but to mold attitudes, create favorable and appropriate images, and influence people. Such persuasional and distortive communication produces resistance. Direct and open flow of information, on the other hand, serves to create an atmosphere which encourages people to share information with those above as well as with those below.

In general, openness and information giving improves the decision-making process, for experience in giving information and expressing feelings enhances consensus; and the more nearly a group can reach consensus on operational issues, the higher the quality of the decision and the greater the group's commitment to the program.

Moreover, participative goal-formation optimizes self-determination and self-assessment. Intrinsic motivations become increasingly relevant and powerful. People explore their own capacities and interests, and try to find or create work for themselves that is satisfying and fulfilling. They enlarge their own jobs, asking for more responsibility and more creative and interesting work. Such work is fulfilling to the person, and extrinsic rewards are secondary to satisfaction in accomplishing the task. Administrators find that people like to work; they "own" their jobs and feel great loyalty and responsibility toward the common goals of the group. People feel little need to escape from the work situation, and the "thank goodness it's Friday" clubs become less enticing. Concerns over salary and merit increases are symptomatic of defensive-leading pressures.

Participative administration creates interdependence and diminishes the problem of authority. For instance, work is allocated by consensus—people assess their abilities and select or create appropriate tasks. Where there is interdependence, conflict and disagreement are openly expressed and can thus ben resolved and integrated into productive work. Where people feel they are working together for a common goal, the organization of work can be flexible, diverse, and informal, with a minimum of written job boundaries and rigid role requirements. Channels of communication are free, open and spontaneous.

These concepts are a challenge to the university. The Ohio State studies, particularly, showed how far behind even the military and industry the university administration is in achieving some kind of more participative and less authoritarian administrative relationships. The headlines today are filled with conflicts. The university is in many ways more susceptible to the pressures which produce fear than is industry, government, or business. The university is at one and the same time vulnerable to attacks from public opinion and also historically inviolate. The products of the university are highly intangible, and it is difficult to apply vigorous controls to the product and to tell if the university is successful in the same way that a business or even the military is with its hard criteria for productivity, profit, or victory. Thus highly vulnerable, the university has preserved a historical isolation from social pressures; and administrative behavior is often medieval and out of touch with the vigorous demands of democratic growth. The university, strangely, is sometimes a citadel for autocratic administrative behavior.

The Ethics of Participation

I should say a word about the implications of this model for ethical behavior. In abstract, this model of leadership specifies a theory of ethics: That behavior is more ethical which is most trusting, most open, most self-determining, and most interdependent. Thus one would look in the university setting for unethical behavior in the areas of distrust, strategic filtering of feelings and ideas (honesty), manipulative abridgement of self-determination, and dependency-producing or rebellion-producing high control behavior.

It seems to me that joint, interdependent, and shared planning is the central concept of the kind of participative, consultative leadership that we are considering. Planning, to be moral, in this framework, to be efficient, and to be growth-producing must be organic to the institution, involve to an optimal degree all of the participants, and must be done interdependently. It is easy to find illustrations on the university campus of buildings in architectural styles that are unrelated to experimental learning theory, fund-raising methods that are planned by a special group of people who are usually collecting funds in ways that would be anathema to other members of the college community, athletic programs that arise from financial need rather than from educational policy, personnel practices that are inherited unabashedly from business institutions, planning as a fragmentary, emergency process engaged in by small groups of people who are often out of touch with the university as a community.

Our assumption is that the blocks to innovation and creativity are fear, poor communication, imposition of motivations, and the dependency-rebellion syndrome of forces. People are innovative and creative. The administration of innovation involves freeing the creativity that is always present. The administrative problem of innovation is to remove fear and increase trust, to remove strategic and distortional blocks to open communication, to remove coercive, persuasional, and manipulative efforts to pump motivation, and to remove the tight controls on behavior that tend to channel creative efforts into circumvention, counter-strategy, and organizational survival rather than into innovative and creative problem-solving.

Valid, direct, authentic, and open communication among all segments of the organic institution is a central process of effective leadership in the model we are examining. Effective leadership grows with communication in depth. Effective leadership is hampered by all forces which inhibit or restrain communication in depth. If emergent or participative leadership were prevalent on the campus, communication programs would become less and less necessary. Defensive administration breeds the conditions that require an increasing escalation of massive communication programs to hopefully alleviate the conditions produced by the defensive leadership.

We are attempting to become as a people and as a culture. We are in the process of discovering and creating models of interdependent, high-trust, self-determining, and open behavior. We are trying to create an interdependent, achieving, free, becoming culture. This has never been done in the world, and the strains of transition are awesome and somewhat frightening. But for those of us who are dedicated to the university as a way of life, the challenge to the college and university administrator and leader is clear. The challenge is there. The road is unclear. The goal is at one and at the same time preservation of certain concepts we hold dear and the achievement of a more free, a more open, a more self-determining, and a more human environment for learning and growth.

Leadership in an Organized Anarchy

Michael D. Cohen and James G. March

THE AMBIGUITIES OF ANARCHY

The college president faces four fundamental ambiguities. The first is the ambiguity of *purpose*. In what terms can action be justified? What are the goals of the organization? The second is the ambiguity of *power*. How powerful is the president? What can he accomplish? The third is the ambiguity of *experience*. What is to be learned from the events of the presidency? How does the president make inferences about his experience? The fourth is the ambiguity of *success*. When is a president successful? How does he assess his pleasures?

    These ambiguities are fundamental to college presidents because they strike at the heart of the usual interpretations of leadership. When purpose is ambiguous, ordinary theories of decision making and intelligence become problematic. When power is ambiguous, ordinary theories of social order and control become problematic. When experience is ambiguous, ordinary theories of learning and adaptation become problematic. When success is ambiguous, ordinary theories of motivation and personal pleasure become problematic....

Leader Response to Anarchy

The ambiguities that college presidents face describe the life of any formal leader of any organized anarchy. The metaphors of leadership and our traditions of personalizing history (even the minor histories of collegiate institutions) confuse the issues of leadership by ignoring the basic ambiguity of leadership life. We require a plausible basic perspective for the leader of a loosely coupled, ambiguous organization.

Such a perspective begins with humility. It is probably a mistake for a college president to imagine that what he does in office affects significantly either the long-run position of the institution or his reputation as a president. So long as he does not violate some rather obvious restrictions on his behavior, his reputation and his term of office are more likely to be affected by broad social events or by the unpredictable vicissitudes of official responsibility than by his actions. Although the college library or administration building will doubtless record his presidency by appropriate portraiture or plaque, few presidents achieve even a modest claim to attention 20 years after their departure from the presidency; and those who are remembered best are probably most distinguished by their good fortune in coming to office during a period of collegiate good times and growth, or their bad fortune in being there when the floods came.

In this respect the president's life does not differ markedly from that of most of us. A leadership role, however, is distinguished by the numerous temptations to self-importance that it provides. Presidents easily come to believe that they can continue in office forever if they are only clever or perceptive or responsive enough. They easily come to exaggerate the significance of their daily actions for the college as well as for themselves. They easily come to see each day as an opportunity to build support in their constituencies for the next "election."

It is an old story. Human action is frequently corrupted by an exaggeration of its consequences. Parents are intimidated by an exaggerated belief in their importance to the process of childrearing. Teachers are intimidated by an exaggerated belief in their importance to the process of learning. Lovers are intimidated by an exaggerated belief in their importance to the process of loving. Counselors are intimidated by an exaggerated belief in their importance to the process of self-discovery.

The major consequence of a heroic conception of the consequences of action is a distrust of judgment. When college presidents imagine that their actions have great consequences for the world, they are inclined to fear an error. When they fear an error, they are inclined to seek social support for their judgment, to confuse voting with virtue and bureaucratic rules with equity. Such a conception of the importance of their every choice makes presidents vulnerable to the same deficiencies of performance that afflict the parents of first children and inexperienced teachers, lovers, or counselors.

A lesser, but important, result of a heroic conception of the consequences of action is the abandonment of pleasure. By acceding to his own importance, the college president is driven to sobriety of manner. For reasons we have detailed earlier, he has difficulty in establishing the correctness of his actions by exhibiting their consequences. He is left with the necessity of communicating moral intent through facial intensity. At the same time, he experiences the substantial gap between his aspirations and his possibilities. Both by the requirements of their public face and by their own intolerant expectations, college presidents often find the public enjoyment of their job denied to them.

The ambiguities of leadership in an organized anarchy require a leadership posture that is somewhat different from that implicit in most discussions of the college presidency. In particular, we believe that a college president is, on the whole, better advised to think of himself as trying to do good than as trying to satisfy a political or bureaucratic audience; better advised to define his role in terms of the modest part he can play in making the college slightly better in the long run than in terms of satisfying current residents or solving current problems. He requires an enthusiasm for a Tolstoyan view of history and for the freedom of individual action that such a view entails. Since the world is absurd, the president's primary responsibility is to virtue.

Presidents occupy a minor part in the lives of a small number of people. They have some power, but little magic. They can act with a fair degree of confidence that if they make a mistake, it will not matter much. They can be allowed the heresy of believing that pleasure is consistent with virtue.

THE ELEMENTARY TACTICS OF ADMINISTRATIVE ACTION

The tactics of administrative action in an organized anarchy are somewhat different from the tactics of action in a situation characterized by clearer goals, better specified technology, and more persistent participation. Nevertheless, we can examine how a leader with a purpose can operate within an organization that is without one.

Necessarily, any presentation of practical strategies suggests a minor Machiavellianism with attendant complications and concerns. There is an argument that strategies based upon knowledge contribute to administrative manipulation. There is a fear that practical strategies may be misused for evil ends. There is a feeling that the effectiveness of the strategies may be undermined by their public recitation.

We are aware of these concerns, but not persuaded by them. First, we do not believe that any major new cleverness that would conspicuously alter the prevailing limits on our ability to change the course of history will be discovered. The idea that there are some spectacularly effective strategies waiting to be discovered by some modern Machiavelli seems implausible. Second, we believe that the problem of evil is little eased by know-nothingness. The concern about malevolent manipulation is a real one (as well as a cliche), but it often becomes a simple defense of the status quo. We hope that good people interested in accomplishing things will find a list of tactics marginally helpful. Third, we can see nothing in the recitation of strategic recommendations that changes systematically the relative positions of members of the organization. If the strategies are effective, it is because the analysis of organization is correct. The features of the organization that are involved are not likely to change quickly. As a result, we would not anticipate that public discussion of the strategies would change their effectiveness much or distinctly change the relative positions of those (e.g., students, presidents) who presumably stand to profit from the advice if it is useful.

As we will indicate later in this chapter, a conception of leadership that merely assumes that the college president should act to accomplish what he wants to accomplish is too narrow. A major part of his responsibility is to lead the organization to a changing and more complex view of itself by treating goals as only partly knowable. Nevertheless, the problems of inducing a college to do what one wants it to do are clearly worthy of attention. If presidents and others are to function effectively within the college, they need to recognize the ways in which the character of the college as a system for exercising problems, making decisions, and certifying status conditions their attempts to influence the outcome of any decision.

We can identify five major properties of decision making in organized anarchies that are of substantial importance to the tactics of accomplishing things in colleges and universities:

1. Most issues most of the time have *low salience* for most people. The decisions to be made within the organization secure only partial and erratic attention from participants in the organization. A major share of the attention devoted to a particular issue is tied less to the content of the issue than to its symbolic significance for individual and group esteem.

2. The total system has *high inertia*. Anything that requires a coordinated effort of the organization in order to start is unlikely to be started. Anything that requires a coordinated effort of the organization in order to be stopped is unlikely to be stopped.

3. Any decision can become a *garbage can* for almost any problem. The issues discussed in the context of any particular decision depend less on the decision or problems involved than on the timing of their joint arrivals and the existence of alternative arenas for exercising problems.

4. The processes of choice are easily subjected to *overload*. When the load on the system builds up relative to its capabilities for exercising and resolving problems, the decision outcomes in the organization tend to become increasingly separated from the formal process of decision.

5. The organization has a *weak information base*. Information about past events or past decisions is often not retained. When retained, it is often difficult to retrieve. Information about current activities is scant.

These properties are conspicuous and ubiquitous. They represent some important ways in which all organizations sometimes, and an organization like a university often, present opportunities for tactical action that in a modest way strengthen the hand of the participant who attends to them. We suggest eight basic tactical rules for use by those who seek to influence the course of decisions in universities or colleges.

Rule 1: Spend time. The kinds of decision-making situations and organizations we have described suffer from a shortage of decision-making energy. Energy is a scarce resource. If one is in a position to devote time to the decision-making activities within the organization, he has a considerable claim on the system. Most organizations develop ways of absorbing the decision-making energy provided by sharply deviant participants; but within moderate boundaries, a person who is willing to spend time finds himself in a strong position for at least three significant reasons:

- By providing a scarce resource (energy), he lays the basis for a claim. If he is willing to spend time, he can expect more tolerant consideration of the problems he considers important. One of the most common organizational responses to a proposal from a participant is the request that he head a committee to do something about it. This behavior is an acknowledgement both of the energy-poor situation and of the price the organization pays for participation. That price is often that the organization must allow the participant some significant control over the definition of problems to be considered relevant.

- By spending time on the homework for a decision, he becomes a major information source in an information-poor world. At the limit, the information provided need have no particular evidential validity. Consider, for example, the common assertions in college decision-making processes about what some constituency (e.g., board of trustees, legislature, student body, ethnic group) is "thinking." The assertions are rarely based on defensible evidence, but they tend to become organizational facts by virtue of the shortage of serious information. More generally, reality for a decision is specified by those willing to spend the time required to collect the small amounts of information available, to review the factual assertions of others, and to disseminate their findings.

- By investing more of his time in organizational concerns, he increases his chance of being present when something important to him is considered. A participant who wishes to pursue other matters (e.g., study, research, family, the problems of the outside world) reduces the number of occasions for decision making to [sic] which he can afford to attend. A participant who can spend time can be involved in more arenas. Since it is often difficult to anticipate when and where a particular issue will be involved (and thus to limit one's attention to key times and domains), the simple frequency of availability is relatively important.

Rule 2: Persist. It is a mistake to assume that if a particular proposal has been rejected by an organization today, it will be rejected tomorrow. Different sets of people and concerns will be reflected each time a problem is considered or a proposal discussed. We noted earlier the ways in which the flow of participants leads to a flow of organizational concerns. The specific combination of sentiments and people that is associated with a specific choice opportunity is partly fortuitous, and Fortune may be more considerate another day.

For the same reason, it is a mistake to assume that today's victory will be implemented automatically tomorrow. The distinction between decision making and decision implementation is usually a false one. Decisions are not "made" once and for all. Rather they happen as a result of a series of episodes involving different people in different settings, and they may be unmade or modified by subsequent episodes. The participant who spends much time celebrating his victory ordinarily can expect to find the victory short-lived. The loser who spends his time weeping rather than reintroducing his ideas will persistently have something to weep about. The loser who persists in a variety of contexts is frequently rewarded.

Rule 3: Exchange status for substance. As we have indicated, the specific substantive issues in a college, or similar organization, typically have low salience for participants. A quite typical situation is one in which significant numbers of participants and groups of participants care less about the specific substantive outcome than they do about the implications of that outcome for their own sense of self-esteem and the social recognition of their importance. Such an ordering of things is neither surprising nor normatively unattractive. It would be a strange world indeed if the mostly minor issues of university governance, for example, became more important to most people than personal and group esteem.

A college president, too, is likely to become substantially concerned with the formal acknowledgement of office. Since it is awkward for him to establish definitively that he is substantively important, the president tends to join other participants in seeking symbolic confirmation of his significance.

The esteem trap is understandable but unfortunate. College presidents who can forgo at least some of the pleasures of self-importance in order to trade status for substance are in a strong position. Since leaders receive credit for many things over which they have little control and to which they contribute little, they should find it possible to accomplish some of the things they want by allowing others to savor the victories, enjoy the pleasures of involvement, and receive the profits of public importance.

Rule 4: Facilitate opposition participation. The high inertia of organizations and the heavy dependence of organizational events on processes outside of the control of the organization make organizational power ambiguous. Presidents sense their lack of control despite their position of authority, status, and concern. Most people who participate in university decision making sense a disappointment with the limited control their position provides.

Persons outside the formal ranks of authority tend to see authority as providing more control. Their aspirations for change tend to be substantially greater than the aspirations for change held by persons with formal authority. One obvious solution is to facilitate participation in decision making. Genuine authoritative participation will reduce the aspirations of oppositional leaders. In an organization characterized by high inertia and low salience it is unwise to allow beliefs about the feasibility of planned action to outrun reality. From this point of view, public accountability, participant observation, and other techniques for extending the range of legitimate participation in the decision-making processes of the organization are essential means of keeping the aspirations of occasional actors within bounds. Since most people most of the time do not participate much, their aspirations for what can be done have a tendency to drift away from reality. On the whole, the direct involvement of dissident groups in the decision-making process is a more effective depressant of exaggerated aspirations than is a lecture by the president.

Rule 5: Overload the system. As we have suggested, the style of decision making changes when the load exceeds the capabilities of the system. Since we are talking about energy-poor organizations, accomplishing overload is not hard. In practical terms, this means having a large repertoire of projects for organizational action; it means making substantial claims on resources for the analysis of problems, discussion of issues, and political negotiation.

Within an organized anarchy it is a mistake to become absolutely committed to any one project. There are innumerable ways in which the processes we have described will confound the cleverest behavior with respect to any single proposal, however imaginative or subjectively important. What such processes cannot do is cope with large numbers of projects. Someone with the habit of producing many proposals, without absolute commitment to any one, may lose any one of them (and it is hard to predict a priori which one), but cannot be stopped on everything.

The tactic is not unlike the recommendation in some treatments of bargaining that one should introduce new dimensions of bargains in order to facilitate more favorable trades. It is grounded in the observation that the press of proposals so loads the organization that... a large number of actions are taken without attending to problems. Where decisions are made through oversight or flight, considerable control over the course of decision making lies in the hands of two groups: the initiators of the proposals, who get their way in oversight, and the full-time administrator, who is left to make the decision in cases of flight. The college president with a program is in the enviable position of being both a proposal initiator and a full-time administrator. Overload is almost certainly helpful to his program. Other groups within a college or university are probably also advantaged by overload if they have a positive program for action, but their advantage is less certain. In particular, groups in opposition to the administration that are unable to participate full time (either directly or through representatives) may wish to be selective in the use of overload as a tactic.

Rule 6: Provide garbage cans. One of the complications in accomplishing something in a garbage can decision-making process is the tendency for any particular project to become intertwined with a variety of other issues simply because those issues exist at the time the project is before the organization. A proposal for curricular reform becomes an arena for a concern for social justice. A proposal for construction of a building becomes an arena for concerns about environmental quality. A proposal for bicycle paths becomes an arena for discussion of sexual inequality.

It is pointless to try to react to such problems by attempting to enforce rules of relevance. Such rules are, in any event, highly arbitrary. Even if they were not, it would still be difficult to persuade a person that his problem (however important) could not be discussed because it is not relevant to the current agenda. The appropriate tactical response is to provide garbage cans into which wide varieties of problems can be dumped. The more conspicuous the can, the more garbage it will attract away from other projects.

The prime procedure for making a garbage can attractive is to give it precedence and conspicuousness. On a grand scale, discussions of overall organizational objectives or over-all organizational long-term plans are classic first-quality cans. They are general enough to accommodate anything. They are socially defined as being important. They attract enough different kinds of issues to reinforce their importance. An activist will push for discussions of grand plans (in part) in order to draw the garbage away from the concrete day-to-day arenas of his concrete objectives.

On a smaller scale, the first item of a meeting agenda is an obvious garbage can. It receives much of the status allocation concerns that are a part of meetings. It is possible that any item on an agenda will attract an assortment of things currently concerning individuals in the group; but the first item is more vulnerable than others. As a result, projects of serious substantive concern should normally be placed somewhat later, after the important matters of individual and group esteem have been settled, most of the individual performances have been completed, and most of the enthusiasm for abstract argument has waned.

The garbage can tactic has long-term effects that may be important. Although in the short run the major consequence is to remove problems from the arena of short-term concrete proposals, the separation of problem discussion from decision making means that general organizational attitudes develop outside the context of immediate decisions. The exercise of problems and the discussion of plans contribute to a building of the climate within which the organization will operate in the future. A president who uses the garbage can tactic should be aware of the ways in which currently irrelevant conversations produce future ideological constraints. The same tactic also provides a (partly misleading) device for the training and selection of future leaders of the organization. Those who perform well in garbage can debates are not necessarily good leaders, though they may frequently be identified as potential leaders. Finally, the tactic offers a practical buffer for the organization from the instabilities introduced by the entry and exit of problems that drift from one organization to another. In recent years universities have become an arena for an assortment of problems that might have found expression in other social institutions. Universities and colleges were available and accessible to people with the concerns. Although the resulting strain on university processes was considerable, the full impact was cushioned by the tendency of such problems to move to decision-irrelevant garbage cans, to be held there until they could move on to another arena in another institution.

Rule 7: Manage unobtrusively. If you put a man in a boat and tell him to plot a course, he can take one of three views of his task. He can float with the currents and winds, letting them take him wherever they wish; he can select a destination and try to use full power to go directly to it regardless of the current or winds; or he can select a destination and use his rudder and sails to let the currents and wind eventually take him where he wants to go. On the whole, we think conscious university leadership is properly seen in third light.

A central tactic in high-inertia systems is to use high-leverage minor actions to produce major effects—to let the system go where it wants to go with only the minor interventions that make it go where it should. From a tactical point of view, the main objection to central direction and control is that it requires an impossible amount of attention and energy. The kinds of organizations with which we have been concerned are unable to be driven where we want them to go without making considerable use of the "natural" organizational processes. The appropriate tactics of management are unobtrusive and indirect.

Unobtrusive management uses interventions of greater impact than visibility. Such actions generally have two key attributes: (1) They affect many parts of the system slightly rather than a few parts in a major way. The effect on any one part of the system is small enough so that either no one really notices or no one finds it sensible to organize significantly against the intervention. (2) Once activated, they stay activated without further organizational attention. Their deactivation requires positive organizational action.

Given all the enthusiasm for elaborating a variety of models of organizations that bemoan bureaucracy and the conventional managerial tools associated with bureaucratic life, it is somewhat surprising to realize that the major instruments of unobtrusive management are bureaucratic. Consider the simple act of committing the organization by signing a piece of paper. By the formal statutes of many organizations, some people within the organization are conceded authority to sign pieces of paper. College presidents tend, in our judgment, to be timid about exercising such authority. By signing a piece of paper the president is able to reverse the burden of organizing the decision-making processes in the system. Many people have commented on the difficulty of organizing the various groups and offices in a college or university in order to do something. What has been less frequently noted is that the same problems of organization face anyone who wants to overturn an action. For example, the official charter of an institution usually has some kind of regulation that permits a desired action, as well as some kind of regulation that might be interpreted as prohibiting it. The president who solicits general organizational approval for action is more likely to obtain it if the burdens of overcoming organizational inertia are on his opposition. He reverses the burden of organization by taking the action.

Major bureaucratic interventions lie in the ordinary systems of accounting and managerial controls. Such devices are often condemned in academic circles as both dreary and inhibiting. Their beauty lies in the way in which they extend throughout the system and in the high degree of arbitrariness they exhibit. For example, students of business have observed that many important aspects of business life are driven by accounting rules. What are costs? What are profits? How are costs and profits allocated among activities and subunits? Answers to such questions are far from arbitrary. But they have enough elements of arbitrariness that no reasonable business manager would ignore the potential contribution of accounting rules to profitability. The flow of investments, the utilization of labor, and the structure of organization all respond to the organization of accounts.

The same thing is true in a college or university, although the process works in a somewhat different way because the convenient single index of business accounting, profit, is denied the university executive. Universities and colleges have official facts (accounting facts) with respect to student activities, faculty activities, and space utilization. In recent years such accounting facts have increased in importance as colleges and universities struggled first with the baby boom and now with fiscal adversity. These official facts enter into reports and filter into decisions made throughout the system. As a typical simple example, consider the impact of changing the accounting for faculty teaching load from number of courses to student credit hours taught. Or, consider the impact of separating in accounting reports the teaching of language (number of students, cost of faculty) from the teaching of literature in that language at a typical American university. Or, consider the impact of making each major subunit in a university purchase services (e.g., duplication services, computer services, library services) at prices somewhat different from the current largely arbitrary prices. Or, consider the consequences of allowing transfer of funds from one major budget line to another within a subunit at various possible discount rates depending on the lines and the point in the budget year. Or, consider the effect of having students pay as part of their fees an amount determined by the department offering the instruction, with the amount thus paid returning to the department.

Rule 8: Interpret history. In an organization in which most issues have low salience, and information about events in the sytem is poorly maintained, definitions of what is happening and what has happened become important tactical instruments. If people in the organization cared more about what happened (or is happening), the constraints on the tactic would be great. Histories would be challenged and carefully monitored. If people in the organization accepted more openly the idea that much of the decision-making process is a status-certifying rather than a choice-making system, there would be less dependence on historical interpretation. The actual situation, however, provides a tactically optimal situation. On the one hand, the genuine interest in keeping a good record of what happened (in substantive rather than status terms) is minimal. On the other hand, the belief in the relevance of history, or the legitimacy of history as a basis for current action, is fairly strong.

Minutes should be written long enough after the event as to legitimize the reality of forgetfulness. They should be written in such a way as to lay the basis for subsequent independent action—in the name of the collective action. In general, participants in the organization should be assisted in their desire to have unambiguous actions taken today derived from the ambiguous decisions of yesterday with a minimum of pain to their images of organizational rationality and a minimum of claims on their time. The model of consistency is maintained by a creative resolution of uncertainty about the past.

Presidents and Tactics

As we observed at the outset, practical tactics, if they are genuine, will inevitably be viewed as somewhat cynical. We will, however, record our own sentiments that the cynicism lies in the eye of the beholder. Our sympathies and enthusiasm are mostly for the invisible members of an organized anarchy who make such tactics possible. We refer, of course, to the majority of participants in colleges and universities who have the good sense to see that what can be achieved through tactical manipulation of the university is only occasionally worth their time and effort. The validity of the tactics is a tribute to their reluctance to clutter the important elements of life with organizational matters. The tactics are available for anyone who wants to use them. Most of us most of the time have more interesting things to do.

But presidents, as full-time actors generally occupying the best job of their lives, are less likely to have more interesting things to do. In addition, these tactics, with their low visibility and their emphasis on the trading of credit and recognition for accomplishment, will not serve the interests of a president out to glorify himself or increase his chances to be one of the very few who move up to a second and "better" presidency. Instead, they provide an opportunity chiefly for those who have some conception of what might make their institution better, more interesting, more complex, or more educational, and are satisfied to end their tenures believing that they helped to steer their institutions slightly closer to those remote destinations.

The Study of Educational Leadership

Ralph M. Stogdill

Significant studies of educational leadership are concerned less with the personality traits, and more with the behaviors, of leaders. Research growing out of the Ohio State Leadership Studies (Shartle, 1950) is representative of the trend toward a behavioral orientation. The Leader Behavior Description Questionnaire (Hemphill and Coons, 1957) consists of two factorially defined scales that were identified as Consideration and Initiation of Structure in Interaction (Halpin and Winer, 1957). The LBDQ has been widely used in studies of educational leadership.

Hemphill (1955) reported results obtained in a study of 21 college departments, the chairmen of which were each described by several department members. When faculty members rated their department high in administrative effectiveness, they tended to describe their chairman high in both Consideration and Initiating Structure. Furthermore, the smaller the discrepancy between a faculty member's conception of ideal leader behavior and the actual behavior of his chairman, the more highly he rated the administration of his department.

Excerpted from Ralph M. Stogdill, "The Trait Approach to the Study of Educational Leadership." In Luvern L. Cunningham and William J. Gephart (Eds.), *Leadership: The Science and the Art Today.* Itasca, IL: F.E. Peacock, 1973. Copyright © 1973 by Phi Delta Kappa. Used with permission.

Halpin (1956) studied the leadership of 64 school superintendents who were described by staff members, school board members, and self on both the "real" and "ideal" forms of the LBDQ. The superintendents were described higher in Initiating Structure by board members than by staff or self. They were described lower in Consideration by staff than by board members or self. Board members expected the superintendent to be more considerate than considered ideal by the staff. There was a non-significant tendency for board members to expect more Initiation of Structure than staff members or superintendents considered ideal. Superintendents who were evaluated as most effective by board members and staff tended to score high on both Consideration and Structure.

In a second study of 50 superintendents (Halpin, 1966), a similar research design was used. In all three groups (board members, staff members, and superintendents) the ideal superintendent was regarded as one who scored high on both Consideration and Structure. Superintendents thought they should be more Considerate than board or staff members considered ideal. Staff members required less Consideration than board members set as a standard. Board members expected more Initiating Structure than was expected by staff members or superintendents. Staff members in turn, preferred less Structure than superintendents thought they should initiate.

Luckie (1963) asked staff members and superintendents to describe 53 directors of public instruction. Staff members and superintendents expected more Initiating Structure than directors considered ideal, but exhibited less Consideration than expected by staff and superintendents.

Carson and Schultz (1964) obtained descriptions of junior college deans by student leaders, college presidents, department heads, and the deans themselves. The greatest discrepancies between ideal and observed behavior were found between student leaders and college presidents. These discrepancies in expectation were regarded as providing a potent source of role conflict for the deans.

Sharpe (1956), in a study of school principals, found that teachers and staff members perceived principals to deviate less from the ideal norms than did the principals themselves. Fast (1964) found that the actual Consideration and Structuring scores of principals were positively related to teacher satisfaction, but ideal scores were not. The smaller the discrepancy between expected and observed principal behavior, the greater the satisfaction of the teachers. Seeman (1957; 1960), reported that evaluations of school principals' leader effectiveness are positively related to teacher descriptions of Structure, Consideration, Communication, and Willingness to Change.

A remarkable set of studies involving very large samples has been conducted in Canada. It was found by Greenfield and Andrews (1961) that both the Consideration and Structuring behaviors of teachers, as described by pupils, are positively and significantly related to pupil scores on province-wide examinations on academic subjects. Keeler and Andrews (1963) also found that the Consideration and Structure of principals as described by teachers are significantly related to pupils' scores on the province-wide examinations. One might expect the behavior of teachers to have a direct impact on the performance of students. It comes as a surprise, at least to the writer, to find that the leader behavior of principals also exerts a significant effect on pupil performance. These are exciting findings, indicating that positive leader behavior has a payoff in student achievements.

Stogdill (1965) has shown in a study of 27 organizations that leader Consideration tends to be associated with group drive and freedom of action. Leader Structuring of Expectations tends to be associated with group cohesiveness and support of the organization. Thus, both Consideration and Structure provide for two essential ingredients of organization.

A word needs to be said about democratic and autocratic forms of leadership behavior. When Anderson (1959) surveyed some 60 studies of democratic and autocratic leadership in the classroom, the evidence failed to demonstrate that either pattern of behavior is consistently related to achievement or productivity. There was a qualified tendency for morale to be higher under democratic than under autocratic leadership. Anderson concluded that "the democratic-authoritarian construct provided an inadequate conceptualization of leadership behavior."

IMPLICATIONS FOR EDUCATIONAL LEADERSHIP

Any realistic discussion of leadership practice in education should take into account a factor that has received very little attention by researchers. This is the factor of leadership philosophy. Conviction, value systems, and philosophical inclination tend to influence overt behavior.

The author's interviews with educational leaders, and particularly with professors of educational philosophy, lead him to believe that there is a pervasive commitment throughout the profession to a laissez-faire style of leadership, as defined by Lippitt and White (1943) and promulgated by a popular program of sensitivity training (Bradford, Gibb, and Benne, 1964). This pattern of philosophy and practice appears to be based on the assumptions that (1) leadership should be entirely permissive of and receptive to examination and challenge, and (2) any attempt to structure expectations is not only autocratic, but suppresses sensitivity to group processes.

Educational leaders vary widely in the extent to which they are considerate and structure expectations (Hemphill, 1955; Halpin, 1956). But a highly permissive philosophy seems to prevail as an ideal. Leaders and their superiors sometimes advocate higher degrees of Consideration than followers desire (Halpin, 1956).

Research results obtained by Stogdill (1965) suggest that if the leader is extremely high in Structure and low in Consideration, his organization is likely to be high in loyalty and cohesiveness, but low in drive. If, on the other hand, the leader is extremely high in Consideration at the expense of Structure, his organization is likely to be high in drive, but low in cohesiveness and member loyalty. The latter seems to be exactly the situation that numerous educational leaders have created for themselves. They find a high degree of drive directed against themselves, and few followers come to their support.

The leader who emerges in group interaction is accorded leadership status because he reinforces the expectation that he will maintain role structure and group movement in accord with the group norms and purpose. Members who join an organization because they are in sympathy with its purpose and the benefits it confers expect the appointed leader also to maintain role structure and operations that are in conformity with existing norms and goals.

Some interesting questions now arise. Are the majority of followers who have committed themselves to a longstanding norm and purpose the people who are most capable of judging what is good for themselves? Is the leader under any obligation to maintain the normative integrity and survival of the organization? Or does he have a higher obligation to his own values that justifies his use of the organization as an instrument for instituting new norms and programs?

Research cannot tell a leader what his morality ought to be. It can, however, provide him with information on the consequences of decisions that he may make. If a leader fails to structure expectation[s] around the basic norms and purpose of the organization, he is likely to lose the loyalty of a majority of its members. Without their support, the leader is highly vulnerable to attack by dissident subgroups within the organization. The survival of the leader is dependent upon the survival of the organization. If he is willing to sacrifice the organization for an ideal, he is likely at the same time to sacrifice any chances of implementing the ideal. Change programs require organizations and institutions as instruments for implementation. When the organization collapses, the leader falls and his program goes with him.

The practicalities of organizational life suggest that a leader has a better chance of survival when he lets the followers know (1) that he identifies himself with the purpose of the organization, and (2) that in doing so he is working for the welfare of the follower group. This means that change programs—designed to improve the organization, produce a better service, or cope with environmental demands—must be shown to be consonant with the purpose of the organization and the norms of the members.

In times of change and social ferment, the leader may be faced with a difficult choice. Will he support the organization and its more conservative majority, or will he support one or another minority that is demanding change? In making his decision, he should be aware of the fact that a call for change often involves a demand for power—the power to determine role structure and goal direction. In other words, a demand for change is easily converted into a direct attack upon the leadership positions. Thus, the leader who is committed to an ideal of social change may find it difficult to identify himself with the conservative majority which is likely to support the continued functioning of the organization as a provider of valued services. The minorities that welcome change, and might be expected to support the progressive leader, may be the very ones that are seeking his overthrow.

One leadership trait that the educational leader might use to advantage is the trait of verbalism. Bass (1954) and others have shown that the member of a group who talks the most tends to emerge as a leader. However, he needs to say the right things and get followers to listen to him. Here again, the factor of normative values comes into play. Followers are most likely to support the leadership of the individual who most clearly verbalizes their own norms and values. It is at this point that leader Consideration comes into play. Consideration contains a strong component of listening to followers and showing receptivity to their ideas and suggestions. A truly considerate leader will know whether a highly vocal minority is accurately voicing the norms and values of the silent majority whose support he needs.

The leader who is out of touch with his followers can at least begin questioning and listening. He should know what the follower norms are before he attempts to become a spokesman for the group. He must know what their aspirations are if he is to succeed in structuring the expectations of followers in terms of the basic purpose of the organization. Without such structure, followers remain uncertain, confused, and receptive to almost any form of leadership that makes itself available. The appointed leader is expected to maintain the leadership role. The practice of unmitigated permissiveness and the failure to structure expectations constitute a surrender of the leadership role.

References

Anderson, R.C. Learning in Discussions—A Resume of the Authoritarian-Democratic Studies. *Harvard Educational Review*, 1959, 29, 201-215.

Bass, B.M. The Leaderless Group Discussion. *Psychological Bulletin*, 1954, *51*, 465-492.

Bradford, L.P., Gibb, J.R., & Benne, K.D. *T-Group Theory and Laboratory Method.* New York: John Wiley, 1964.

Carson, J.O., & Schultz, R.E. A Comparative Analysis of the Junior College Dean's Leadership Behavior. *Journal of Experimental Education*, 1964, 32, 355-362.

Fast, R.G. Leader Behavior of Principals as It Relates to Teacher Satisfaction. Master's thesis, University of Alberta, 1964.

Greenfield, T.B., & Andrews, J.H.M. Teacher Leader Behavior. *Alberta Journal of Education Research*, 1961, 7, 92-102.

Halpin, A.W. *The Leader Behavior of School Superintendents.* Columbus, OH: Ohio State University, College of Education, 1956.

Halpin, A.W. *Theory and Research in Administration.* New York: Macmillan, 1966.

Halpin, A.W., & Winer, B.J. A Factorial Study of the Leader Behavior Descriptions. In R.M. Stogdill & A.E. Coons, *Leader Behavior: Its Description and Measurement*. Columbus, OH: Ohio State University, Bureau of Business Research, 1957, Monograph No. 88.

Hemphill, J.K. Leadership Behavior Associated with the Administrative Reputations of College Departments. *Journal of Educational Psychology*, 1955, *46*, 385-401.

Hemphill, J.K., & Coons, A.E. Development of the Leader Behavior Description Questionnaire. In R.M. Stogdill & A.E. Coons, *Leader Behavior: Its Description and Measurement*. Columbus, OH: Ohio State University, Bureau of Business Research, 1957.

Keeler, B.T., & Andrews, J.H.M. Leader Behavior of Principals, Staff Morale, and Productivity. *Alberta Journal of Educational Research*, 1963, *9*, 179-191.

Lippitt, R., & White, R.K. The Social Climate of Children's Groups. In R.G. Barker, J.S. Kounin, & H.F. Wright, *Child Behavior and Development*. New York: McGraw-Hill, 1943.

Luckie, W.R. Leader Behavior of Directors of Instruction. *Dissertation Abstracts*, 1960; 1963, *25*.

Seeman, M. A Comparison of General and Specific Leader Behavior Descriptions. In R.M. Stogdill & A.E. Coons, *Leader Behavior: Its Description and Measurement*. Columbus, OH: Ohio State University, Bureau of Business Research, 1957, Monograph No. 88.

Seeman, M. *Social Status and Leadership: The Case of the School Executive*. Columbus, OH: Ohio State University, Bureau of Educational Research and Service, 1960.

Sharpe, R.T. Differences between Perceived Administrative Behavior and Role-Norms as Factors in Leadership Evaluation and Group Morale. *Dissertation Abstracts*, 1956, *16*, 57.

Shartle, C.L. Studies of Leadership by Interdisciplinary Methods. In A.G. Grace (Ed.), *Leadership in American Education*. Chicago: University of Chicago Press, 1950.

Stogdill, R.M. *Managers, Employees, Organizations*. Columbus, OH: Ohio State University, Bureau of Business Research, 1965.

The Impact of Situational Leadership in an Educational Setting

Paul Hersey, Arrigo L. Angelini, and Sofia Carakushansky

Situational Leadership Theory (Hersey & Blanchard, 1982) has been widely used in management training worldwide, in organizations of all sorts, for over a decade. Only recently, however, have substantial research reports begun to appear, evaluating the effects of this type of leadership training (see for example, Beck,[1] Peters,[2] Raynor,[3] and Hambleton & Gumpert, 1982). The present study goes further in two respects. First, the concepts of Situational Leadership are applied to the educational or training process itself, rather than examined in terms of their effects when applied by trained managers. Thus, it is the leadership role of the trainer or teacher that is under examination in the present study. Second, this study reports the results of a specific experimental application of the theory to classroom instruction. Thus, rather than train teachers and later determine whether they correctly and successfully applied Situational Leadership Theory, the leadership behaviors of instructors were consciously controlled, according to the theory. The results were judged in terms of student performance.

Reprinted from Paul Hersey, Arrigo L. Angelini, and Sofia Carakushansky, "The Impact of Situational Leadership and Classroom Structure on Learning Effectiveness," *Group & Organization Studies*, Vol. 7, No. 2 (June 1982), pp. 216-224, © Sage Publications, Inc. Used with permission.

BACKGROUND

According to Situational Leadership, there is no single best method of influencing the behavior of subordinates. Rather, the task-relevant maturity levels of individuals or groups in a given situation tends to determine which leadership styles are likely to achieve the highest results.

The Situational Leadership Model (Figure 1) provides leaders with a diagnostic procedure for assessing the maturity of followers regarding specific tasks; it is a prescriptive tool for selecting the leadership style with the highest probability of success.

Each of the four leadership styles—telling, selling, participating and delegating—in the "prescriptive curve" is a combination of task behavior and relationship behavior, the two major dimensions of leader behavior that were first clearly identified by researchers at Ohio State University in the early 1950s (Stogdill & Coons, 1957). Task behavior is the extent to which the leader provides direction for people, setting goals and defining their roles (for example, telling people what to do, when, where, and how to do it). Relationship behavior is the extent to which the leader engages in two-way or multiway communication, facilitation behaviors, and socioemotional support behaviors.

The task-specific maturity of followers is a matter of degree. Some benchmarks of maturity are provided on the maturity continuum shown at the bottom of Figure 1. These range from very low (M1) to very high levels of maturity (M4). The appropriate leadership style for each of the four levels of maturity is prescribed in the model itself, which illustrates the proper combination of task and relationship behavior to be used by the leader.

Having determined the maturity level of an individual or group to accomplish a given task or responsibility, the leader reads directly above the maturity continuum to select the appropriate leadership style along the prescriptive curve. The four leadership styles are as follows:

Telling (S1) is for low maturity (M1). People who are both unable and unwilling to perform a specific task need clear directions and close supervision. In emphasizing high task/low relationship behavior, Style One requires the leader to define roles and to tell people what, where, when and how

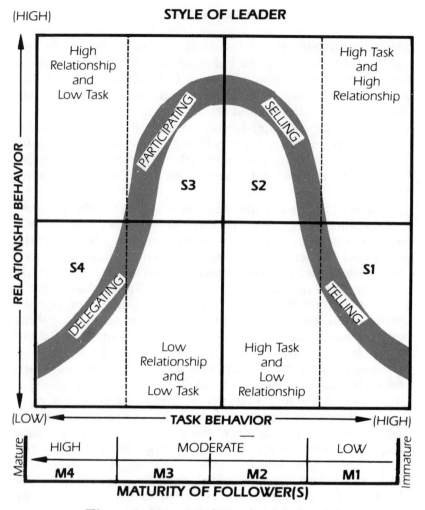

Figure 1. Situational Leadership Model

to perform tasks. At the same time, supportive behavior is minimized (but not completely omitted) in order to avoid being perceived as permissive or rewarding of poor performance.

Selling (S2) is for low to moderate maturity, that is, people who are willing but unable to take responsibility for a specific task or function (M2). In this high task/high relationship style, leaders still need to display very directive behavior, but should also provide strong supportive behavior to reinforce the followers' willingness and enthusiasm. Style Two is called "selling" because most of the direction is provided by the leader, who now uses two-way communication to explain decisions and gain follower support.

Participating (S3) is for moderate to high maturity. Followers at this level (M3) have the ability to perform the specific task but lack confidence or enthusiasm. Leaders using this high relationship/low task style need to reduce or de-emphasize the importance of their own structuring behaviors while maintaining a high level of supportive behavior, including two-way communication and active listening. Style Three is called "participating" because the leader and follower share decision-making, with the primary role of the leader shifting to facilitating and communicating.

Delegating (S4) is for high maturity people who are both able and willing to perform the specific task (M4). Leaders using this low task/low relationship style demonstrate little directive or supportive behavior, because the followers are self-motivated and are capable of self-direction.

In addition to simple, direct applications—judging subordinate maturity and behaving accordingly—leaders can use the model to help followers develop in maturity by adjusting their own leadership behavior through the four styles along the prescriptive curve. This developmental cycle is accomplished through a series of two-step processes: First, the leader reduces directive behavior to encourage the follower to assume greater task-relevant responsibility; second, as soon as performance improvement is noted, the leader rewards the follower by increasing supportive behavior as positive reinforcement; finally, as the follower reaches higher levels of maturity (M3 and M4), the leader responds by decreasing both task and relationship behavior, to provide these very mature people with autonomy rather than socioemotional support.

Conversely, the leader can arrest and reverse tendencies toward declining performance in followers by reassessing their maturity level and moving backwards through the prescriptive curve to provide the necessary amounts of task and relationship behavior.

The present study extends the Situational Leadership Theory to the educational process. The authors considered leadership goals in a teaching environment, where the leader works with and through followers (participants) to accomplish the goal of learning. The study was conducted at Centro de

Produtividade do Brasil (São Paulo) to explore the compatibility of Situational Leadership with classroom instruction, using the following assumptions:

1. Groups facing a new subject tend to be relatively "immature" regarding that subject (M1 and M2), and require highly directive behavior on the part of the leader (Telling and Selling).
2. Group maturity will tend to increase from M2 to M3 as the leader reinforces participant contributions by increasing supportive behavior, and decreasing task structure (Selling to Participating).
3. When the group begins to provide a more significant role in determining its own directions (M3), members are likely to be able to self-manage (M4) if the leader maintains a supportive and consultative posture (Participating to Delegating).

In accordance with these assumptions, the study involved changing not only the verbal and nonverbal behavior of the leader, but also the physical arrangement of the classroom, as the participants' level of task-relevant maturity increased.

METHOD

Included in the study were 60 executives with university degrees in economics, business administration, or civil engineering. Two separate experiments were conducted with these managers, who attended a management training course on transactional analysis. In each experiment the managers were divided into experimental and control groups as follows:

First Experiment	A	Experimental group (N = 15)
	B	Control Group (N = 15)
Second Experiment	C	Experimental group (N = 15)
	D	Control group (N = 15)

All four groups were provided the same material, to maintain as much continuity in content as possible.

Control groups attended courses administered under a conventional teacher-student format, in which the material was presented through various combinations of lectures, audiovisual aids, group discussions and other techniques. Experimental groups encountered an atmosphere in which structural changes compatible with Situational Leadership were used to augment the leader's style and methods. The situational approach was applied in four stages which reflected the increasing levels of maturity of students and the corresponding need for changes in instructors' leadership style.

Stage One

At first the participants' maturity was relatively low in terms of the specific subject matter. Some individuals—perhaps coerced by their managements to attend the course—tended to be unable and unwilling to take responsibility for the learning task (M1). Most were enthusiastic, but lacked significant experience in this subject matter (M2), even though they may have been high in maturity within their areas of expertise, such as accounting, finance, marketing or production. The leader therefore needed to provide specific instructions (Telling) and/or to explain his directions and content while giving participants opportunities for clarification (Selling).

At this stage the classroom was physically structured in a conventional manner. Participants' tables were arranged in a herringbone style, with the leader's desk at the front of the room. Facing the group, the leader used a structured style to specify procedures (S1); he then increased his relationship behavior to reinforce group actions that were positive toward objectives (S2). He controlled deadlines for activities, time limits for tests and rules for group discussions; he supervised closely as participants performed, keeping individual records and giving detailed appraisals. He was also careful to identify and praise all positive contributions by participants.

Stage Two

Whenever the group or individual participants would show improvement—in terms of increased knowledge, ability to perform learning tasks, and behaviorally expressed willingness to learn—the leader rewarded them immediately with praise, friendly behavior, humor, and so forth. In applying the developmental cycle of Situational Leadership, the leader was taking calculated risks: decreasing task structure and positively reinforcing changes in the desired direction (Selling to Participating). Since the participants were maturing (M2 to M3), they received increases in responsibility, such as self-supervision of reading assignments and deadlines. Of course, if at any time the participants had not handled the new responsibilities, the leader would have reassumed control and waited for an opportunity to facilitate growth in maturity.

During this stage the physical structure of the classroom was altered to reflect the participants' growth and to promote further progress. Participants' tables were arranged in an open U-shape, with the leader's desk at the opening—much closer to the group but still separate and distinct from them. As participants demonstrated their ability to function at the higher levels, the leader increased praise and reinforcement, and continued to lessen task structure as long as the participants showed growth in maturity.

Stage Three

The leader had his desk removed and began to sit among the participants, whose seating arrangement had been changed from the U-shape to a circular layout. Task structure was reduced even further. Participants were now determining correct answers to questions, dividing themselves into smaller groups for discussion, appointing their own moderators, and replacing reading assignments with participant-led activities.

At this point, with each new success the participants were increasing their ability to provide self-motivation (M3 to M4). As a result, their dependence on the leader began to diminish; feedback and encouragement from the leader became their rewards. The leader began to change his position at random—although always away from the "head of the class" location—to various nondominant positions among the participants.

Stage Four

As the group began to demonstrate self-management in determining its direction (M4), the leader altered his style from Participating to Delegating. Participants were developing commitment and self-confidence as they demonstrated the ability to set challenging but realistic goals and to solve their own problems.

The leader had his desk moved to the back of the room, where he spent his time working on other projects while remaining available for consultation. By this time, responsibility for managing the learning process had been turned over to the participants (Participating to Delegating). The leader's confidence in their ability and willingness appealed to the participants' sense of competence and stimulated further activities which demonstrated high levels of maturity.

RESULTS

At the close of training, all 60 participants completed a final examination designed to measure understanding of the material presented. The results for the various experimental and control groups are shown in Table 1. These results show that the experimental groups demonstrated significantly higher levels of learning than did the control groups.

Table 1. Final Examination Results

Groups	Experiment 1 Mean	SD	Mean Diff.	Experiment 2 Mean	SD	Mean Diff.
Experimental	9.3	1.43		9.8	2.28	
			0.8[a]			1.0[b]
Control	8.5	.50		8.8	1.30	

[a] $t = 2.12$, $p < .05$.
[b] $t = 3.08$, $p < .05$.

Other results were observed but not quantitatively measured or tested: a higher level of enthusiasm seemed to appear in experimental groups; the leader was praised more often by experimental group members, from whom he felt he received closer cooperation; absenteeism was higher in control groups; and efforts to clarify intragroup relations were more frequently necessary in control groups.

The relatively narrow spread in test scores among all four groups may be due primarily to the nature of the participants. All were highly motivated, successful executives; all 60 participants had demonstrated academic achievement well above the average prior to the study. It is suggested that with larger and less homogeneous populations, differences in performance would be greater between those receiving instruction based on Situational Leadership Theory and those receiving traditional forms of instruction.

DISCUSSION

Results of this study indicate that leadership and structural changes can have a positive influence on learning environments, with implications not only for management training, but in any learning situation. In terms of both quantitative and qualitative student performance measures, proper applications of Situational Leadership Theory resulted in better student performance outcomes, as compared with identical learning situations in which no attempts were made to apply the theory.

Situational Leadership Theory may well be as applicable to all types of training situations, then, as it appears to be to managerial leadership situations. It often seems to be the case that trainers, like so many professionals, fail to practice what they preach. The present study gives evidence that suggests it may be quite beneficial for trainers and group facilitators to apply Situational Leadership Theory to their own leadership behavior in a teaching/training context.

Notes

[1]Beck, J.D.W. *Leadership in education: A field test of Hersey and Blanchard's Situational Leadership Theory.* Doctoral dissertation, School of Education, University of Massachusetts, May 1978.

[2]Peters, L.G. *Some aspects of leader style, adaptability and effectiveness among western Massachusetts principals.* Doctoral dissertation, School of Education, University of Massachusetts, September 1974.

[3]Raynor, M.R. *A study of the relationship among knowledge of leadership theory, behavior, and effectiveness.* Doctoral dissertation, School of Education, University of Massachusetts, 1976.

References

Hambleton, R.K., & Gumpert, R. The validity of Hersey and Blanchard's theory of leader effectiveness. *Group & Organization Studies*, 1982, 7(2), 225-242.

Hersey, P., & Blanchard, K.H. *Management of organizational behavior: Utilizing human resources.* Englewood Cliffs, NJ: Prentice-Hall, 1982.

Stogdill, R.M., & Coons, A. (Eds.). *Leader behavior: Its description and measurement.* Columbus, OH: Bureau of Business Research, Ohio State University, 1957.

Community Leadership

Introduction to Part 4: Community Leadership

Over the past century, the nature and structure of American communities has changed substantially. Their relative importance as useful subunits of society has been challenged in both popular and academic circles by a variety of authors (e.g., Hunter, 1975; Warren, 1972).

Certain fundamental changes have occurred that clearly alter the social relevance of communities. Increased specialization and division of labor has led to proliferation of associations based on specialization of function. These associations have important impacts on individual and collective behavior, often at the expense of community viability. The new associations have been generated through development of changed forms of organization, communication, and transportation. Changes cut across community boundaries, lessening the functions of single communities and increasing the importance of extra-community systems.

In Warren's (1972) judgment, the diminished role of communities is generated in part by the mobility of residents:

> The constant moving back and forth across the country in search of the better job or as a result of the company's planned policy of personnel rotation, or for whatever reason, puts a premium on the tree which can survive with shallow roots.... (p. 18) There is increasing association of people on the basis of common occupational or other interests rather than on the basis of locality alone.... (p. 17) The individual is oriented toward specialized, vertical systems as the important reference groups in relation to which he forms his self-image. (p. 84)

This implies that communities are less likely than before to provide the focus of interest for the most able leaders, who are often more concerned with a "community of interest" related to professions or specialized organizations than with the geographic community. The remaining community "leaders" often fail to recognize the changed community circumstance or may be ill-equipped to deal with new leadership requirements.

Community leaders may not be conscious of the inability of many existing community institutions to meet public needs; their perspectives and experience may be too limited to solve the most pressing problems. If community concerns are to attract the interest and time of capable people, and if a new kind of more adequate "community" is to emerge, local leadership must learn how to use outside resources in solving problems and in capitalizing on opportunities.

Nix summarizes and interprets studies of community leadership that relate the nature of leadership to the type of community. He emphasizes the importance of studies that go beyond mere description of organizational interest groups, associations, and leadership roles; it is essential to understand the relationships among leaders and subunits of the community. He identifies "exchange" and "coordination" as two important types of relationship. Central concepts required to understand community leadership are noted: social power, hierarchies, functional classifications of leadership, general or specialized leadership, and task or social leaders. He concludes that community structure tends to be (a) focused or unitary, (b) split or bifactional, (c) multifactional, or (d) amorphous. Finally, Nix suggests that the core leadership patterns are the cross-community linkage groups and the degree of competition or collaboration between them.

Lassey and Sashkin focus on requirements for improving community leadership performance, with specific attention to increasing pluralism and broadening participation. They discuss areas in which knowledge is needed and the characteristics of an effective community leadership structure.

External consultants often are important contributors to new initiatives within communities when the local leadership base is inadequate. Lassey and Sashkin also discuss some of the useful roles that consultants can play in helping community leaders to organize effective development programs. The leadership behaviors used by effective consultants are also noted, as are characteristics of the consultation process. Finally, six general principles are presented as basic considerations for both consultants and local leaders.

Warner emphasizes external and internal organizational variables that affect professional consultant effectiveness as well as professional roles specific to community development. He offers a very useful analysis of the types of "clientele" with which a community development consultant is likely to work. Although Warner does not make specific reference to "Situational Leadership" as it is presented in earlier discussions, his presentation of the context in which a professional community developer must work has a comparable emphasis.

Weir and Howell describe and evaluate a major educational program for community leaders. Four states (Pennsylvania, Michigan, Montana, and California) received W.K. Kellogg Foundation grants to undertake demonstration programs in development of leadership competence in public affairs. The characteristics common to each of the four programs are summarized, as are the unique aspects of the programs.

A formal assessment indicates that the training programs were effective in expanding leader participation in public affairs. The demonstration programs provided the basis for development of ongoing training programs in several additional states, and a region-wide program focused on development of women leaders is underway in the Western United States.

Leadership in educational institutions is considered unique because of their "loosely-coupled" nature. This factor also is present, possibly in larger measure, at the community level of social organization. A contemporary community consists of enormously varied groups and organizations that are often linked very loosely indeed. The role of the leader, whether a member of the community or a development consultant, appears to involve creation or activation of forces that can bind these loosely-coupled units more tightly as they jointly pursue development goals.

References

Hunter, A. The loss of community: An empirical test through replication. *American Sociological Review*, 1975, *40*, 537-552.

Warren, R.R. *The community in America*. Chicago: Rand McNally, 1972.

Concepts of Community
and Community Leadership

Harold L. Nix

The growing body of literature on community power, decision making, and action has demonstrated at least four basic points. First, social power is present and is exercised in patterned ways in all social systems, including communities. Furthermore, certain individuals play key roles in the exercise of community leadership. Second, community leaders can be identified by using certain techniques. Third, only a very small percentage of the citizens of a community becomes actively involved in the decision-making process. One author has concluded that no more than one per cent of the population is involved in community decision-making in most American cities.[1] Fourth, successful community action depends, in large measure, upon finding and involving the key community leaders. Gamson reported in his study of eighteen communities that the side supporting change won only 30 percent of the time without the united support of reputational leaders but two-thirds of the time with it.[2] These basic findings or generalizations focus upon the increasing need for change agents to understand more about the nature of the community and its leadership structure.

Reprinted with permission from *Sociology and Social Research*, 1969, 53(4), 500-510. (This article is a version of a paper read at the Rural Sociological Society meeting in Boston, August, 1968. The work on which the article is based was supported by grants from the Office of Urban Environmental Health of the National Center for Urban and Industrial Health and the Georgia Department of Public Health.)

The purposes of this paper are twofold. The first is to offer a conceptual clarification of the nature of community. The second is to present a set of concepts and classifications relating to community leadership. These concepts and classifications include types of social power, a classification of community leaders, and forms of community leadership.

A CONCEPT OF COMMUNITY

One can categorize all the individuals and study the internal structure of all the special-interest groups and organizations in an area and still have little notion of the nature of a community. The view is taken here that the social facts of which communities are made are the relationships between the various special-interest groups and organizations within a locality. According to Bates and Bacon, these "interstitial" or "inbetween" relationships may be viewed as two basic types.[3]

The first type may be referred to as exchange relationships, in which individuals, groups, and organizations exchange their specialized goods or services. Typical of this type of relationship is the merchant-customer or professional-client relationship. It is hypothesized that individuals tend to gain (or lose) potential community power by the nature and extent of exchange relationships.

The second type of community relationship has been labeled coordinative. The function of coordinative relationships is to manage the relationships among two or more groups or organizations which have differing and potentially conflicting interests. These relationships occur in what has been called "coordinative interstitial groups."[4] Examples are a local chamber of commerce, a community development council, and an informal decision-making clique. Members of such organizations represent the interests of several different special-interest groups, such as: a hardware store, a bank, a realty company, a law firm, or an industrial firm. Though community power appears to be gained through exchange relationships, it is believed that the exercise of community power is primarily through coordinative relationships. That is, a person may gain great potential power in his exchange relationships, but unless he becomes actively engaged in the key coordinative group or organization in his community, he is not likely to be in a position to exercise effective influence on community affairs. Research nearing completion at the University of Georgia supports this thesis.[5]

Two basic types of community relations have been discussed—exchange and coordinative, respectively, which occur in "exchange interstitial groups" and "coordinative interstitial groups." Both types are quite different from the special-interest groups and organizations, such as: the Jones family, the Johnson Hardware Company, the Ideal Mop Handle Company, and the Edison County Elementary School, in which the role behavior of their members is culturally or ideally reciprocal and where each member is supposed to be oriented to the basic goal of the group or organization he represents. On the other hand, in the role behavior in community type interstitial groups, both exchange and coordinative, the relationship is basically conjunctive or competitive:[6] as customer and merchant meet and as representatives of various special-interest groups meet in the local chamber of commerce, they are basically oriented to different goals. That is, they are expected to defend the interests of the...interstitial organizations or groups they represent.

The purpose of the preceding paragraphs has been twofold: first, to show that if one wishes to understand the community, he should focus his attention upon the interstitial groups and organizations which are made up of representatives of the various special-interest groups and organizations; second, to dispel the notion that communities are basically systems of cooperating individuals, groups, and organizations. The basic orientation or relationship in both exchange and coordinative interstitial groups [is] conjunctive or competitive. Hence, the force which underlies community-wide cooperation is not as often a common goal as it is interdependence brought about by the increasing specialization in society.

Based on these assumptions, we may define community as a social system whose function is to manage the competition and conflict which arise out of the necessity to exchange goods and services which, in turn, arise out of (1) the division of labor in society and (2) the scarcity of goods and services.[7]

If the preceding analysis is accurate, the adaptive community is not one with complete harmony and consensus, but one whose specialized leaders and group representatives realize that their interdependency requires an organized approach to compromise and a system of conflict management. Furthermore, the need for an organized or patterned leadership structure for controlling competition and conflict becomes greater as the community grows larger, more complex, and more interdependent.

CONCEPTS OF COMMUNITY LEADERSHIP

Social Power

The basis of leadership is social power, which in turn may be defined as "the capacity to determine the action of others." This social power may or may not be used. If it is used, leadership is exercised.

In terms of the source of social power, a three-way classification has been broadly accepted: *authority, influence,* and *unlegitimized coercion.* A part of an individual's power is based on the authority vested in the offices or positions he holds in groups and organizations. Authority is the right that anyone who occupies a particular position in a group has to control other members of that particular group. Authority is more characteristic of special-interest groups and organizations and their associated reciprocal relationships than of community-type (exchange or coordinative) groups.[8]

Another part of a person's social power is associated with no particular office but resides within the individual. This type is called influence. The degree of an individual's community influence is the result of his personal qualities, such as: appearance, age, family background, reputation, special skills, and communication abilities; his control of or access to scarce resources, such as: jobs, land, goods, services, power, and prestige; and the cumulative influence growing out of all the positions or offices held. Community influence is not the right but the ability of an individual to control the behavior of others in intergroup and interorganizational relationships. In other words, exchange and coordinative relationships are characterized by the exercise of influence rather than of authority.

The third type of social power is through unlegitimized coercion, such as taking the property of others at gun point.

Types of Community Leaders

In the study of leadership in communities and other types of groups or organizations, increasing attention has been given to the types of leaders, especially to the functional types.[9] This focus has been brought about, in part, by the realization that the different techniques used in identifying leaders tend to uncover different functional types of leaders. A brief attempt will be made to summarize some of the types of community leaders under three broad classes based on different dimensions. These dimensions are (1) level and function, (2) scope of influence, and (3) basic orientation.

Hierarchical Level and Functional Classification of Leaders

The first four types to be discussed are considered subtypes under a hierarchical level and functional classification of leaders.

1. *Legitimizers.* The first of this classification may be called legitimizers. These top community influentials also have been called gatekeepers, key leaders, influentials, and institutional leaders. Such leaders, as the names imply, are the individuals whose approval is usually needed if a proposed community action project is to succeed. They may or may not become actively involved in the endeavor, but their approval explicitly or implicitly is usually needed before the support of the next level of leadership is obtained.

These persons who have the reputation of being top leaders in their community are easily identified by asking, "Who are the most influential or powerful people in this community?" They tend to hold top positions in the largest and most active financial, business, industrial, governmental, professional, educational, religious, and labor organizations.[10] However, for various reasons, one cannot automatically assume that top positional leadership coincides with reputational leadership. First, people with authority in top organizations may or may not choose to use the influence it yields in community affairs and participate in the key coordinative interstitial group of the community. Second, influence tends to be cumulative; that is, a person may not presently hold a top position, but through previous positions he has built up influence and a reputation which he now chooses to exercise.

2. *Effectors.* A second type leader based on level and function have been called effectors. Effectors are often called second-level leaders or lieutenants. In medium-sized to large cities, the effectors may be the more active workers in community decision making. Freeman describes them in the Syracuse study as follows: "Many of the most active effectors are government personnel and professional participants; and the others are the employees of the large private corporations directed by the Institutional Leaders."[11] Such leaders tend to hold key positions which are vital in the planning of community change, and they possess technical and professional competency in various specialized areas. Such leaders tend to be identified most readily by studying participation in the decision-making processes and by asking knowledgeables to name leaders in specialized areas, such as: education, public health, city development, recreation, and industrial development. Persons classified in this second level of leadership may be in regular touch with one or more of the influentials. However, effectors appear to operate often on their own except for the guidance of policies of their organization.

In large cities, effectors appear to carry the main burden of initiating and effecting community change, except for the approval and prestige lent by the legitimizers for important projects. In small communities, the effectors and the legitimizers appear to be the same people.[12]

3. *Activists.* A third type leader based on level and function are often called activists. These types are also called doers and joiners. These are the people who can be identified by determining who are the active workers and officeholders in community, civic, and service clubs. In the larger communities, activists usually lack the power base and technical skills required to be involved in important legitimization or decision making. They appear to function more as a means through which to diffuse information, educate the public, and gain support on decisions already made. They also act at times to bring public pressures upon the decision makers.

It must be emphasized that the differentiation between these three hierarchical levels and functional types of leaders becomes less realistic as the size and diversification of the community decreases.

4. *General Public.* The discussion of the small percentage of people in a community who may be classified as legiti-

mizers, effectors, and activists should not be interpreted to mean that they make up the total leadership structure. Each person, no matter how insignificant, has some direct or indirect influence on the behavior of others. Prisoners in cells as well as voters at the polls can and do contribute to the rise and fall of leaders as they choose whether or not to follow their lead.

All the people in a geographic-political area are a part of the leadership structure, and many persons outside the area are in a social sense tied into the network of community decision making. This may be illustrated by the authority and influence of district, state, and national public health officials upon the local health officials, the health programs, and ultimately, the total community.

General Versus Specialized Leaders

Another way to classify leaders is in terms of degree of generality of their influence. Does a specific leader exercise influence "across the board" in community affairs, or is he involved in decision making only when his specialized area of competency is involved? The earlier studies[13] based on the reputational approach tended to conclude that communities contain a relatively small number of key leaders whose influence is general. Later studies, using the decision-making approach, emphasized the pluralistic and specialized nature of leadership.[14] More recent comparative approach studies[15] indicate that the truth lies between the extreme positions of the advocates of the reputational approach and the advocates of the decision-making approach.[16]

Perhaps by asking both general and specific questions, one can more clearly assess the truth. In three medium-sized Georgia cities, an attempt was made to determine the degree of overlap between general leadership and specialized leadership.[17] This was done by asking knowledgeables to name the persons who have the most influence in general community affairs and those most influential in specialized areas, such as: business and industry, government, education, religion, and health. The findings indicate that most of the overlap between specialized leaders and general leaders was with business and industrial leaders and political leaders. That is, 75 per cent of both those named as "business and industrial" leaders and "political" leaders were also named as general community leaders. On the other hand the percentage of persons named as leaders in other specialized areas who were also named as general leaders was much less. This is indicated by the following list of specialized areas and the percentages of these type leaders who were also named as general community leaders: religion, 33 per cent; education, 16 per cent; health, 15 per cent; welfare, 9 per cent; and recreation, 7 per cent. In addition, persons named as leaders in the specialized areas of religion, education, health, welfare, and recreation, as well as in general community affairs, were named relatively few times as general community leaders. Not only were persons who were nominated a relatively large number of times as general community leaders in the three Georgia communities likely to be from the areas of business, industry, or politics; they were also likely to be very active in the key coordinative-interstitial organizations in their respective communities.

Regarding the degree to which leaders in a community are generalists or specialists, the demands of a more complex society, the increase in size of cities, and the diversification of the economic and occupational base all appear to be associated with a shift toward a more pluralistic leadership structure made up of more individuals with more specialized skills.[18] Even the more general leader in a large, complex community tends to be a specialist of a type; that is, he tends to be an expert in finance, administration, or human relations.

"Task" Leaders Versus "Social" Leaders

A third way of classifying leaders is in terms of their basic orientation, that is, their relative interest in task performance or in group maintenance. Is a leader more concerned with performing basic tasks or the objectives of his group, or is he more concerned with the solidarity and strength of the social relations within the group?

Studies of small groups, organizations, and communities reveal an interesting situation. Usually where there is both a high degree of consensus as to who the leaders are and a high degree of adjustment, we find not one but two basic types of leaders. Referring only to communities, there are "task-oriented" leaders who are usually specialists at something. They see conditions in the community which, by their expert standards, need improving, and so they drive hard to change the community in some technical way. In the well-organized, adjustive community, there is also the "social" leader, the "harmonizer," or the "process" leader. He is the leader who is more concerned with people and groups and their relationships to each other. Whereas the "task" leader tends to create tension and destroy the social system as he promotes physical and technical change, the "social" leader reduces friction, improves relationships, and maintains the community social system.

The community, as is true of other social systems, needs both types of leaders. Warren states it this way:

> What we see...is a perpetual process of new achievement and consolidation, coupled with a process of tension induction and reduction, and we have seen that in this multiple process there are roles in our communities both for the man whose eye is on the task accomplishment, and for the man whose eye is on the relationships existing among people. It may be just as well, given these diverse needs and this pulsating process, that not all people choose the same way to serve.[19]

Perhaps closely related to the "social" leader is a type of leader which may be called a "go-between." These are the people who serve as linkage between opposing groups or factions in a community. Go-betweens who are more communicators than power leaders may be overlooked by asking knowledgeables to name only community influentials. This is because strong leadership in either of the opposing camps would negate a person's effectiveness as a go-between.

FORMS OF COMMUNITY LEADERSHIP

The accumulating evidence indicates the existence of a broad range of leadership forms or patterns in different communities and in the same communities through time. This being the situation, Bonjean has stated that the focus is now shifting to a concern with the range of possible leadership structures, the important dimensions that differentiate the various structures, and the manner in which these dimensions can be measured. He further suggests that the important dimensions which appear to be involved in two ideal types—"covert power elite" and "legitimate pluralism"—are legitimacy, visibility, scope of influence, and cohesiveness.[20] Rather than elaborating on the various possible combinations which would result from this four-dimensional model, efforts will be directed toward a brief description of some of the more common forms described in the literature on community power and observed in Georgia communities.[21] The forms or structures will be grouped for convenience into four categories which may be labeled (1) focused or unitary, (2) split or bifactional, (3) multifactional, and (4) amorphous.[22]

Focused or Unitary

The focused or unitary classification of community leadership patterns includes communities whose leadership is pyramidal in form. At the apex of power is a person, group, or organization which unquestionably exercises power in a patterned way through the descending levels of leadership. The *first* type of this focused classification is often referred to as "bossism." Here power is centered in one person (or family) who exercises power through his "lieutenants." This form appears to be most often associated with small communities, slow-growing or declining communities, and communities with a narrow economic base, such as an agricultural or a one-industry town.[23]

The *second* focused type of structure has been called the "informal clique." This is the type of structure in which a small informally organized power elite controls the policy-making, coordination, and direction of the affairs of the community. This type of structure has been found in some Georgia communities to be an intermediate stage between bossism and the following type.[24]

A *third* type of power structure in this classification may be called an "organized pluralistic" structure. At the apex of this pyramid of power is a formally organized group, usually a voluntary lay organization, such as a local chamber of commerce, a community development council, or a local civic club. In a larger community, such an organization usually has rather broad representation which relates it to the various groups, organizations, political subdivisions and factions. Such an organization has the reputation for being the organization whose involvement is needed in relation to major change proposals for the community. Both these types of formal organizations and the community directing "informal cliques" described above are types of coordinative interstitial groups.

Split or Bifactional

A second broad classification of leadership structures may be labeled "split" or "bifactional." These double-pyramid community patterns are characterized by major splits or cleavages, such as: city-county, white-colored, or labor-management. It suffices to say here that each of the two factions in a cleavage may be characterized by bossism, informal cliques, or organized pluralistic patterns.

Multifactional

In addition to the focused and split patterns of power, some studies have revealed what might be termed multifactional structures. There may be more than one basic and continuing cleavage within a community and consequently more than two factions. Each faction may have its own type of organization. In all factional communities, a major concern for the change agent is the identification and involvement of the leaders of each faction. Concern should be given to discovering the individuals and groups which serve as linkages between factions as well as to the usual procedures used in relating representatives of the competing factions.

Amorphous

The last theoretical type of community leadership to be mentioned has been called "amorphous" or disorganized. Barth[25] described two communities in which no structure of leadership was identified. This condition was thought to be associated with absentee ownership and the dominance exerted over the community by a metropolitan regional center.

The distinction between the multifactional and the amorphous community leadership structure would be very difficult to delineate where factions approach the point of being difficult to recognize.

In summary, an attempt has been made in this paper to first, focus attention upon the interstitial or in-between groups and organizations in the community, as well as the conjunctive or competitive nature of the relationships within them. Second, an effort is made to offer some modifications to the many classifications of types of community leaders and forms of community power.

Notes

[1]Robert Presthus, *Men at the Top: A Study in Community Power*. New York: Oxford University Press, 1967, 105.

[2]William A. Gamson, Reputation and Resources in Community Politics, *American Journal of Sociology, 72* (September, 1966), 30.

[3]Frederick L. Bates and A.L. Bacon, Community as a Social System: A Theory of Community Structure. (Paper read at the annual Southern Sociological Society meeting, Atlanta, Georgia, 1965), 10-12.

[4]*Ibid.,* 6.

[5]Charles J. Dudley, Harold L. Nix, and Frederick L. Bates, Community Power Structure: A Structural Approach. (Paper read at the annual Southern Sociological Society meeting, New Orleans, Louisiana, April, 1966); Donald J. Shoemaker, An Analysis of Community Power Structure Utilizing the Concepts of Exchange and Coordinative Relationships. (Unpublished Master's thesis, The University of Georgia, Athens, 1968), 105-111.

[6]Frederick L. Bates and A.L. Bacon, *op. cit.,* 9.

[7]This definition of community is a modification of the following definition given by F.L. Bates and A.L. Bacon in the paper cited in footnote number three above: "...Community is a social system whose function is to manage the conflict and competition which arise out of the necessity to exchange functions (goods and services) which arise out of the division of labor in society."

[8]This statement does not mean that certain political offices are not vested with the authority to control certain types of behavior of members of all groups within their political jurisdiction. However, all members of all groups and organizations in a political jurisdiction are all members of one encompassing group—the "political" group.

[9]Harold L. Nix, Jennie McIntyre, and Charles J. Dudley, Bases of Leadership: Cultural Ideal and Estimates of Reality, *Southwestern Social Science Quarterly, 48* (December, 1967), 423-432.

[10]Linton C. Freeman, *et al.*, Locating Leaders in Local Communities: A Comparison of Some Alternative Approaches, *American Sociological Review, 28* (October, 1963), 797-798.

[11]*Ibid.*

[12]*Ibid.*

[13]Floyd Hunter, *Community Power Structure: A Study of Decision Makers.* Chapel Hill, NC: University of North Carolina Press, 1953.

[14]Robert A. Dahl, A Critique of the Ruling Elite Model, *American Political Science Review, 52* (June, 1958), 463-469.

[15]Illustrative of these comparative studies are: Freeman, *loc. cit.;* Presthus, *op. cit.,* 421-426; and M. Elaine Burgess, *Negro Leadership in a Southern City.* Chapel Hill, NC: University of North Carolina Press, 1960.

[16]Charles M. Bonjean and David M. Olson, Community Leadership: Directions of Research, *Administrative Science Quarterly, 9* (December, 1964), 289.

[17]Harold L. Nix and Charles J. Dudley, *Community Social Analysis of Savannah-Chatham County* (Community Social Analysis No. 1. Institute of Community and Area Development, University of Georgia, Athens, and Georgia Department of Public Health, Atlanta, 1965); Harold L. Nix, *Community Social Analysis of Macon-Bibb County* (Community Social Analysis No. 2. Institute of Community and Area Development, University of Georgia, Athens, and Georgia Department of Public Health, Atlanta, 1966); Harold L. Nix and Charles J. Dudley, *Community Social Analysis of Augusta-Richmond County* (Community Social Analysis No. 3. Institute of Community and Area Development, University of Georgia, Athens, and Georgia Department of Public Health, Atlanta, 1966).

[18]Harold L. Nix and Charles J. Dudley (No. 3), *op. cit.,* 43-44.

[19]Roland L. Warren, Toward a Reformulation of Community Theory, *Human Organization*, *15*(2) (published by The Society for Applied Anthropology, Summer, 1956), 8-11.

[20]Charles M. Bonjean and David M. Olson, *op. cit.*, 289-295.

[21]Ernest A.T. Barth, Community Influence Systems: Structure and Change, *Social Forces*, *40* (October, 1961), 58-63; Robert O. Schulze, The Bifurcation of Power in a Satellite City, in Morris Janowitz (Ed.), *Community Political Systems*. New York: The Free Press, 1961, 50-53; Bonjean and Olson, *op. cit.*, 294-295; and footnote number 19, *supra*.

[22]Harold L. Nix, Donald J. Shoemaker, and Ram Singh, *Community Social Analysis of Ogelthorpe County* (Community Social Analysis No. 5. Institute of Community and Area Development, University of Georgia, Athens, and Georgia Department of Public Health, Atlanta, 1967), 36-43.

[23]*Ibid.*

[24]*Ibid.*

[25]Ernest A.T. Barth, *op. cit.*, 58-63.

Leadership and Community Development

William R. Lassey and Marshall Sashkin

Most communities would benefit from improved quality of leadership, focused on developing a pluralistic or more broadly based leadership structure. Leadership training can enhance pluralism, broaden leadership structure, and increase the effectiveness of a community. No community is likely to be totally transformed through participation in such activities, but substantial improvement has proven to be possible in a variety of locations.

Current attempts to improve leadership in communities seem to be based on certain assumptions. First, we assume that participative decision making is more productive than centralized decision making (Maier, 1963; Sashkin, 1982). Second, it is assumed that planned change involving widespread participation by all affected parties is possible and is more desirable than unplanned or ad hoc change (Lassey, 1977). Third, we believe that the process that produces planned change can be learned and used by a variety of people who are interested in improving the quality of their community (Lippitt, Watson, & Westley, 1958; Lippitt, Hooyman, Sashkin, & Kaplan, 1979). Fourth, it is assumed that potential leadership competence is present throughout

This article is an extensive revision of an article in the second edition of this volume that was co-authored with Richard R. Fernandez. The original article was adapted from "Community Development Theory and Practice" by William R. Lassey, in William R. Lassey and Anne S. Williams (Eds.), *Community Development in Montana: Resources, Methods, Case Studies.* Bozeman, MT: Big Sky Books, 1970.

the population of most communities and can be activated through the acquisition of knowledge, skill training, and leadership experience (Cottle, 1969).

Some key areas for learning and development of skills by potential community leaders, identified by Zaltman and Duncan (1977), include: problem identification and refinement, planning and problem-solving processes, decision-making processes, location and acquisition of resources, program management, and action implementation processes. Community residents who have acquired knowledge and developed skills in the areas listed generally will be more effective in helping their communities to identify and take advantage of opportunities for development.

The acquisition of knowledge and development of skills usually is best accomplished through experience. Learning is likely to occur most rapidly and profoundly if the knowledge and skills are put directly to work through significant community programs.

CHARACTERISTICS OF A POTENTIALLY EFFECTIVE COMMUNITY LEADERSHIP GROUP

If broad community leadership competence is to be increased, certain types of individuals need to be involved (Ross, 1968). These include:

1. persons with advanced educations who represent a variety of occupations;
2. individuals who represent the variety of socioeconomic and ethnic groups in the community;
3. those with historic family roots in the community as well as persons who may have been born elsewhere but who have lived in the community for a substantial period of time;
4. newcomers to the community;
5. citizens involved in formal local government, both elected and appointed; and
6. people who have demonstrated strong, long-term commitment to community progress through their past behaviors and community involvement.

It will usually not be possible to achieve such widespread involvement at the beginning of a new community development program. As the program's leadership base is broadened, however, the potential for further involvement is increased.

Although leadership development will prove to be valuable in facilitating community progress, it may also be important to continue some reliance on outside assistance for many activities. Certain critical professional skills and knowledge may not be available in the local community, and an outside consultant can directly contribute to resolving key problems or obstacles.

THE ROLE OF EXTERNAL CONSULTANTS

Outside consultants or educational facilitators may be needed to assist local citizens in updating their knowledge, skills, and experience. Consultants can perform several roles in developing local leadership skill and community competence (Rothman, 1974):

1. *Catalyst.* Helping community members to recognize problems and opportunities while generating their interest in the improvement of local ability to achieve new development.
2. *Process helper.* Assisting local citizens in designing and implementing the processes required to improve leadership skills.
3. *Resource linker.* Helping local citizens to locate resources (i.e., financial and technical assistance, new knowledge, government programs) and establishing links between the local community and sources of outside assistance.
4. *Expert.* Having the knowledge, skills, and experience that are directly applicable to the solution of the community's problems, or the realization of its opportunities, and assisting the community most efficiently by sharing understanding or abilities.

The role of outside expert might be appropriate in implementing a leadership training program. Most of the local leadership activities would fit comfortably under the catalytic, process-helper, or resource-linker roles—each of which can be learned by selected local citizens. Representatives of public or private agencies or organizations in the community may already command considerable knowledge, skill, and experience in one or more of the roles.

Several classifications of community development "consultants" have been delineated: (a) the professionally trained community-process specialist, who may be a university professor, a chamber of commerce employee, an extension specialist, a church worker, a social welfare worker, or a public health worker; (b) the institutional administrator who directs or guides several field workers; (c) the private planning or development consultant, employed by a professional firm; (d) the consultant who is hired full time by the community to direct planning and development programs, or (e) state or federal representatives assigned to work with a group of communities (Christenson & Robinson, 1980).

A consultant may help to initiate a development program or may simply be requested to assist an effort already underway. Development programs that become vital to the participants should achieve a momentum of their own and should become increasingly the responsibility of the people involved. An effective consultant can help a program remain operational through periods of crisis and may contribute important knowledge about program content and method of approach.

Consultant Knowledge, Skills, and Characteristics

The consultant must be able to strike a proper balance between exerting influence and encouraging local initiative and participation. The consultant's initiative usually is greater in the early stages and then tapers off as the local citizens gain confidence and competence.

To some extent, the knowledge and skills required of an effective community development consultant are obvious. Technical knowledge and skill in the process and content of community planning and development are needed, as are basic organizational and administrative abilities. The consultant must understand local politics, the nature of community power structures, and the dynamics and characteristics of the community with which he or she is involved. Effective communication skills are necessary in order to understand and communicate with local leaders and community members. Finally, the community development consultant must value and believe in the potential for local self-help and productive community development (Zaltman & Duncan, 1977).

The community consultant must be willing to accept and respect the unique wants, beliefs, needs, customs, values, worth, and priorities of local citizens. This attitude is basic to openness in seeking contributions of local ideas. Citizens usually are ready to cooperate with consultants if they are treated as partners in the change process and given the opportunity to do as much as possible for themselves (Lassey, 1977).

Willingness to accept lay citizens unconditionally is not a trivial stance. The consultant must relate to them with due respect for their individuality and must seek to understand and respect their images of themselves, even when these images do not appear to be very realistic.

The consultant cannot hope to remain unclassified. Local people will want to place outsiders in their frames of reference. They will tend to interpret everything from their image of an appropriate outsider role in the community. In this sense, it is better for the consultant to expose his or her value biases and hope to be accepted on that basis.

Consultants must understand the likelihood of conflict over development priorities and the potential difficulty of achieving cooperation and collaboration within the community through accepted political and power channels. Failure to communicate effectively with influential citizens and leaders of public opinion can only lead to serious problems in implementation. Confrontation with the establishment may occasionally be called for, if establishment leaders are behaving contrary to clearly established development requirements.

Obsolescence of local organizations may be a primary reason for lack of effective development. It is extremely important for the consultant to have a clear understanding of organizational alternatives and possible new organizational designs. It also would be helpful to understand the process through which an organization can be modified or a new organization can be initiated (Beckhard, 1969).

CHARACTERISTICS OF SUCCESSFUL CONSULTATION

Although various authors and researchers have attempted to identify the personal characteristics of successful consultants, the results of such studies generally have not been enlightening, usually producing lists of desirable and undesirable traits that are based more on beliefs and impressions about effective consultants than on research findings. It has been suggested, for example, that the effective consultant is an extrovert, has considerable interpersonal skills, is creative and takes risks, has the ability to conceptualize and present ideas clearly, and is good at organizing activities. It would be hard not to agree with such a list. Unfortunately, this is not based on firm evidence or data.

Havelock and Sashkin (1982) have, however, been able to identify a set of factors characteristic of effective *consultation*, based on an extensive review of the research literature. These factors are characteristic of the way the consultant manages the process of change, rather than of personality or general behavioral attributes.

Homogeneity implies that the more alike the consultant and clients are, the more likely it is that the effort will be successful. When the consultant is more like the clients, the clients are far more likely to *accept* the consultant and to *participate* effectively in the development process. Moreover, the consultant is more likely to *understand* the clients.

Empathy is the skill of understanding the feelings and thoughts of another person and can be learned; it is not only a personal characteristic of the consultant. Empathy leads to improved communication and understanding between the consultant and the clients.

Linkage is the degree of collaboration between the consultant and the clients; the extent to which they are linked to one another, as equal participants in the development process directly affects the chance that the development effort will succeed.

Proximity refers to the accessibility of the consultant and clients to one another. Increased proximity obviously makes it easier to develop collaborative linkages. Such access also facilitates the development of empathy between the consultant and the clients.

Structuring refers to the ability of the consultant and clients to clearly plan and organize their activities with respect to the development effort. When the development effort is clearly outlined and presented, it is more likely to be mutually agreed on and, thus, more likely to be effective. Structured organization also facilitates implementation of the change approach in a straightforward manner.

Capacity is actually a characteristic of the client system, the community. It refers to the capacity of the clients to provide the resources needed for success. When resources that are important are seriously lacking, attention must be directed toward ways of obtaining these resources.

Openness is the degree to which the consultant and clients are open to one another, that is, open to one another's ideas, needs, and feelings. The preceding six factors all can facilitate the development of such openness or, when absent, they can effectively hinder the development of openness between the consultant and clients.

Reward refers to the potential benefits of the change for the clients and the consultant. Ideally, development efforts should be designed so that, in both the long and the short-run, the clients are rewarded for changing. When short-term rewards are low, this may be overcome by focusing on the clients' need for change; not changing may be even less rewarding than changing. Long-range benefits also should be emphasized.

Energy is the amount of effort that both the consultant and clients have available to put into the development activity. It is not unusual for consultants to be "spread thin" across many communities. When this is the case, all the clients may suffer from a lack of energy on the part of the consultant. Similarly, when other problems are so pressing that they take all of the local citizens' energy, it is unlikely that they will be capable of generating the effort needed to make the development effort successful.

Synergy results from the positive reinforcement that each of the preceding nine factors exerts on the others. Synergy means that the whole is more than the sum of its parts. The more favorable each of the preceding nine factors is, the more synergy there will be to contribute to the success of the development effort.

BASIC PRINCIPLES OF LEADERSHIP FOR COMMUNITY DEVELOPMENT

Community development leadership has been experienced and observed more than it has been researched. Guidelines have been developed from many community development projects and programs. It appears that failures occur not because the principles are inapplicable but because local leaders or consultants do not understand how to apply them (Christenson & Robinson, 1980).

I: A Systems Perspective. It is critical that leaders and consultants be aware that the community and its surrounding environment form an integrated social system and that this fact be recognized in specific action programs. Community development is more likely to be effective when decisions and actions involve established, informal, primary groups as well as formal councils, boards, and commissions.

II: A Local Perspective. The structures of community organizations must be developed according to the characteristics and needs of the local situation. Organization imposed by outside consultants or by leaders acting without the involvement of community members neglects unique local factors and is likely to be inappropriate and inadequate for meeting the community's needs.

III: Community Involvement. Members of the community must be active partners with the consultant in the development process. This means that while the consultant may suggest, advise, and propose, the decisions must be made by the community members, not on the consultant's initiative. A community development program is most likely to succeed when the knowledge and skills possessed by the community members are tapped and used effectively.

IV: Awareness of Community Culture. Both consultants and community members should have a thorough knowledge of the main values and principal features of the community's culture. This often requires the collection of detailed information. A development program is much more likely to succeed when ideas and actions are in tune with the social, political, economic, and ecological systems of the community.

V: Minimal Conflicts. The probability of conflict is inherent in any community development program, because any change is likely to conflict with some existing condition and some people are likely to prefer the existing condition. However, conflict is less likely to occur if local leaders and consultants take certain factors into account. Most obviously, the leaders should try to determine whether the program is incompatible with the beliefs, attitudes, values, status, or expectations of community members. A more sophisticated approach would be to try to identify any threats to vested interests that might develop as a result of planned changes.

VI: Relevance to Local Needs. Community development activities are more likely to succeed when they grow out of some strongly felt need, interest, or problem. It is desirable that the program's goals promise relatively high returns for the amount of effort and work invested by participants.

CONCLUSION

Community development leadership has been examined in terms of the knowledge, skills, and practices required for success. The leader or consultant is most likely to succeed when community development is treated as a planned, participative process.

In the broadest sense, community development is an educational endeavor. It is a process that involves members of the community, community leaders, and consultants in learning how to create needed, desired, and effective changes in the social and biophysical environments.

References

Beckhard, R. *Organization development: Strategies and models*. Reading, MA: Addison-Wesley, 1969.

Christenson, J.A., & Robinson, J.W., Jr. *Community development in America*. Ames, IA: Iowa State University Press, 1980.

Cottle, T.J. Bristol Township schools: Strategy for change. *The Saturday Review*, September 20, 1969, pp. 70-82.

Havelock, R.G., & Sashkin, M. HELP SCORES: A guide to promoting change in groups and organizations. In H. Blumberg, A.P. Hare, V. Kent, & M. Davies (Eds.), *Social groups and social interaction* (Vol. 2). London: John Wiley, 1983.

Lassey, W.R. *Planning in rural environments*. New York: McGraw-Hill, 1977.

Lippitt, R., Watson, J., & Westley, B. *The dynamics of planned change*. New York: Harcourt Brace Jovanovich, 1958.

Lippitt, R., Hooyman, G., Sashkin, M., & Kaplan, J. *Resourcebook for planned change*. Ann Arbor, MI: Human Resource Development Associates, 1979.

Maier, N.R.F. *Problem solving discussions and conferences*. New York: McGraw-Hill, 1963.

Ross, M. *Community organization*. New York: Harper & Row, 1968.

Rothman, J. *Planning and organizing for social change*. New York: Columbia University Press, 1974.

Sashkin, M. *A manager's guide to participative management*. New York: American Management Associations, 1982.

Zaltman, G., & Duncan, R. *Strategies for planned change*. New York: John Wiley, 1977.

Professional Leadership Roles in Community Development

Paul D. Warner

If community development is the process whereby those in a community arrive at group decisions and take actions to improve their well-being, community developers are the professional workers who help these changes to come about. They are sometimes called change agents, planners, resource persons, educators, consultants, organizers, and various other titles. The roles of CD professionals are as varied as the groups they work with and the development strategies utilized.

This chapter presents an overall framework for understanding the role of the CD professional. Previous attempts to specify and categorize the different roles have usually centered on "what the person does" or on specific philosophies or strategies of development. In the first ten volumes of the *Journal of the Community Development Society*, at least six different classification schemes are presented. These typologies are helpful but they are limited in that most consider only a single criterion and often end in attempts to justify why one approach is superior to another.

It seems futile to attempt to refine the existing schemes without adding relevant criteria. Answering the question, What do CD professionals do? is not enough in itself. Other

Reprinted by permission from *Community Development in America* by James A. Christenson and Jerry W. Robinson, editors. © 1977 by The Iowa State University Press, Ames, Iowa 50010.

questions of importance include, What types of knowledge and skills do they possess? What organization or agency do they represent? Who is the clientele being served? The CD practitioner model presented here comprises the interrelationship of four elements: individual factors (I), organizational factors (O), task functions (T), and the nature of clientele being served (C).

$$\text{CD role} = f(I_{a,b,c,..}\ O_{g,h,i,..}\ T_{m,n,o,..}\ C_{s,t,u,...})$$

The CD professional's role thus is seen as a function of all four variables. Each of the four, in turn, represents a group of factors ($a, b, c, . . .$) that relates to the organization, the person, the task, and the clientele.

THE INDIVIDUAL

Each CD professional has a unique set of skills, experiences, and attitudes. These intellectual and personal characteristics are specific to the person and impact the role. It follows that a community organizer needs an educational and experience base in social organization and leadership, and a health planner needs to have technical knowledge of the field of health services and the planning process. These skills are obviously required for employment. In addition, the specialist also brings a style and philosophy of work, personality traits, physical appearance, initiative and imagination, motivation, sensitivity, established relationships and contacts, a status position and reputation in the community, and a capacity for making decisions. Mark Cohen (1980) concludes that the essential traits of a successful community developer are tolerance of ambiguity, common sense, perseverance, and humility. The professional comes to the job with all the strengths and weaknesses of the human personality.

We might conclude that such characteristics as friendliness, enthusiasm, intelligence, decisiveness, persistence, and courage are desirable traits in successful professionals; however, as in trait-oriented research on leadership, rarely could we find two persons who would agree as to which are essential (Stogdill, 1974). Individual factors are not unimportant; they are crucial in the understanding of the CD role. But a single set of traits that fits all situations is too simplistic. Rather, a multitude of personal characteristics need to be considered as important in defining the professional role.

The CD professional interacts within a work environment and is influenced by the structure and dynamics of the organization in which he or she works and by client groups served. At the same time, the professional is influencing these groups. And the relationship is constantly changing, adjusting, and adapting.

THE ORGANIZATION

The CD role is influenced to a considerable extent by the organizational context, which represents a whole set of conditions. Some of these characterize the organization's influence on the individual CD professional and others relate to the organization's relationship to its environment.

The organization possesses certain goals, purposes, and philosophy concerning development, which in turn are generally subscribed to by their [sic] employees. For example, Hamilton (1978) cites the definition and approach to community development that has been clearly specified by the Cooperative Extension Services' National Committee on Organization and Policy. Organizations may espouse one of the three approaches to development as presented earlier: self-help, technical assistance, or conflict. The role expectations for the CD worker would vary accordingly. The goals of the organization may be specific or very general, short term or of long duration (for example, to build a new park or to improve the social and economic well-being of the people). Employees tend to pattern their roles according to the framework established by the organization.

To function effectively an organization requires some degree of shared beliefs and practices that unite the members, some agreement on important values. This normative system consists of the dos and don'ts that govern the actions and imply the sanctions and rewards for group members. An organization establishes patterns of interaction among its members and places them in various positions of authority in relationship to other members. Differing levels of responsibility and status are thus conferred by the organization. This status level, in turn, carries over into the community in the form of titles, prestige, etc. In addition to these relations between individuals within the organization, the status attributed to the organization itself is also important. It may be a new and struggling consulting firm of three members or a century-old university of 1,000 faculty.

Functional specialization within and among organizations has increased over the years. Developmental problems are generally complex in nature, requiring the input of many specialists. Most development efforts require, at a minimum, specialists in planning, financing, design, and organization. Increased specialization has made it necessary for the CD worker to interact across the boundaries of organizational subsystems and with other organizations and agencies. At the same time, large organizations have the capacity for possessing many specialists on call to address specific needs. One could conclude, therefore, that increased specialization has made the CD professional's role more complex but it also has the potential for providing the CD worker with more specialized support.

The interorganizational climate in a community can impact the CD professional role. Ecologists have generally distinguished between two basic types of relations: symbiosis and commensalism (Hawley, 1950, p. 36-39). The former refers to relations of mutual dependence and advantage, while the latter describes competition for the same scarce resources. Because developmental problems often require the input of many organizations, cooperation among agencies and agency representatives is crucial (symbiosis). Formal and informal linkages between organizations, in turn, set the framework in which the professionals work. If the organizations are competing for the same resources (commensalism), recognition, or domain, joint efforts of the workers will be severely hampered.

TASK FUNCTIONS

In attempting to define the CD worker's role in terms of the task performed, one is struck by the wide range and diverse activities commonly identified with the role. Ross (1967, p. 40) suggests many of the task functions when he defines community organization as "a process by which a community identifies its needs or objectives, orders these needs or objectives, takes action with respect to them, and in doing so extends and develops cooperative and collaborative attitudes and practices in the community."

The most basic specialization of functional roles focuses on content versus process (Cebotarev and Brown, 1972). Content refers to the provision of technical subject-matter information with a task orientation, whereas process deals with strategies for developing a capacity in individuals and groups for decision making and action (Mahan and Bollman, 1968); the "what" versus the "how." These two concepts are often presented as if they represent a continuum.

More specific functions have been delineated in reference to identifiable professional roles. From the social perspective, Gallaher and Santopolo (1967) identified four roles that link the change agent to the client system: analyst, advisor, advocator, and innovator. From this point of view the CD worker is seen as a specialist in process skills and a generalist in technical subject matter. These functions approximate the tasks identified in Hamilton's study of community developers in the Cooperative Extension Service.

From a city and regional planning perspective, Meyerson (1956) delineates the following five task functions: central intelligence, pulse-taking, policy clarification, detailed development plan, and feedback review. The central intelligence and pulse-taking functions serve to facilitate the orderly growth and development of the private and public sectors of the community. The policy clarification function is the statement and revision of community objectives. Preparing the technical plan is the function most widely identified with the planner role. In addition, the planner is expected to evaluate program consequences as a guide to future action (feedback review).

The Cooperative Extension Service has defined six functions as appropriate for the CD professional (ECOP, 1966): (1) providing technical and analytical assistance, (2) helping identify community problems and development goals and objectives, (3) identifying consequences of development alternatives, (4) fostering liaison with outside individuals and groups, (5) stimulating community interaction, and (6) bringing together diverse groups.

Other efforts to define the role of the CD worker according to the task performed resemble the basic concepts in the change agent, planning, and extension roles. For example, Morris (1970) specifies four work roles: field agent, advisor or consultant, advocate, and planner. A more general level of approach is suggested in Cary's (1972) terms of enabler, activist, advocate, and community organizer.

In an attempt to synthesize the various listings of functions attributed to the CD role, Bennett (1973) developed a classification scheme based on five principal functions: process consultant, technical consultant, program advocate, organizer, and resource provider. The process consultant role focuses on the "hows" of problem solving, decision making, organizing, enabling, and implementing rather than on the particular group action outcomes; strategies for facilitating change are the process consultant's areas of expertise. The technical consultant, on the other hand, "provides information, know-how, and perspective to the community in relation to specific programs of change" (Bennett, 1973, p. 64). Supplying accurate technical information to a community is a vital part of development; therefore information-giving and analysis concerning developmental alternatives are central to this role. The CD professional is seen as an expert in certain subject matter areas.

When CD workers propose a specific course of action, they are performing in the role of advocate. The professional analyzes the situation and decides what the best alternative is for the community. In this case the professional goes beyond presenting the alternatives to the community for their [sic] action and recommends a specific alternative as the best solution for the problem.

The organizational role is concerned with the formulation and renewal of an organizational structure that can deal with community problems. With this approach, the CD worker helps a community organize for action. This role has often been utilized in neighborhood settings through the use of the Alinsky approach (1969). The organizer focuses on bringing individuals together in a group setting so they can have a voice in community affairs. The process consultant role is then involved in seeing that the organization continues to function.

The fifth role presented by Bennett is that of resource provider. He defines this function as the channeling of financial resources to the community. Ratchford (1970) and Ross (1967) also cited this role, though (contrary to Bennett) they did not limit the concept of resources to money, but rather focused on the role of the professional in the identification of a community need for outside help and how to go about securing it.

Though different categorical names are used by the various typologies, the Bennett scheme appears to include most of the important tasks generally attributed to CD professionals. A worker may perform one or more of the five tasks, all of which are important for community development.

CLIENTELE

Professionals work with a wide variety of clientele. The appropriate individual or group will be largely determined by which decisions are to be made, what actions are to be taken, and who will enter that process. The most general level of clientele involvement is the public-at-large. Some developmental goals impact most or all citizens; for example, programs of general education and awareness would come under this heading. However, most CD professionals tend to have regular, direct contact with a limited number of people. In this case, the client group is the segment of the public who is seen as the primary consumer of the services offered by the CD worker. The CD professional generally works through these individuals or groups for the ultimate benefit of the community residents.

Whether the approach to development be self-help, confrontation, or technical intervention, a basic assumption of the relationship between professionals and clients is that decisions are expected to be governed not by the professionals' own self-interests but by their judgment of what would serve their clients' interests best. Of concern is that professionals may fail to serve their clients' best interests because of a preoccupation with their own status or career or, on the other hand, become subservient to client interests at the expense of objective professional judgment.

The CD professional may work with individuals or groups. The nature of the professional assistance provided determines the setting, and the skills needed by the professional differ accordingly. For example, the worker may be responding to a very specific request of one person or helping a group through a decision-making process.

The clientele may be local *lay leaders*. Such persons are generally voluntary, unpaid individuals working for the good of the community. These persons possess a wide variety of preparation and skills, as well as time and effort that they contribute. They are from the local community and may be self-appointed, designated, or elected and may have a locally recognized status and following (Bilinski, 1969). Working through voluntary lay leaders offers the professional an established linkage into the existing social structure of the community, though the volunteer leader may be limited in training and experience in CD efforts and lack sufficient time. In this case the professional needs to offer informal support, training, and information to these individuals within a very flexible time frame. In Hamilton's (1978) study of CD professionals in the Cooperative Extension Service, lay leaders proved to be the clientele group with which the most time was spent.

Local officials make up another important client group. They are usually elected or appointed and are charged with the responsibility of caring for specific governmental functions. Some are unpaid but most receive some compensation, either on a part- or full-time basis. Like volunteer leaders, their knowledge, skills, and experience vary substantially. Also, their areas of responsibility and interests may be communitywide or very specialized. The success of the CD professional, to a great extent, lies in the professional's ability to support these officials without competing with them and thus threatening their power position in the community. The CD professional can provide such help as general awareness education and assistance in problem-solving and planning, as well as providing specific factual information. A prime example of professionals serving this client group is planners, who provide assistance to governmental officials in the areas of problem identification, data collection and analysis, plan formulation and implementation, and feedback.

Civic and development organizations are often directly or indirectly involved in carrying out or encouraging development. Many lay leaders work through these organizations. The goals of these groups may or may not be limited to development and their involvement may be in a specific aspect of development (e.g., industry, health, education). The members are volunteer and their backgrounds and experiences are varied. Though sometimes the organizations' interests are very specific and the group process may be slow, they have had and will continue to have a great impact on the development of communities because of their ability to draw on a wide range of skills and experiences of their members and to exert influences to mobilize resources.

Many *developmental agencies and organizations* have paid professional staff in communities. These professionals are supported from outside the community and usually work with a local advisory board or group. They are professionally trained in specialized subject areas, and their status is derived principally from their professional position in the parent organization rather than from the community. Instances of this arrangement can readily be found in such federal agencies as the Economic Development Administration; Housing and Urban Development; Health, Education, and Welfare; and the Farmers Home Administration.

Because of the independent nature of the many development organizations and individuals, the possibility for an uncoordinated, fragmented approach to development definitely exists.

Bilinski (1969, p. 162) describes the professional as possessing a feeling of "competition with other professionals trying to promote their segmental interests at the expense of the rest of the program of community development." The overall success of the developmental effort, as well as that of professionals, depends on a cooperative attitude of the professionals sharing information and working together while working toward the good of the community.

References

Alinsky, S.D. *Reveille for radicals.* New York: Random House, Vintage Books, 1969.

Bennett, A. Professional staff members' contributions to community development. *Journal of the Community Development Society,* 1973, 4 (Spring), 58-68.

Bilinski, R. A description and assessment of community development. In Luther T. Wallace, Daryl Hobbs, and Raymond D. Vlasin (Eds.), *Selected perspectives for community resource development.* Raleigh, NC: North Carolina State University, Agriculture Policy Institute, 1969.

Cary, L.J. Roles of the professional community developer. *Journal of the Community Development Society,* 1972, 3 (Fall), 36-41.

Cebotarev, E.A., & Brown, E.J. Community resource development: An analytic view of work strategies. *Journal of the Community Development Society,* 1972, 3 (Spring), 40-55.

Cohen, M. Professional roles: As a community psychologist. In James A. Christenson and Jerry W. Robinson, Jr. (Eds.), *Community development in America.* Ames, IA: Iowa State University Press, 1980.

ECOP Report. Community resource development. Washington, DC: United States Department of Agriculture, Cooperative Extension Service, 1966.

ECOP Report. Community development: Concepts, curriculum, training needs. Washington, DC: United States Department of Agriculture, Cooperative Extension Service, 1975.

Gallaher, A., Jr., & Santopolo, F.A. Perspectives on agent roles. *Journal of Cooperative Extension*, 1967, *5*, 223-30.

Hamilton, V.E. Survey of state CES community development leaders. Raleigh, NC: North Carolina State University, 1978.

Hawley, A.H. *Human ecology*. New York: Ronald Press, 1950.

Mahan, R.A., & Bollman, S.R. Education on information giving. *Journal of Cooperative Extension*, 1968, *6*, 100-108.

Meyerson, M. Building the middle-range bridge for comprehensive planning. *Journal of the American Institute of Planners*, 1956, *22*, 58-64.

Morris, R. The role of the agent in the community development process. In Lee J. Cary (Ed.), *Community development as a process*. Columbia, MO: University of Missouri Press, 1970.

Ratchford, C.B. The CD profession in today's society. *Journal of the Community Development Society*, 1970, *1* (Spring), 5-13.

Ross, M.G. *Community organization: Theory, principles, and practice* (2nd ed.). New York: Harper & Row, 1967.

Stogdill, R. *Handbook of leadership: A survey of theory and research*. New York: Free Press, 1974.

Leadership Development in Community and Public Affairs

Ivan Lee Weir and Robert E. Howell

Studies of leaders and leadership development in communities have examined several dimensions of leadership, including traits, status, and roles of leaders, and the environments that are conducive to the exercise of leadership. Recent attention has been focused increasingly on the development of leadership for the public good. To this end, four experimental, statewide, leadership development programs were established between 1965 and 1971 for the purpose of achieving two common goals.[1] One goal was to increase participation in public affairs among program recipients. The second was to improve participants' problem-solving skills and leadership capabilities.

In 1978 an evaluation[2] was made of the four programs to discover whether the desired effects were being achieved and, if so, why. This paper summarizes the basic design features of these programs while also describing the effects of the programs on increasing participation in public affairs.

This article was specifically requested by the editors as an original contribution to the Third Edition. Used by permission of the authors.

PROGRAM PARTICIPANTS

Between 1965 and 1976, more than 700 young men and women, largely from rural areas, participated in the statewide public-affairs leadership development programs conducted by educational institutions in Pennsylvania, Montana, Michigan, and California. The Pennsylvania and Montana programs enrolled both men and women, while Michigan and California limited participation to men. Participants were largely between the ages of twenty and forty-five years. Although selection criteria varied among the programs, most participants were chosen in part because of a demonstrated potential for leadership. Table 1 shows a comparison of selected participant characteristics.

Table 1. A Comparison of Selected Characteristics of All Respondents in the Four Leadership Development Programs

Characteristic	State Programs			
	Pennsylvania N = 294	Montana N = 72	Michigan N = 124	California N = 143
Income (median)	$14,329	$17,307	$22,656	over $30,000[a]
Age (mean)	31.7	42.0	39.0	36.0
Sex (percent male)	68.3	63.9	100.0	100.0
Marital Status (percent married)	78.9	83.3	98.4	88.1
Occupation (percent farmers and farm managers)	30.5	29.2	88.7	68.1
Education (percent college degree or more)	54.4	61.1	28.2	81.2

[a]The specific median income could not be calculated for California respondents because the highest income category was "Over $30,000," and just over 50 percent of California respondents indicated that their income was over $30,000.

EDUCATIONAL PROGRAM CHARACTERISTICS

The educational programs included classroom training, "live-in" workshops, and travel seminars. The workshops were similar to conference-style executive-development programs, lasted from three to five days each, and occurred over a one- to three-year period. Both workshops and travel seminars were targeted at providing participants with an understanding of social, economic, cultural, and political dimensions of public problems; insight into the mechanisms by which public policy is developed; and knowledge of the means by which group action is initiated and carved out in order to resolve pressing public concerns. Specific seminars were designed to develop individual and group communication skills; sharpen problem-solving capabilities; increase knowledge of governmental processes; and broaden the participants' understanding of important local, national, and international issues. The seminars were conducted by university faculty members, government officials, and leaders of business and industry. Although there were substantial differences among the programs in style, delivery, participants, and resource persons, many characteristics were similar. Table 2 illustrates the curricula used in one or more of the four programs.

The three-year programs were structured so that participants concentrated on local and state-wide issues during their first year of training, regional and national issues during the second year, and international issues during the third year. Throughout the first-year program, the emphasis was on enhancing the ability of participants to analyze public problems and to communicate effectively. Through workshops and simulations, participants were encouraged to make decisions and test their ideas with resource persons and fellow participants. They were encouraged to raise questions and to enter into discussions as they would in actual, public, problem-solving situations. Problems identified by the participants, such as the provision of public transportation in rural areas and the delivery of improved rural health-care services, were analyzed in task-force groups during classroom sessions and travel seminars. Task-force group meetings with state and Federal government officials provided opportunities to become familiar with resources and technical assistance available to community leaders, as well as public policy processes.

Table 2. An Illustration of Program Topics Included in the Four Leadership Development Programs

General Area	Selected Specific Topics		
	Year 1	Year 2	Year 3
Government	Local government as a problem solver; Rural legal assistance; Taxation	Federal executive, legislative and judicial branches of government; State constitutions; Public policy issues	International interdependency; European economic community; United States and European foreign policies
Economics	Socio-economic changes in rural areas; Local fiscal planning and management; Money and banking; the Federal Reserve system; Elements of pricing systems	Labor structure and determinants; United States monetary and fiscal policies	Comparative economic systems; State relationships to national and international economics; Price stability and economic expansion; International economic development issues
Politics	Political parties; Role of farm organizations in politics; Urban and rural land use planning	Comparative political systems; Political leadership styles; Practical politics	Development of foreign policy; Rich nations—poor nations and moral responsibility
Sociology and Social Problems	Public problem analysis; poverty in America; Inner city problems; Demography; Leadership: Working with groups	Welfare systems; Social action processes; Contemporary native American problems	Problems of developing nations; World hunger
Communications	Parilmentary procedures; influencing community groups; Public speaking; Writing	Effective communications; Farm organization communications	Language problems
Travel Seminar Preparation	Natural resources	Urban sociology; Geography	History and culture of the countries to be visited
Arts, Religion, etc.	Music; Symphony; Light opera; Visual arts	History of United States music and art; Shakespeare's plays	World religions; Architecture; Sculpture; Communism as a religious force

During the state travel seminars, participants met with legislators and received overviews of the legislative, judicial, and executive branches of state government. They also visited selected major industries and learned about other industrial-economic sectors that have an impact on their own professions as well as United States production systems as a whole.

The international program topics included price stability, balance-of-payments problems, problems of developing nations, international development strategies, and the culture and history of the countries to be visited. The international travel seminar generally exposed participants to both highly developed and developing nations.

After an initial trial period, the three-year program evolved into a two-year pattern, with the second-year program being devoted to topics concerning domestic and international issues.

UNIQUE CHARACTERISTICS OF EACH PROGRAM

Michigan. The Kellogg Farmer's Study Programs (KFSP) began in Michigan in 1965 and continued until five three-year programs had been completed. The program's curriculum included issues related to agricultural policies, economics, other social sciences, and the humanities. Discussions of important social issues were held, focusing on alternative methods of solving public problems. The largest difference between KFSP and the other state programs was the larger emphasis given to an economic perspective. Some of the formal topics presented included elements of pricing systems, banking and the Federal Reserve System, U.S. monetary and fiscal policies, the European economic community, and trade and economic development. The program was conducted by faculty members from Michigan State University's Department of Agricultural Economics.

Pennsylvania. The Public Affairs Leadership Program (PALP) was initiated in Pennsylvania in 1970, continued for six consecutive years, and included programs ranging from one to three years in length. Although many participants were farmers or employed in agriculturally related occupations, a substantial number came from urban areas and earned their living in many types of employment. The program was conducted by faculty members from Pennsylvania State University's Department of Agricultural Economics and Rural Sociology.

Travel seminars were an especially important segment of the Pennsylvania programs. Participants examined the problems of a major city (Philadelphia) firsthand. A one-day personalized field experience was included in the urban seminar, in which individual group members met with professionals who were working on inner-city problems. These experiences ranged from walking the beat with a policeman to spending the day with a case worker in a low-income housing project. Travel seminars during the second year included a visit to a Southern state to examine problems such as rural poverty and inadequate rural health-care facilities and services, which are similar to those encountered in Pennsylvania.

Participants visited Western European countries during the third year to view alternative forms of government and innovative rural-development programs. The groups also visited Southern Europe and North Africa to view the problems of developing nations and to become more sensitive to the problems faced by people living under conditions of extreme poverty.

Montana. The Kellogg Extension Education Project (KEEP) began in Montana in 1971 under the leadership of personnel from Montana State University's Cooperative Extension Service. Like the Pennsylvania program, KEEP included both men and women; followed a "live-in" seminar format; and included a statewide, national, and international travel-seminar format. In addition to many of the topics listed in Table 2, a unique aspect of the KEEP programs was the use of summer institutes involving participants' families, which created a family-support component for community leadership activity.

California. The Agricultural Leadership Program (ALP) began in 1970 as a special educational program in public affairs for California farmers and persons employed in occupations and professions related to agriculture. ALP was administered through a nonprofit foundation, but the curriculum was divided among four land-grant universities, each specializing in a particular group of topics. For example, topics in economics were taught at the University of

California, Davis; politics and government were presented through California State University at Fresno; communications at California Polytechnic State University at San Luis Obispo; and sociology, arts, religion, and rural-urban studies were taught through California State Polytechnic University at Pomona. The national travel seminar included visits to other rural areas, selected major cities, and Washington, D.C. Many different countries were visited during the international travel seminars. One additional component of ALP was the inclusion of industry-sponsored seminars by organizations such as Safeway Corporation, Security Pacific Bank, and Tenneco Corporation.

METHODS USED TO ASSESS PROGRAM IMPACTS

Participation in voluntary associations and other nonprofit organizations may be viewed as a method for influencing all levels of government.[3] Such participation also provides opportunities for individuals to influence decisions related to community affairs.[4] Although de Tocqueville described America as "a nation of joiners," recent surveys tend to qualify this notion as applicable primarily to identifiable leaders and persons who demonstrate leadership behaviors.[5] Studies in mobilization theory reinforce the importance of leadership in voluntary associations and nonprofit organizations by arguing that increased involvement stimulates men and women to become more politically active, which, in turn, prepares people to assume larger leadership roles.[6]

As a test of whether the educational programs led to increased participation in public affairs, data were collected on membership affiliations with nonprofit organizations and voluntary associations.[7] Pre-program measures of organizational affiliations were obtained from application forms completed by all prospective program participants from all states. Post-program data were collected through a questionnaire that employed the total-design method for mail surveys (Dillman, 1978). The "post-test" was administered to program participants two years after program completion (Howell, Weir, & Cook, 1979) and to comparison group members two years after completion of the "pre-test." Data were obtained from 294 participants in the Pennsylvania program during the years 1971-1976, and from seventy-six members of a similar but nonequivalent comparison group. Similar data were collected from seventy-two Montana participants, 124 Michigan participants, and 143 California participants. Data for comparison groups were not available from the latter three states.

EFFECTS OF PROGRAM PARTICIPATION

Table 3 displays the proportion of increase or decrease in affiliation with voluntary and nonprofit organizations before and after program participation. The largest percentage gains (24 percent to 71 percent) were found for participation in "instrumental-type" organizations, as defined in Table 3. The Pennsylvania comparison group showed a slight decrease (–4 percent) in instrumental organizational affiliations. Relatively smaller gains of 1 to 10 percent were found for the category of "expressive-type" organizations, with a very slight decrease (–1 percent) for the comparison group.

Table 3. Measures of Before to After Program Participation Showing Proportion of Change in Memberships in Instrumental- and Expressive-Type Organizations.

State	Proportion of Change by Organizational Type		
	Instrumental[a]	Expressive[b]	Total
	%	%	%
Pennsylvania	31	5	36
Comparison	–4	–1	–5
Montana	24	10	34
Michigan	29	1	30
California	71	7	78

[a]Instrumental classification categories were defined as: government and quasi-governmental public service organizations; voluntary public service organizations; economic associations and professional societies; political parties; and general political-interest groups.

[b]Expressive classification categories were defined as: religious organizations; veterans and patriotic organizations; fraternal organizations (lodges) and nationality groups; and social clubs, athletic and sports organizations, hobby and avocational organizations.

CONCLUSIONS

The characteristics of the leadership programs considered to be essential for their success included: (a) an "intensive" and "extensive" educational program that focused on the analysis of public problems, (b) participants who demonstrated a potential for leadership and an interest in agriculture and public affairs, and (c) substantial commitment on the part of public and private sponsoring institutions.

Given the widespread interest in increasing the participation of women in public affairs, it is important to note that in the two state-wide programs that included women, Pennsylvania and Montana, separate analyses revealed that women showed gains equal to or greater than those of the men, especially in public service organizations.

Although both theoretical and empirical data indicate that the educational model used in the four leadership development programs will lead to increased participation in public affairs, there is no certainty that the model will work under every condition and for populations with less leadership potential. Since the results of the public-affairs leadership-development program evaluation were released in 1979, a national conference on the public-affairs leadership-development program concept was held for the purpose of communicating the results of the evaluation and the nature of the program model. Subsequently, new educational programs for agricultural and rural leaders were established in several states, and a regional program began in the Northeast.

Notes

[1]Financial support for the programs was provided by the W.K. Kellogg Foundation and by various public and private sources.

[2]The complete results of this evaluation are reported in Robert E. Howell, Ivan Lee Weir, and Annabel Kirschner Cook, *Public Affairs Leadership Development: An Impact Assessment of Programs Conducted in California, Michigan, Montana, and Pennsylvania* (Pullman, WA: Washington State University, 1979); and Robert E. Howell, Ivan Lee Weir, and Annabel Kirschner Cook, *Development of Rural Leadership: Problems, Procedures, and Insights* (Battle Creek, MI: W.K. Kellogg Foundation, 1982).

[3]See Kornhauser, 1959; Zimmer and Hawley, 1959; Lipset, Trow, and Coleman, 1956.

[4]See Smith and Freedman, 1972; Babchuk and Booth, 1973; Babchuk and Edwards, 1965.

[5]See Hyman and Wright, 1971; Hawley and Zimmer, 1970; Aggar and Ostrom, 1956; and Verba and Nie, 1972.

[6]See Olsen, 1976; and Rogers, Bultena, and Barb, 1975.

[7]See Howell et al. (1979), for a thorough description of the methods used in evaluating the leadership development programs. To identify members of the Pennsylvania comparison group, reference persons named by participants on their program applications were asked to identify two individuals who were of the same age, sex, marital status, socio-economic status, and who had similar opportunities for leadership as persons whom reference persons had previously recommended for the leadership development program. Each identified person was asked to complete a questionnaire that was identical to the one completed by program participants. The persons who responded became members of the comparison group.

References

Aggar, R.E., & Ostrom, V. Political participation in a small community. In E. Heintz, S.J. Eldersveld, and M. Janowitz (Eds.), *Political behavior*. Glencoe, IL: The Free Press, 1956.

Babchuk, N., & Booth, A. Voluntary association membership: A longitudinal analysis. *Social participation in urban society*. Cambridge, MA: Schenchman, 1973.

Babchuk, N., & Edwards, J.N. Voluntary associations and the integration hypothesis. *Sociological Inquiry, 35*(2), 1965, 149-162.

Dillman, D.A. *Mail and telephone surveys: The total design method*. New York: Wiley Interscience, 1978.

Hawley, A.H., & Zimmer, B.G. *The metropolitan community: Its people and government*. Beverly Hills, CA: Sage, 1970.

Howell, R.E., Weir, I.L., & Cook, A.K. *Development of rural leadership: Problems, procedures, and insights*. Battle Creek, MI: W.K. Kellogg Foundation, 1982.

Howell, R.E., Weir, I.L., & Cook, A.K. *Public affairs leadership development: An impact assessment of programs conducted in California, Michigan, Montana, and Pennsylvania*. Pullman, WA: Washington State University, 1979.

Hyman, H.H., & Wright, C.R. Trends in voluntary association memberships of American adults: Replications based on secondary sample surveys. *American Sociological Review*, 1971, *36* (April), 191-206.

Kornhauser, W. *The politics of mass society*. New York: The Free Press, 1959.

Lipset, S.M., Trow, M., & Coleman, J.S. *Union democracy*. New York: The Free Press, 1956.

Olsen, M.E. Interest association participation and political activity in the United States and Sweden. *Journal of Voluntary Action Research*, 1976, *4* (Fall), 17-33.

Rogers, D.L., Bultena, G.L., & Barb, K.H. Voluntary association membership and political participation: An exploration of the mobilization hypothesis. *Sociological Quarterly*, 1975, *16* (Summer), 305-318.

Smith, C., & Freidman, A. *Voluntary associations*. Cambridge, MA: Harvard University Press, 1972.

Verba, S., & Nie, N.H. *Participation in America: Political democracy and social equality*. New York: Harper & Row, 1972.

Zimmer, B., & Hawley, A.H. Significance of membership in associations. *American Journal of Sociology*, 1959, *65* (September), 196-201.

Social Movement
and Political Leadership

Introduction to Part 5: Social Movement and Political Leadership

Social movements and political dynamics are different from the ordered activity in complex organizations, educational systems, and communities. The basic concepts presented in Part I have some application here, but not as much as they did in Parts II, III, and IV. Yet, if this volume is to attempt to be comprehensive, it cannot ignore the topic of social and political leadership. Although there is considerable literature on the subject, we found only four perspectives that seemed usefully related to the themes introduced earlier. These four selections are current, pertinent, and thought provoking.

Eichler argues that to understand the nature of leadership of social movements, we must examine whether membership in the movement is open or closed. Examples of open membership are the women's liberation movement (typified by membership in the National Organization for Women, which is open to all interested persons) and a nineteenth century religious sect, the Millerites. Closed-membership movements include the Nazi party under Hitler and the Manson family. In Eichler's definition, closed-membership movements are led by charismatic leaders who make all decisions and give all orders, while open-membership movements typically do not have a strong leader and are usually characterized by widespread participation.

Eichler's argument is interesting, but far from obvious or well-tested. Although closed-membership movements always involve charismatic leaders, social movements with charismatic leaders are not necessarily closed. For example, Martin Luther King was widely acknowledged as a charismatic leader, yet his followers—both blacks and whites—were part of an open-membership social movement. MENSA is a social organization that only admits people with IQs of 130 or higher and is, therefore, a closed-membership movement, yet it has no strong, charismatic leader. We note also that Eichler's examples of closed membership are disreputable groups, while her examples of open membership are, at worst, neutral. Despite the weakness of the categorical boundaries defined in the article, because research on leadership of social movements has been limited, Eichler's analysis is a useful addition to the literature of leadership.

The second article examines the social structure of local political leadership, rather than the personal characteristics or actions of leaders. In a classic, in-depth study of a small college town, Wildavsky traces a pattern of participative political and social leadership. A wide range of leaders are drawn into the process of local political leadership; some are "specialists" working in one area (such as housing), while others are "meteors," rising to work with only one problem, then returning to anonymity.

Wildavsky presents an engaging account of the manner in which one of two major political factions was successful in attaining power and influencing policies. He identifies the nature of available and useful resources and then shows how they were used to attain political success. However, Wildavsky modifies the nearly Utopian political picture he has painted when he notes that without the presence and perseverance of one person—one "great leader"—the story might have been very different.

Pye evaluates the "great leader" issue in depth. The focus is on one of the most successful charismatic leaders of all time, Mao Tse-tung. Pye's analysis of Chairman Mao illustrates the psychoanalytic approach to charismatic leadership. In Freudian theory, charismatic leadership is a matter of "the relationship between [the leader's] own psychological needs and the psychological needs of masses of people...." Pye develops an interesting outline of this relationship, rooted in the dependency needs of followers and the narcissistic needs of leaders. When such needs are pronounced, it is possible for a leader with appropriate skills and traits to exploit masses of followers by convincing them that they will reach complete fulfillment of all their needs. This exploitation may be mutual; many followers may know that the leader's promises are masks for insecurity and fear. By playing their parts and maintaining the illusion that the leader will provide for them, the followers exploit the image of the charismatic leader to maintain their own self-image.

Some scholars in the field of leadership dismiss the psychoanalytic approach as unscientific. We should, however, remember that in many respects—and especially with regard to the theory of ego development—Freudian theory has not only held up over time but has, in many respects, proven accurate in scientific research studies (See Kline, 1981, or Fisher & Greenberg, 1977).

The final article is an analysis of presidential leadership written by a former general, presidential counselor, and Secretary of State, Alexander Haig. The president's role as a "moral leader" is emphasized. But Haig views presidential leadership as primarily a matter of maintaining balance in the governmental system. It is the President's responsibility to maintain balance between the Executive Office and Congress. A second balance must exist between operation of the Executive Office and subordinate units, especially at the cabinet level. Still another balance must be struck between the public's expectations and presidential actions. Haig argues that the social institution of the American presidency is viable only if the incumbent is able to perform as a "balance wheel" at the hub of a complex sociopolitical mechanism.

Although Haig expresses faith in the institution of the presidency, he wonders about the qualities of past incumbents. In his judgment, few presidents have understood the central importance of "moral" and "balancing" leadership roles.

Leadership in social movement and political arenas is complex and not well understood. Charismatic leaders seem to have the greatest visibility, and some degree of charisma may be required for effectiveness. Nonetheless, charisma without certain critical skills can be a source of social instability and, occasionally, outright destructiveness to the sociopolitical systems through which our local and national values and goals are pursued.

References

Fisher, S., & Greenberg, R. *The scientific credibility of Freud's theories and therapy.* New York: Basic Books, 1977.

Kline, P. *Fact and fantasy in Freudian theory* (2nd ed.). London: Methuen, 1981.

Leadership in
Social Movements

Margrit Eichler

Social movements are one of the major vehicles for social
change and as such have been studied since the beginning of
the social sciences as sciences. Yet, in spite of a long-standing
recognition of the importance of social movements, we have
not yet satisfactorily answered the most elementary question
of all: namely, what is a social movement?[1] We are all likely to
recognize a social movement when we see one, yet it seems
peculiarly difficult to identify the boundaries of a social
movement in terms of time, membership, and the geographical area affected.[2] This lack of delimitation may be partially
due to the fact that special movements are by their nature
transient phenomena which tend to go through shifts in their
structure, membership, ideology, and tactics. For instance, as
a movement grows or contracts, so its membership and the
geographical area affected grow or contract. Or a movement
may be successful and become established, or seize power if it
is a revolutionary movement, thus ceasing to be a social
movement and instead becoming some other type of social
organization such as a political party, a business corporation,
or an established church. Social movements in one country
may spark off or start concomitantly with similar movements
in other countries, and we are faced with the question whether
the international Student Movement or the international

Reprinted from Margrit Eichler, "Leadership in Social Movements," *Sociological
Inquiry*, 1977, *47*(2), 99-107. Copyright © 1977 University of Texas Press. Used by
permission of the author and publisher.

Women's Liberation Movement (WLM) or the international Watchtower Movement are one movement each or many. And at what point of time do we start to call a movement a movement? At a time when it is still a local group (if that is how it started)? Is it still the same movement when it spreads around an entire country, or to more than one country?

For some questions an exact delimitation of a social movement in terms of time, membership, geographical area, and from other types of social organizations such as parties, churches, pressure groups, corporations, communes, etc., may be irrelevant. However, when our concern is leadership in social movements, an understanding of the boundaries is crucial, or else how can we determine who a leader is and what the structure of the decision-making process is?

In the case of some movements it is easy to identify the primary leader (defined as the person who most contributes to group locomotion). The primary leader of the early Christians was Christ; of the Mormons, Joseph Smith; of the Millerites, William Miller; of the Nazis, Adolf Hitler; of the Shakers, Mother Ann Lee, etc. But who is the leader, or who are the leaders, of the New Left? Of the WLM? Depending on whether we define the beginning of the WLM in the United States with the activities around the establishment of the Presidential Commission on the Status of Women, with the founding of the National Organization of [sic] Women (NOW), or with the women's caucus at the Chicago Congress of the New Left, we will place the beginning of the WLM in 1961, 1966, or 1967, respectively, and identify entirely different women as leaders. To confuse matters further, groups concerned with sex equality started in several European countries in the mid-sixties. Depending on where and when we locate the beginning and whether we define the WLM as one international or many national movements, we will come up with different names and different statements about the structure of the decision-making process. Let us for the moment simply recognize the boundaries of a social movement as a problem and turn to the question of leadership.

The most common approach to the problem of leadership in social movements is to construct types of leaders and then identify particular leaders as belonging to a specific type. The basis on which such types are constructed varies, but a frequent basis is the type of function that leaders perform for their movements. The focus is often on the leader(s) as person(s)—perhaps because leaders of social movements tend to be colorful people and are therefore intrinsically interesting to observers and analyzers of a movement. Nevertheless, we should note that sometimes movement members perceive such a focus as a basic misinterpretation of movement structure. The WLM is a case in point. Basically the WLM sees itself as anti-hierarchical and "leaderless." Although "leaderlessness" is, sociologically speaking, an impossibility, since there will be informal or formal spokespersons and office holders, we should take a claim of "leaderlessness" as an important descriptive statement about the decision-making structure of a movement. A leader is only a leader if (s)he has followers. Followers are people who commit themselves to follow something or somebody. It might therefore be profitable to examine the leadership structure of social movements from the standpoint of commitment of the followers since, after all, social movements are voluntary organizations which will neither come into being nor continue to exist without commitment. The complement to commitment is the source of legitimacy which provides the reason for commitment.

It was Max Weber who introduced the claim to legitimacy as a basis for the elaboration of his three types of authority, one of which is charismatic authority. There is probably no better indicator of the conceptual and theoretical problems of the discussion of leadership in social movements than the debate concerning the concept of the charismatic leader. We shall, therefore, briefly review the historical development of the concept.

THE CHARISMATIC LEADER

Originally, the concept of *charisma* (grace) was introduced into the sociological literature by Max Weber (1956) who, in turn, borrowed the concept from the theologian Troelsch. Other concepts, such as Cohn's (1970: 62-65) *propheta*, are identical in their meaning. Weber (1968: 215) distinguished three types of authority on the basis of their claims to legitimacy: rational-legal authority, traditional authority, and charismatic authority. In the case of rational-legal authority, the claims to legitimacy are based on "rational grounds— resting on a belief in the legality of enacted rules and the right of those elevated to authority under such rules to issue commands.... ." The claims to legitimacy of traditional authority are based on "traditional grounds—resting on an established belief in the sanctity of immemorial traditions and legitimacy of those exercising authority under them . . . ." The claims to legitimacy of charismatic authority, finally, are based on "charismatic grounds—resting on devotion to the exceptional sanctity, heroism or exemplary character of an individual person, and of the normative patterns or order revealed or ordained by him . . . ." Weber then defined "charisma" as follows:

> Charisma shall denote a quality of personality which is believed to be extraordinary (originally, as well in the case of prophets as therapeutics, as law-sages, as leaders of hunt, as war heroes: magically caused) and because of which he is gifted with supernatural or superhuman or at least extraordinary forces and qualities which are not available to everybody or who is judged to be sent by God or to be a model and, therefore, a 'leader.' How the respective quality *would* have to be judged from any ethical, aesthetic or other standpoint as 'objectively' correct is of course conceptually entirely irrelevant: only that is important how it *is* actually judged by those who are charismatically ruled, namely the 'followers' (Weber, 1956: 140, my translation, Weber's emphasis).

Weber furthermore enumerated several typical dependencies of a charismatic claim to legitimacy. According to Weber, in cases of charismatic authority, the congregation is an emotional community. Officials are appointed according to the revelations of the charismatic leader who determines their realm of competency for them. They are not formally reimbursed but live with their leader in a form of love communism. There is no rational legislation but only creation of law from case to case in the original sense of charisma: through revelation to the charismatic leader. Its acceptance by the followers is compulsory. Any charismatic authority rejects a traditional or rational economy which is geared towards the continuing economic activity. It is typically an uneconomic way of life (Weber, 1956: 111-112).

The major problems with the concept, after more than half a century of usage, can be identified as follows:

1. In spite of Max Weber's emphasis of the relational aspects of leadership and in spite of his elaboration of typical dependencies which accompany a charismatic claim to legitimacy, the concept has been largely utilized to denote a personality type rather than a specific follower-leader relationship.

2. Weber constructed his three types of authority with nation-states in mind. He apparently intended his three types to be exhaustive. By definition, rational-legal and traditional authority are not applicable to social movements (which are emergent social realities and therefore have neither written laws nor traditions). Consequently, some people drew the conclusion that charismatic leadership is the only type of leadership in social movements. This is clearly erroneous. The First International Socialist Movement, for example, was an important social movement which was not charismatically led—Marx and Engels, while certainly vibrant, important, and fascinating figureheads and ideologues were not charismatic leaders in terms of the typical dependencies as outlined by Weber.

3. Due to the first two problems, the concept has been used so widely and so indiscriminantly that it now resembles a coat that has been worn by hundreds of people for hundreds of different purposes. Try as (s)he may, the original slim owner can no longer make it fit. The concept should thus be discarded, as has been proposed by Worseley (1968: liii). However, this suggestion should be applied only to the label that has been used, not to what the label originally stood for.

If we retain legitimacy and add commitment as a basis on which to develop types of leaders, we can ask ourselves what adherents of movements that are not charismatically led (such as the WLM) are committed to, what the source of their legitimacy is, and how it varies from the source of legitimacy of a charismatically led movement. We can thus create another type of leadership parallel to Weber's charismatic leadership.

OPEN AND CLOSED ACCESS LEADERSHIP

We concluded above that the term charismatic leadership is no longer a useful concept since it has been used too indiscriminantly. We therefore need to attach another name to the phenomenon. We also want to identify the crucial difference that distinguishes the leadership style of a charismatically led movement from the leadership style of a movement such as the WLM. If we phrase the question in terms of commitment of the adherents as well as in terms of the source of legitimacy, we find that followers of charismatically led movements are committed to a person who is perceived as the only channel through which a follower has access to the source of legitimacy while adherents of a movement such as the WLM are committed to a principle or ideology. In the latter case, the source of legitimacy is open and accessible to anybody while in the former case access to the source of legitimacy is monopolized by one person.

I am here suggesting that on the basis of simply knowing whether access to the source of legitimacy is open or closed, which implies that the primary loyalty of adherents of a movement is, in the first case, directed towards a principle or ideology, or, in the other case, towards a person who controls the access to the source of legitimacy, we can predict the essential features of the decision-making process.

In a closed access (CA) movement, the ideology is revealed to the CA leader in a personalized manner—in the form of a personal revelation or illumination which is not repeatable by anyone else. On the basis of such revelation (the content of which is immaterial for its structural consequences—compare Hitler with Christ, Father Divine, or Charles Manson, all CA leaders), the CA leader claims the personal allegiance of his or her followers. Followers become followers by virtue of believing in the essential correctness of the revealed ideology and the monopoly of the CA leader's access to the source of legitimacy. Closed access to the source of legitimacy has two major structural consequences: the CA leader exerts total personal control over his or her followers, and the followers are totally committed to the CA leader personally. We must assume that people who are unwilling to totally commit themselves to a person will not become or remain adherents of a CA movement and, concomitantly, that only a person who desires total personal control will become a CA leader. Total personal control of the CA leader has several structural consequences:

- Decision-making power is centralized in the hands of the CA leader. In order to maintain the centralization of power, the CA leader will engage in all or some of the following tactics:
- He or she will personally appoint, maintain, promote or demote people in positions of secondary leadership. By consequence, winning, maintaining or losing a position of secondary leadership will depend primarily

on winning, maintaining, or losing the trust of the CA leader rather than on impersonal procedure or on convincing a portion of the membership of the correctness of one's interpretation of the ideology.

- The CA leader will strive to keep an element of uncertainty in terms of policy, which may express itself either in quick, unnegotiated, unilaterally imposed shifts in policy or in the pronouncement of new revelations that have consequences for group behavior, and/or by controlling and restricting the flow of information from the top down.

Total personal commitment of the followers and its enforcement by the CA leader also have several structural consequences:

- The relationship between the CA leader and the followers is seen as a primary one and other primary relationships, especially family and sexual relationships, are seen as dangerous competition. Therefore, the CA leader will actively seek to destroy and/or control family and sexual relationships and other primary relationships of his/her followers.
- Due to the personal tie of each follower with the CA leader, disgruntled followers will find it hard to collect a group of other disgruntled persons around them in order to organize a schism. Instead, disillusioned members will tend to leave the movement as individuals rather than in groups.

By contrast, a movement that legitimates itself with reference to a principle or ideology which is open and accessible to anybody will have a very different leadership structure.[3] First, the OA leader of such a movement will be the primary leader not by virtue of some personal and private illumination, insight, or revelation but by virtue of being the acknowledged interpreter of the ideology of the movement. He or she is, therefore, only *primus inter pares* rather than an absolute ruler.

Since primary allegiance of movement members is not to a person but to some principle or ideology, several consequences for the leadership structure of the movement emerge:

- Decision-making power will be decentralized and dispersed through various groups in the movement.
- Positions of secondary leadership depend on winning over members of the movement to a particular interpretation of the prevailing ideology; consequently,

demotion, promotion, or maintenance of a position of secondary leadership do not depend on losing, winning, or maintaining the trust of the primary leader. Indeed, there may be open animosity between various leaders of the same movement, or at least open competition for leadership positions.

- Shifts in policy are likely to be negotiated and widely discussed since nobody has sufficient power to unilaterally institute them.
- The flow of information will not be successfully controlled by the primary leader.
- There will be no total commitment to any person (although there may be a total commitment to what a person stands for).
- Primary relationships will not be seen as dangerous by the OA leader, although constant association with non-movement members may be seen as dangerous. In that case, the effort will not be directed towards destroying the primary tie, but towards converting the unconverted or else disassociating the converted from the renegate [sic]. In any case:
- The primary leader will not make any efforts to destroy and/or control family and sexual ties of the followers.
- Ideological debate is a means to power since leaders become leaders by convincing other members of the movement of the correctness of their interpretation of the ideology (this is not so in CA movements). Schisms are therefore likely to occur, by disgruntled secondary leaders winning over a minority of followers to their interpretation. In case of a serious ideological rift, the group will split as a group rather than as several individuals who leave the movement at the same time but separately.

TYPES OF LEADERSHIP AND THE BOUNDARIES OF SOCIAL MOVEMENTS

We started the paper with the observation that social movement theory lacks a commonly accepted definition that delimits social movements in terms of time, membership, and geographical space. We then proceeded to propose a typology of social movement leaders on the basis of the access to the source of legitimacy. It will be noticed that the proposed typology of leaders is also a typology of movements and that it defines, at the same time, the boundaries of the movements.

In the case of CA movements, time boundaries are determined by the emergence of the CA leader as a leader (i.e., with the leader winning some personal followers). All individuals who are totally committed to the CA leader are members, and the geographical spread of the movement coincides with the membership distribution. Organizationally, we can speak of a movement for as long as there are members totally committed to the CA leader, even though this commitment may formally be practised [sic] within the framework of some other type of organization such as a political party, a religion, or a utopian community.

In the case of OA movements, time boundaries are determined by the emergence of organized group support for a particular principle or ideology, and membership includes all those people who claim to support the principle or ideology of the movement and who in some way act together with other people towards the implementation of the principle. Geographically, boundaries are again defined by membership spread.

As can be seen, the definition of boundaries varies in each case and varies greatly in terms of specificity by type of movement. It is much easier to establish who is a member of a CA movement than who is a member of an OA movement. For instance, CA movements can be international only if a particular CA leader elicits personal loyalty in more than one country (not if people refer to him or her as an ideologue—e.g., Rosa Luxemburg—or use his or her principles as guides for action—e.g., Gandhian non-violent principles—but only if they are personally committed to him or her). International CA movements are quite unlikely since constant interaction between CA leader and followers is required, or else the movement will become an OA movement. Within the general framework of a particular movement tradition we may find both OA and CA movements. Christianity provides a good example. It started out as a CA movement and became an OA movement after Christ's death. In principle, the source of legitimacy—the Bible—is open and accessible to everybody. However, within this general movement tradition, many new CA movements started in which people claimed personal revelations that perpetuated and augmented the revelations contained in the Bible. In turn, some of these became OA movements or established churches after the death of their

CA leaders, or withered away like the Shakers. In the case of an OA movement, there may be groups claiming allegiance to the same legitimating principle which come into contact only after their independent formation. This is one of the things that make a discussion of the structure of OA movements so very difficult.

If we take this approach towards defining the boundaries of social movements, we are defining movements in terms of commitment and legitimacy, rather than in terms of some organizational criterion.[4] This allows us to accept the statement of an OA movement such as the WLM about the absence of leaders as an informative statement; there are, indeed, no leaders in the sense that movement members are personally committed to any one "leader"—there are, of course, leaders in the sense that some people more than other[s] contribute to group locomotion and define the ideology of the movement.

Constructed types order otherwise disparate data. They cannot be right or false, they can only be more or less useful. In the types proposed above, we have constructed two types of leadership style (which imply two types of social movement, CA and OA movements) and made a number of specific predictions about structural consequences of the open or closed access to the source of legitimacy. One very concrete prediction is that in the case of CA movements, the CA leader will attempt to destroy and/or control all pre-existing primary ties of his or her followers whereas no such attempts will be discernible in the case of OA leaders. How, in practise, control over primary ties will be carried out in CA movements may, of course, vary greatly. One possibility is to regulate the sexual contacts of movement members by determining who may have sexual contacts with whom in what way and when. This was the approach taken by Noyes in the Oneida Community through his Complex Marriage arrangement. A functional equivalent is to forbid sexual contacts altogether. This was the approach taken by Mother Ann Lee of the Shakers.

The predictions made are all empirically testable. In the following, we shall examine a few selected examples and determine whether or not the predictions are confirmed. Due to space restrictions, this will be an exceedingly brief examination although every effort will be made to avoid a caricature.[5] For the first two examples of CA movements, I have selected both a very large and a very small one to indicate that size— like the content of the ideology—is irrelevant for the essential features of the leadership structure, although, of course, the tactics of a particular CA leader in assuring personal control are affected by the size of the organization (s)he heads.

APPLICATION OF THE TYPES

1. Example of a Closed Access Movement: The Nazis

The precursor to the NSDAP (Nationalsozialistische Deutsche Arbeiter Partei, abbreviated Nazis) was founded in 1919 under the name of Deutsche Arbeiter Partei. Hitler joined the party in 1920, when it had about 40 members, and was immediately elected into the steering committee. In 1923 he staged a putsch in Munich which failed. Hitler was sentenced to prison and served nine months. During his prison sentence, the party was banned and split into two groups. After his release, Hitler entirely reorganized the party and immediately set himself up as unquestioned dictator of the party. Membership increased from 27,117 members at the end of 1925, to 1,414,975 members at the end of 1932 (Volz, 1939: 21). In January 1933 Hitler, after an election victory, was appointed chancellor of Germany and changed the country into a totalitarian state within a few months.

In terms of leadership structure, we find that the power is indeed centralized in the hands of the CA leader—Adolf Hitler. In the process of acquiring absolute personal control, two events are of particular importance. In 1921 the original founder of the party made an attempt to curtail Hitler's power. Hitler resigned from the party and set an ultimatum which included the following point: "The present acting committee of the party renounces all offices, for the new election I demand the post of the first chairman with dictatorial authority for the immediate formation of an action committee which will carry out the ruthless purification of the party from alien elements which have invaded it today" (cf. Franz-Willing, 1962). His ultimatum was accepted.

In this first public speech after his release from prison, Hitler asked that the movement accept him as its unconditional leader for one year with the words: "I am not willing to accept any conditions. Once again I take the responsibility for everything that happens in this movement" (Orlow, 1969: 54). Overall, in spite of repeated challenges to his authority, it is no exaggeration to state that the decision-making process was formally vested in Hitler, most explicitly expressed by his formally acknowledged right to overrule any decisions made by anybody in the movement at any time. Nor was there ever any pretense that followers had any say in policy matters. At a party congress in 1929, for instance, arguments developed about a matter of policy. They were silenced by one of Hitler's deputies who told the delegates: "I don't know why [all of you] wish to speak, comrades. After all, we are not in a Parliamentary gossip hut...here, with discussions, votes, and agendas. You know you can't make decisions here. You came here to hear the opinion of the Führer; [and] I have told you that. Now act accordingly" (quoted after Orlow, 1969: 169, brackets his).

From 1921 on, Hitler appointed all the chairmen and major functionaries of all important administrative bodies. These functionaries were always directly responsible to Hitler. In his appointments, Hitler did not follow any prescribed procedures, although as a rule he appointed extremely capable men. For instance, a secondary leader might not even be a member of the party prior to being appointed to an office by Hitler (as happened, for example, in the case of Max Aman). Secondary leaders who publicly registered disapproval of Hitler were expelled from the party (e.g., Otto Strasser). In cases in which a secondary leader opposed Hitler's will in some important matter of policy, he was cast into the role of a black villain who had been subversively active during all of his membership in the movement. The two most notorious cases of this kind are those of Gregor Strasser and Walter Stennes. All attempts to organize schisms failed, and the organizers either left the party or were expelled.

Between Hitler and his followers, including all his secondary leaders, a mythical unity was claimed, expressed in poetry and ritual (cf. Gamm, 1962). For instance, after an abortive attempt by a secondary leader to separate the SA from Hitler, Hitler expressed their relationship as follows: "I am the SA and the SS and you [the members] are members of the SA and the SS as I am within you in the SA and SS" (quoted after Orlow, 1969: 218). All SA leaders were then required to submit loyalty declarations to Hitler, which they did. SS men swore an oath that they were willing to forfeit their lives for Hitler's cause. As of 1932, Hitler regulated explicitly their sexual and family lives by requiring all SS men to submit their brides to the scrutiny of the party before permitting them to marry (the marriage order is reprinted in d'Alquen, 1939: 9-10).

While this is an excessively brief treatment of the commitment and control of Nazi members we can state that the Nazis exhibited the predicted structural traits of the CA type of leadership style.

2. Example of a Closed Access Movement:
The Manson Family

The term Manson Family refers to a group of people who, in the late 1960's assembled around Charles Manson, an ex-con and parolee from the American West Coast, to form one family with him as their center. The group ideology included some millenarian beliefs about the imminent end of the world (Helter Skelter) which the family would escape by descending into a hole in the desert. The group first roamed the countryside together and finally settled in a movie farm and engaged in several killings. Several group members, including Manson, were convicted for the killings in the early 70's. Members of the group regarded Manson as their saviour and killed at his bidding.

The power was clearly centralized in the hands of Charles Manson, who employed various mechanisms to keep everybody under total control. When a new member joined the group, he or she was immediately relieved of his or her I.D. card, driver's license and credit cards which were held centrally in one place and only handed back for special, approved excursions (Sanders, 1972: 207). Manson strictly controlled the flow of information. When he discussed a criminal activity with one of the members, "No one would know about it but them—for that was a rule; you didn't discuss anything Charlie talked about with you, unless he said it was okay to speak" (Sanders, 1972: 187-188).

Manson's control over movement members extended to minute details of their living arrangements, such as when, what, and how to eat, how to wear one's hair, when to speak or not to speak [women, for instance, were not permitted to ask questions, the word 'why' was banned, food was offered to the dogs before the women themselves ate (Sanders, 1972: 193)]. Men were not permitted to grow beards—only Manson himself wore one.

"One day in July Charlie was late for chow so the family started to eat without him, a sin. He got really angry when he arrived and stormed out of the house. Tex, Bobby, Clem and

Bruce followed him out, begging forgiveness. Soon they all came back and Charlie played the guitar and they held a songfest" (Sanders, 1972: 211).

Movement members totally submerged themselves in Manson, they experienced a mystical unity with him. "They were all Charlie and Charlie was they" (Sanders, 1972: 206).

From time to time Manson would have a new revelation and would announce a new venture or new group practices. Instant obedience was required. At least one group member (Gary Hinman) was killed when he refused to sell all his things and follow Manson (Sanders, 1972: 237-238).

Sexual relations were a very important aspect of the family. Manson seems to have slept with most or all the women, and there are repeated statements that Manson totally controlled who had sexual relations with whom. Women were required to submit instantly to any man whom Manson had put on the "grope list" (Sanders, 1972: 192) and if Manson wanted a man to conform to his wishes he would take him off the grope list, thus refusing him sexual access to the women.

Overall, we find that the Manson Family exhibits the predicted structural traits of the CA leadership style, and that the parallels between the Nazis and the Manson family in terms of leadership style are startling in spite of vastly differing size, ideology, organizational structure, and aims of the movements. In both movements the members believed the CA leader to be inspired. They experienced a mystical unity with him, committed themselves totally to him and were totally controlled by him. In both movements, the CA leader supplanted existing primary ties and controlled the emergence of new ones.

Let us now consider two open-access movements, chosen to be maximally different in overall organization, ideology, and aims.

1. Example of an Open Access Movement: The Millerites

The Millerites, a millenarian religious movement in the first half of the 19th century, were especially prominent in Upper New York State although there were adherents elsewhere. Miller believed that the millenium would commence in 1843. People who accepted this as true and flocked to his and other peoples' sermons on the subject constituted the movement membership. Millerism developed in two phases, the "1843" phase which lasted from 1838 to 1844, and the "seventh-month phase" which lasted from August 1844 to October 1844. Core believers of Millerism have been estimated to number around 50,000 (Tyler, 1944: 74). During the seventh-month period of the movement, about 500 preachers and 1,500 lecturers laboured for the Millerite cause. Important vehicles of communication were sixteen general conferences held during 1840-1842, and a great number of local conferences and some publications.

Miller has often been referred to as a charismatic leader— in fact, nothing could be further from the truth in terms of the leadership structure of the Millerite movement, although Miller did have a strong and fascinating personality. Miller was widely recognized as the major proponent and initiator of the movement, but consensus on the ideology was established through discussions at the general conferences. The first report of the General Conference, for instance, states: "In presenting this work to their constituents, and to the public, the Publishing Committee have allowed each author to express his own views in his own way; and it is a matter of surprise, that articles prepared without consultation or mutual acquaintance of their writers...would accord in doctrine... both among themselves and with the great body of the Conference" (General Conference, 1841: 3). Of course, an unconscious editorial policy was operative since contributions were invited. The basic pattern of deciding on the content of the ideology was always the same: a specific interpretation of the ideology was proposed by some member of the movement, propagated in various ways (through publications, in mass meetings) and incorporated into the ideology if it was accepted by a majority of the audience.

The most illustrative example of Miller's lack of control was the seventh-month movement. Miller had set a date for the arrival of Christ which had been disconfirmed. After that, Miller did not set an alternative date, but Snow, a relative newcomer to the movement, did, which initiated the seventh-month movement which swept through most of the country. The process has been described by a participant as follows:

"At first the definite time was generally opposed, but there seemed to be an irresistible power attending its proclamation, which prostrated all before it.... The lecturers among the Adventists were the last to embrace the views of the time, and the more prominent ones came into it last of all" (Froom, 1954: 803). The OA leader, Miller, was also the last to accept the ideological innovation (Froom, 1954: 819-820).

All major organizational decisions were made at the general conferences, the first four of which Miller could not even attend because of illness. His absence was noted, but the conferences proceeded unimpeded. Secondary leaders, if they could convince a sufficiently large portion of the membership of the correctness of their interpretation, as did Snow, could define the ideology even against the active and passive resistance of the OA leader. This would be unimaginable in a CA movement.

The core followers of the Millerite movement were as dedicated to their beliefs as were the core members of the Nazis and of the Manson Family—they gave up their possessions, settled their debts, and awaited the end of the world as it existed then (Sears, 1924). However, they were not in any sense personally committed to Miller. They honoured him as an important interpreter of their ideology, but did not regard his words as absolute truth and, indeed, followed in general their own course of thought and behavior. Some schisms did occur.

There is no indication whatsoever that Miller, or any other leader of the movement, tried to rupture existing primary ties except that they urged the members to try to convert their families. There is no indication of any attempts to control or regulate sexual relations among the followers. Overall, we can conclude that the Millerites exhibit the structural traits of an OA movement.

2. Example of an Open Access Movement: Women's Liberation

Membership in the WLM is, as in the case of the Millerites, essentially based on self-definition; whoever accepts the basic premises of women's liberation and defines herself as a movement member is a member. The women's liberation movement started in the Sixties with the general aim to eliminate unnecessary sex differences and to ensure the social, economic, and political equality of women and men. There is no single OA leader who can speak for the entire movement, but there are some recognized opinion leaders who are generally regarded as spokespersons for the movement. In principle, an OA leader in the WLM becomes a leader by publishing interpretations of the women's liberation ideology and/or by giving public speeches. The movement is decentralized, with various groups throughout North America and Europe engaging in specific action programmes. Within groups, resources are usually allocated by group consensus, i.e., movement members must convince other members that, for instance, their proposed usage of funds is worthwhile. In Canada, various groups are funded through government grants (such as rape crisis centers, health centers, research and study groups, publication collectives) and need to adhere to formal accounting procedures, nevertheless, as a rule, allocation of resources seems to proceed on a consensual basis. Groups have no formal way of influencing each others' activities, although informal links do exist.

With respect to the destruction or maintenance of primary ties, the WLM sets an interesting problem. Like all other sexual reform movements (e.g., Gay Liberation) the WLM concerns itself greatly with sexual relations, the family structure, and the nature of interpersonal relations in general. Depending on what group a person belongs to, there may be some group pressure to behave in a certain manner. For instance, lesbianism vs. heterosexuality is a recurrent issue in the WLM, with representatives of both groups charging each other with attempts to silence them, or pressure them into conformity. Nevertheless, the movement structure conforms to the OA type. There is no assumed mystic tie between any one leader and other movement members. Concern about sexual relations is a general rather than a personal concern. If dissensus about the appropriate nature of sexual relations continues at the group level, an individual is free to leave that particular group and join another with a different orientation *while still defining herself as a member of the WLM.*

Schisms are frequent, and there is some public animosity among different leaders. One of the more prominent examples of this are the allegations of the Redstockings that Gloria Steinem was at one time a CIA agent. This needs to be seen in the context that *Ms.* magazine is regarded as too bourgeois by the more radical publication outlets of the movement. Personal accusations are only one of the means of trying to win ideological domination within the movement.

Overall, we can conclude that the WLM exhibits the structural traits of an OA movement.

CONCLUSION

We started with the observation that social movement theory has, so far, not been able to come up with a definition of social movements that satisfactorily identifies the time and social boundaries of a movement. By constructing two types of leadership styles on the basis of membership commitment and open or closed access to the source of legitimacy, we provided at the same time a definition not only of two types of movement leaders, but also of two types of movements which allows us to identify the social and time boundaries of these movements.

On the basis of distinguishing between open or closed access to the source of legitimacy, we made several predictions about the movement structure, including the type and amount of control that the primary leader has over the decision-making process of the movement, the type and degree of commitment the members have towards the primary leaders, and whether or not a leader will attempt to destroy and/or control primary ties of movement members, including sexual contacts.

The two constructed types were then applied to four historical and contemporary cases: the Nazis and the Manson Family as examples of closed access movements, the Millerites and Women's Liberation as examples of open access movements. The hypotheses were confirmed.

The basic distinction between open and closed movements therefore seems to be a fruitful one. Other deductions from this basic distinction that might profitably be explored include the relationship of secondary leaders among themselves, the relationship of movement members to each other, and the relationship of secondary leaders to ordinary movement members.

The analysis attempted in this paper places the importance not on any organizational factors, but where movement members themselves place it: at the level of their commitment and the reason for their commitment—the source of legitimacy. This seems to be a worthwhile effort. One wonders how many other things might be learned by placing priorities where subjects of sociological analysis themselves place them.

Notes

[1]The basic thoughts of this paper were first developed in my dissertation (Eichler, 1971). I therefore owe a debt of thanks to my dissertation committee, especially to Edward A. Tiryakian and John Wilson. I also wish to thank Andrew Effrat and an anonymous reviewer of an early draft of this paper for their helpful comments.

[2]Of course, there are as many definitions of social movements as there are authors writing about them. The following ones are some typical examples: "Social movements can be viewed as collective enterprises to establish a new order of life" (Blumer, 1946: 199). "A value-oriented movement is an attempt to restore, modify or create values in the name of a generalized belief" (Smelser, 1962: 313). ". . . social movements are emergent ideological realities given social significance during periods of a consciousness of dysfunction, which provide referents for mobilization to bring about desired changes within and/or of the social system" (Rush and Denisoff, 1971: 252). ". . . a large-scale, widespread, and continuing elementary collective action in pursuit of an objective that affects and shapes the social order in some fundamental aspect" (Lang and Lang, 1961: 440). The examples could easily be extended. The problem with such definitions is that while they include movement phenomena, they are not well suited to allow us to identify the time and social boundaries of social movements.

[3]Open access movements are not, by implication, "good" movements in any sense of the word. They may take as their source of legitimacy an ideology or principle of sex equality (women's liberation) or male superiority (Pussycats), race equality (NAACP) or white superiority over blacks (KKK) or black superiority over whites (Rastafarians). The *content* of the ideology is therefore irrelevant to the determination of the decision-making structure of a social movement—it is the open or closed *access* to the source of legitimacy that matters.

[4]One of the anonymous reviewers of an early draft of this paper pointed out as the major problem in the paper (and thereby brought it into focus for me) that "the abstractness of ideal-type analysis is compounded by the fact that the ideal-type here is based on an ideology dimension ("legitimacy"), not on features of organizational or societal structure. On the whole I prefer to see ideology explained by structure and not vice versa." This, to me, pinpoints the problem. The structure of social movements is fluid, and varies greatly from one type to the other. Perhaps it is therefore a *bad* starting point from which to try to understand the dynamics of the leader-follower relationship. Instead, it seems more fruitful to start with what is primary to movement adherents themselves: their commitment, what they see as the legitimating principle, and who has access to it. Of course, in order to understand why movements emerge (or why leaders find followers) we need to turn to societal conditions which elicit commitment at specific points in time in specific places under specific circumstances to specific persons or principles. That, however is a different question.

[5]For a somewhat more detailed examination of two of the examples selected here (Nazis and Millerites) and two other examples (Münster Anabaptists and Spartakists) as well as some other cross-national examples, see my dissertation (Eichler, 1971). One *caveat* should be noted: there is no claim that the typology proposed is exhaustive. It is quite possible—and detracts in no way from the utility of the types proposed—that there are movements which legitimate themselves in other ways and the commitment of whose members is directed neither at a principle nor at a person. One possibility is that commitment may be directed toward a particular structure which might be the case in some masonic and monastic orders.

References

d'Alquen, G. *Die SS*. Berlin: Junker und Dünnhaupt, 1939.

Blumer, H. Social movements. In A.M. Lee (Ed.), *New outline of principles of sociology*. New York: Barnes & Noble, 1946.

Cohn, N. *The pursuit of the millenium*. (2nd ed.). New York: Harper & Row, 1970.

Eichler, M. *Charismatic and ideological leadership in secular and religious millenarian movements*. Unpublished Ph.D. Dissertation, Duke University, 1971.

Franz-Willing, G. *Die Hitlerbewegung*. Hamburg, Berlin: Decker's Verlag G. Schenck, 1962.

Froom, L.E. The prophetic faith of our fathers (Vol. IV). *New world recovery and consummation of prophetic interpretation*. Washington, DC: Review and Herald, 1954.

General Conference of Christians Expecting the Advent of the Lord Jesus Christ. *The first report*. Boston: Joshua V. Himes, 1844.

Gamm, H.J. *Der braune Kult*. Hamburg: Rütten und Loenig, 1962.

Lang, K., & Lang, G. *Collective dynamics*. New York: Thomas Y. Crowell, 1961.

Orlow, D. *The history of the Nazi party: 1919-1933*. Pittsburgh, PA: University of Pittsburgh Press, 1969.

Rush, G.B., & Denisoff, R.S. *Social and political movements*. New York: Appleton-Century-Crofts, 1971.

Sanders, E. *The family*. New York: Avon, 1972.

Sears, C.E. *Days of delusion*. Boston and New York: Houghton Mifflin, 1924.

Smelser, N.J. *Theory of collective behavior*. New York: Free Press, 1962.

Tyler, A.F. *Freedom's ferment*. Minneapolis, MN: University of Minnesota Press, 1944.

Volz, H. *Daten zur Geschichte der NSDAP* (10th ed.). Berlin, Leipzig: A.G. Ploetz, 1939.

Weber, M. *Wirtschaft und Gesellschaft* (4th ed.). J. Winckelmann (trans.) Tübingen: Mohr, 1956.

Weber, M. *Economy and society*. New York: Bedminster Press, 1968.

Worseley, P. *The trumpet shall sound* (2nd ed.). New York: Schocken Books, 1968.

Political Leadership in a Small Town

Aaron B. Wildavsky

IDENTIFYING THE LEADERSHIP PATTERN

If we find that the same participants exercise leadership in nearly all significant areas of decision, that they agree, and that they are not responsible to the electorate, we conclude that a power elite rules. If we discover that a majority of citizens are influential in all or most cases, the proper conclusion is that the community is ruled by the people as a mass democracy. And if we find that the leaders vary from one issue area to the other, with such overlap as there is between issue areas concentrated largely in the hands of public officials, we must conclude that there is a pluralist system of rule. Once having arrived at the correct conclusion, it will become possible for us to attempt to explain why this particular power structure exists, to account for changes over time, and to go into the dynamic aspects of how decisions are made in the community.

Following Dahl's procedure, we set up a Leadership Pool consisting of all those who participated in a particular decision and could conceivably be candidates for leadership. Then we separate out those who lost, who got nothing of what they wanted. This leaves us with a Leadership Elite—those who in

---

Adapted from Aaron Wildavsky, *Leadership in a Small Town*. Totowa, New Jersey: Bedminster Press. Copyright © 1964 Bedminster Press, Inc. Reprinted with permission.

some way helped secure an outcome they deemed to be favorable. Within this broad category, we seek to distinguish among those who initiated, vetoed, or gained consent for a policy proposal.

Rarely is it possible to trace the first origins of an idea. To initiate a policy in our terms means to seize upon an idea, develop a policy proposal, and pursue it to a successful conclusion. To veto a proposal means either to secure its defeat entirely or to modify or reject a part. To gain consent one must secure the assent of others for a favorable policy outcome. These categories are further divided in order to give some idea of the degree of leadership. This is inevitably somewhat arbitrary and we have sought to do as little violence to reality as is possible by restricting ourselves to three broad degrees—high (implying a major role in initiating, vetoing, or gaining consent), low (a discernible but minor role), and moderate (a residual category).

For analytical purposes we examined seven issue areas— housing, utilities, welfare, industrial development, zoning, education, and nominations and elections. After describing leadership in these decisions, we compared them to discover the extent of overlap between issue areas and the kind of individuals who exercise influence in more than one area.... .

RESULTS

We find a clear outline of a pluralist system. There is no person or group which exerts leadership in all issue areas. To the extent that overlap between issue areas exists, it is held predominantly by public officials—the City Manager, Mayor, and City Council members—who owe their positions directly or (in the case of the Manager) indirectly to expressions of the democratic process through a free ballot with universal suffrage. One exception is the co-editor of the local newspaper, who owes his prominence with regard to a utility plant issue to membership on the Public Utilities Commission, who has the kind of dispensable occupation which permits time for leadership, and whose job encourages, if it does not demand, rather wide participation in community affairs.... .

Although the individuals we identified, who combine public office with unusual activity, are clearly outstanding leaders, none of them has all the influence there is to have in any case. They all require the consent of others.... .

The number of citizens and outside participants who exercise leadership in most cases is an infinitesimal part of the community. This is necessarily the case since the total number of all those who participate at all in any way is quite small. "Meteors" who participate in only one or two cases (and that sporadically), and specialists, who confine their participation to one or two issue areas, make up the bulk of influentials. The ability of citizens who devote much time and effort to a single case or issue area to become leaders is clearly indicated as is the initiative and support provided by generalist public officials. . . .

Although leadership is diffused, the outcomes of community decisions are not merely random occurrences but fall instead into a rather well-defined pattern. From inspection of the leaders in the cases we have studied, it appears that a rather broad coalition of interests, though its members occasionally disagree and suffer defeats, has been victorious on most issues of importance. This combination of cooperative association members, some college people, out-of-town businessmen, and Negro leaders has, for the sake of convenience, been called "the planners."

THE BASIS FOR SUCCESSFUL LEADERSHIP

The major analytic tasks confronting us are, first, to account for the success of the planning coalition and, second, to explain why the more oligarchic power structure of the past gave way to the pluralist system we found. The explanatory factors we shall employ include differential rates of participation, the structural conditions created by the non-partisan ballot, the existence of several independent centers of influence, and, most important, the more active and skillful exploitation of key bases of influence by the planners (see Table 1).

Table 1. Explanatory Factors in Pluralistic Political Leadership

- Differential rates of participation
- Structural conditions—a non-partisan ballot
- Several independent centers of influence
- Active and skillful exploitation of issues and friendships

The planning coalition was in part consciously created—cooperative association leaders set out to recruit commuting businessmen, Negroes, and college people—and partly the result of engaging in conflict and discovering who was on what side. As the various planning policies were debated it became obvious that the cost involved and the constant use of government had led to a split among the activists. Many of the local businessmen were directly affected by increased water rates, threatened by the possible influx of competing enterprises, and generally fearful of change which might upset the accustomed patterns of affairs in the community. From conversations it appears that some felt that their middle class status was threatened by increased costs which might compel them to become wage earners and reduce their hard-won standard of living. Others objected to changes in the community introduced without their consent, changes which foreshadowed a deprivation of their customary influence and the deference they felt to be their due. At the same time, the commuting businessmen and college people welcomed policies which had the magic label of "planning" and which showed promise of improving community services. The taxes they paid on their houses did not seem onerous to them and they were more willing to sacrifice a little cash for rewards in terms of better schools, and more attractive housing areas and streets. Negro activists made common cause with the planners not only because of a general sympathy with them but also because they saw new industry and a housing code as means of improving the conditions of their race.

Their eminence within the Negro sector enabled them to overcome some opposition from Negro homeowners who had low incomes and objected to higher costs. Skill in coalition building was exercised by the City Manager in collaboration with a leading council member. They proposed policies meeting widespread preferences, recruited personnel to promote them, provided a rationale for those who chose to agree, and modified opposition where necessary without giving up essential elements of their program.

If its members had to run together as Republicans or Democrats however, the planning coalition probably would have been impossible. Take the case of Charles Mosher, publisher of the *News-Tribune*. He was a Republican State Senator, a career legislator, a person who worked hard at his job and looked forward to advancement within the party. He would have found it exceedingly difficult, if not impossible, to justify supporting Democrats in city elections. His allegiance to the party and the expectations of party officials would have been violated by such an action. Under a nonpartisan system, however, Mosher could and did support Democrats on the ground that their party affiliation was not relevant to local affairs. The commuting businessmen, most of them Republicans, would also have felt uncomfortable at being formally allied with Democrats. Moreover, as is common among middle and upper class individuals, they tend to shy away from active participation as partisans, preferring to avoid the tones of political hostility associated with party strife. They were much more easily recruited under the banner of non-partisan good citizenship than they would have been under party labels.

Central leadership for the planners was provided by tandem, cooperative arrangements between a leading councilman and the City Manager. They helped set the general direction, provided huge amounts of energy, initiated proposals of their own, vetoed some they did not like, and helped gain support for the policies of others with which they agreed. Allied with them on the basis of shared perspectives and mutual agreement were active out-of-town businessmen, the editors of the local paper, some college faculty, a few Negro leaders, members of the Co-op, and a sprinkling of others. The point is not that all people falling within these categories gave their support, but that they provided a corps of activists, mostly specialists, who shared the task of developing policies and gaining public approval. It is doubtful, for example, that the category of out-of-town businessmen numbers more than one hundred individuals. But they provided two-sevenths of the 1959 Council, four of the eleven candidates for City Council in 1961, and a vastly disproportionate share of commission and committee memberships appointed by the Council.

College people performed similar functions. It is probably true that the traditionalists had a substantial minority of support in the faculty, but except for a brief flurry in the 1959 election, these people were not especially active.

Why was the planning coalition successful in getting most of what it wanted? One answer could be that it possessed resources which were superior to those of its opponents. Another answer could be that resources were employed more actively and with greater skill. A third possibility is that it met with no appreciable resistance because others agreed or did not feel strongly enough to bother to challenge the coalition (see Table 2).

Table 2. Potential Reasons for Political Success

- Superior resources: time, energy, official position, knowledge, persuasiveness, political skill
- Active and skillful employment of resources
- Lack of organized opposition

POTENTIAL POLITICAL RESOURCES

Let us survey the major resources (bases of influence) which were employed to control decisions and appraise their degree of dominance over others and the rate and skill with which they were employed. We will see that the planning coalition was superior in its possession and use of time, energy, official position, knowledge, persuasion and political skill. And that resources commonly thought to be dominant, such as money, control of credit, jobs, social standing, and the like were not crucial or were mainly in the losers.... .

The most important or potentially important resources can be placed in five categories, as shown in Table 3.

Table 3. Potential Political Resources

- Wealth
- Financial obligations
- Social standing
- Friendship
- Official position

Most of the *wealth* in town was not used for any political purpose at all. Hence, those who have little but use what they have are not necessarily disadvantaged. And since all participants (except those at the barest margin of financial existence) have a little cash to spare, wealth is not terribly important. No doubt the existence of *financial obligations* may help in getting a few signatures on a petition or in obligating an individual to do some work. But these are effects easily obtained by other means. In the secrecy of the ballot box, no one need fear reprisal. There may be some who fear to participate actively lest they incur the displeasure of the wealthy. Yet we know of no such cases and, if they exist, they have not prevented blatant opposition to policies favored by presidents of both banks and wealthy merchants. The victorious planners are in no position to exert financial sanctions over anyone (College faculty and community businessmen hire few townspeople, lend no money) unless it be a few employees of the Co-ops who are not noticeably active in town politics.

Social standing appears to be an insignificant base of influence. No doubt there are deference relationships but these do not appear to translate themselves into the political realm. There are some families who frequent a club and who hold dances in auspicious surroundings, but most of them are not active at all in the community and the few who do take part are rather equally divided between the opposing factions.

If the activists receive deference, it is due to something other than their social position. To be sure, high social standing may predispose individuals toward activity but no one political group has anything like a monopoly of that resource.

Friendship is a valuable resource which is widespread in the community.... . While it is difficult to say that anyone made much better use of friendship than others, it does appear that the planners had more success in getting their acquaintances to become active in civic affairs than did the traditionalists, with the exception of the 1959 election.

One reason for the greater activity of people identified with the planners is a consequence of another resource at their disposal—*officiality*, the holding of elected or appointed public office. This enabled the planners to recruit kindred spirits for positions on the many city commissions and special committees formed to promote policies like the housing ordinance. As these people began to participate, conversations with many of them reveal that they became more interested and engaged in additional activity. They came to know what was going on, developed new friendships, a taste for political "gossip," and even saw some positive results now and then which further solidified their interest.

Official Position: A Key Resource

The most obvious advantage which officiality brings to a Councilman is a vote and to the City Manager, formal authority. There being few or no effective means of coercion (such as patronage), Councilmen are relatively free agents and can dispose of their votes to secure their preferences. This is evident in the many votes establishing and enforcing housing and zoning ordinances, a new water system, continuing and expanding the light plant, and also in internal bargaining whereby individual members receive concessions, such as modifications of the housing code, in return for their votes. The many examples of the City Manager's use of his office include blocking the construction of certain apartments, exercising discretion in enforcing the housing code, and presenting information unfavorable to another town's offer to supply water. Officiality is limited, of course, by the official's perception of community sentiment and by desire for re-election and reappointment. Indeed, it would be extremely difficult for any faction to secure its preferences in most areas of community policy unless they were able to occupy public office and they are sensitive to the need for popularity which this entails. Nevertheless, in regard to the general run of decisions which do not occasion much interest, officiality is a crucial resource. This is all the more true when it is recognized that officiality provides access to other resources—knowledge and information, popularity, friendship, development of skills, the expectation of activity and the legitimization of attempting to exercise influence.

In a democratic political system, officiality is largely dependent on popularity with the voters as the 1959 election demonstrates. The planners proved to be more popular. But why was this so? Although this question cannot be answered conclusively, it does appear that the traditionalists were considerably less skillful, and less continuously active. Their decision to run as a group concentrated their popularity and enabled their opponents, the planners, to tar them all with the same brush as hidebound and against progress. Time after time they were caught with less than full knowledge of a particular issue and made to appear uninformed. They did not foresee their weakness among college people and Negroes and did little to appeal to these sections of the population. The major difficulty here, it seems, was that they started too late. Their burst of activity at election time could not make up for the continuous activity among the planners to pursue policies which would appeal to college people and Negroes, and, possibly more important, to recruit leaders from among these groups. The opinion leaders in the two communities were overwhelmingly for the planners long before the election, a circumstance which may have made it extremely difficult for the traditionalists to make an impact at election time, as their precinct workers discovered. By contrast, the program of the planners appeared to be considerably more positive and received favorable notice from activists in college and Negro quarters. The slate which the planners put forward was deliberately chosen to make a broader appeal through inclusion of conservative businessmen. As the election returns show, the planners appealed to a much wider section of the community than did their opponents.

As the planners were more popular, so were they more persuasive in a context where ability to persuade others is perhaps the chief resource available to anyone who wishes to influence a community decision. . . .

In part, the greater knowledge of the planners was a function of their officiality—the City Manager, Councilmen and Commission members had a right to demand information, were in an advantageous position to receive it, and were required by their positions to be knowledgeable. The advantages this knowledge confers are evident in virtually all the cases under discussion from the water and light plant decisions, where members of the PUC had little difficulty in showing that opposing proposals were ill formed, to the City Manager's ability to help block the apartment and to further recreation goals by knowing what was happening. To a considerable extent, however, the superior knowledge which the planners possessed was a product of their greater effort to inform themselves. . . .

The Nature of Political Skill

It would be wrong to think of skill as something esoteric or a composition of various tricks. For the most part it consists of rather simple kinds of actions. First, the collection of information so that one is better informed than others. Second, the development of a rationale for approaching those who make the decision. Third, the use of citizens committees and

Council Commissions to test community sentiment, to gather support, and to ward-off opposition. Fourth, open meetings to give opponents a chance to vent grievances, to convince the doubtful, and to comply with feeling of procedural due process so that no one can accurately say that he was not given a chance to present his views. Fifth, ceaseless persuasion through personal contact, the newspaper, and official bodies. Finally, and this is perhaps most subtle, an appreciation of group dynamics and a general sense of strategy which includes pinpointing the crucial individuals and persuading opinion leaders of important groups. . . (see Table 4).

Table 4. Elements of Political Leadership Skill

- Collection of information so one is better informed
- Development of a strategy for approaching decision makers
- Involvement of citizen committees
  -to test support
  -to gather support
  -to ward off opposition
- Open meetings to vent grievances
- Persuasion efforts through multiple channels, including personal contact, the media, and official bodies
- Employment of group dynamics with local influentials

SOURCES OF POLITICAL SUCCESS

The point is not that this general approach reveals the presence of some mastermind but rather that the opponents of the planners had nothing to match it. The traditionalists never quite found a way to combat the use of committees and commissions as strategic instruments. To do so would have required a recognition of the danger they posed and the recruitment of a corps of specialists to compete with them. Only by matching the interest and activity of the planners could they have competed with them on the level of knowledge and persuasion. They did not do so, it appears, partly because they did not think the effort was worthwhile and partly because they could not adjust their thinking to a new type of situation in which participation in public affairs, however limited it might appear, had been significantly enlarged. The planners had pyramided their resources by using officiality, knowledge, skill, time and energy to gain popularity, using this popularity to promote policies expanding their base of support, using this increased support to win an election, using the additional personnel to promote new policies, using time in office to develop more knowledge and skill, and so on. . . .

What emerges most clearly from this discussion of resources is the accessibility of the most effective ones. Most people have time and energy if they care to use it, most can obtain knowledge if they work at it, all have a vote to help determine who holds public office, and virtually anyone who feels he can get support is in a position to run for office. Only a small number take advantage of these opportunities, but they are there. Presumably, if sufficient numbers of people felt sufficiently unhappy about the existing state of affairs they would find these resources available to them and could quickly increase the rate at which they were being employed. True, there are some whose socio-economic position or low education have not provided life experiences which would predispose them toward effective participation. There is reason to believe, for example, that members of the Negro community could benefit themselves if they expanded their participation, even though their responses to our questionnaire do not show that there are issues they would like to promote which are not being debated in town. It is true also that interests they have are being promoted by a few of their leaders and by white people who identify with them so that the benefits they receive are greater than their participation per se would justify. Should a number of new leaders—men who would help formulate and interpret their demands and explain the connections between what they want and what happens in community affairs—arise from within the Negro community, the disabilities they may suffer today might be lessened.

The basic answer to the question of why the planning coalition was successful is that it utilized commonly available resources at a much greater rate and with considerably more skill than its opponents. Time, energy, knowledge, persuasion and skill were all available to others in quantity. The only resource the planners came near to monopolizing was officiality and that for only a limited two-year period, subject to approval by the electorate.

What about "other factors" in the situation which may have been significant but which we have not mentioned? It is hardly possible to exhaust the total range of conceivable explanations. But it is desirable to consider at least three others: rule by businessmen, social changes, and the presence of a "great man" who molded local history in his own image.

Businessmen

Regardless of our previous analysis, the fact remains that most of the influential planners were businessmen and this alone may account for their victory in a capitalist society. Yet as we observe the opposing forces over a wide range of decisions, several issues splitting the community from top to bottom, it becomes strikingly evident that the term businessman is woefully inadequate as a predictor of common interests, complementary strategies, or mutual support. The fact is that men who can all properly be called businessmen have taken opposing sides on most of the controversies. Otherwise, it would be exceedingly difficult to account for the conflicts over the past several years, since most of the activists (with the exception of the City Manager and a few college people) are businessmen of one kind or another. . . .

Social Change

In an attempt to show whether the change in power structure between the 1930's and the later 1950's could be related to changes in the social composition, an investigation was made on census returns since the turn of the century. What they reveal is a remarkably stable community. . . . The safest conclusion would appear to be that although social changes may in some degree be responsible for the success of the planners, the available evidence does not suggest that we can lean too heavily on this kind of explanation.

The "Great Man"

The role of the individual in history has long been the subject of inconclusive debate. Is he a true maker of history or is he merely a manifestation of deeper social currents? The case of Lenin's relationship to the Bolshevik Revolution is instructive on this point. Lenin did not and could not have accomplished the first October Revolution which was a result of such factors as mass upheaval due to a bloody war, breakdown in the Czarist system, and the work of many revolutionaries not including the Bolsheviks. Yet it can be said that without Lenin there would have been no Bolshevik (November) Revolution. For he was the only prominent Bolshevik who was in favor of making the attempt and it was he who convinced his fellow conspirators to go ahead. It can be said, then, that while Lenin could not have created the conditions for Revolution, he was able to seize the strategic moment in a vast cataclysm and turn it to his own advantage. Probably the best that can be done in this famous "chicken-and-egg" controversy is to look upon the conditions of the time as setting broad limits within which the remarkable individual can move, that is, to look upon the remarkable individual as thwarted or assisted in varying degrees by these circumstances.

Had Bill Long come in the 1930's he probably would not have been as successful in community affairs as he was at a later date when his opportunities for gaining allies and pursuing change through planning were greater.... To say this, however, may be no more than to suggest that Long might not have tried to do in the thirties what he found feasible in the fifties.

Yet it does appear that if Long had not been present and active, a number of developments...might not have taken place. At least, and this seems to be a safer statement, the changes that he helped bring about might well have been delayed. It is true that [some issues] had been discussed before he came and became active. Yet if he had not participated in hiring a person like the City Manager nor used great quantities of energy, knowledge and skill in bringing these items up for decision, nor persisted where other men might have stopped, much less would have been done. Of course, Long could not and did not do it alone. But he seized upon and created opportunities which might otherwise have come to naught. Without his presence, the town's political system probably would have been much more fragmented; the existing central direction might have given way to relatively autonomous specialists.

A Psychoanalytic Approach to Charismatic Leadership: The Case of Mao Tse-tung

Lucian W. Pye

By all standards, Mao Tse-tung belongs in the company of the few great political men of our century. Born and raised in the obscurity and restrictions of nineteenth-century rural China, he rose to assume the leadership of the Chinese Revolution, rule the largest population in the world with the most pervasive and intense government known in history, and finally has clung to life long enough to become the last of the political heroes of the great generation of World War II. His life spans the emergence of modern China and his character has shaped the manner and style of the Chinese Revolution.

To say that Mao Tse-tung has been the most revered and the most ecstatically worshiped man of the century may seem like paying him a slight compliment in the light of the awesome statistics of China. With some 800 million Chinese presumably holding Mao Tse-tung in absolute reverence as a demigod, what other mortal of our times can claim to be his competitor in popular appeal? Yet, Mao Tse-tung's appeal has reached far beyond the citizenry of his native land, however large. Few have not been touched by his existence, whether in admiration or hatred, in respect or scorn. His name has

---

Excerpted and reprinted with permission from the *Political Science Quarterly*, *91* (Summer 1976): 219-35.

become the label for revolutionary extremists throughout the world, "the Maoists," yet it is Mao Tse-tung with whom leaders throughout the world seek audiences. The pope in one day admits to his presence more people than Mao Tse-tung grants audiences in a year. When Mao last appeared publicly, more than a million people expressed tumultuous joy, and since then the occasions for allowing a select few into his presence have been newsworthy throughout the world. The announcement that the American secretary of state has had a couple of hours of discussion with the chairman is a signal to all that the secretary has been favored, indeed, honored; and, of course, when a trip to China does not include a visit with the chairman, the universal interpretation is that favor is being withheld.

The extraordinary appeal of Mao Tse-tung is hard to identify. Some may suggest that it lies less in the man and more in the nature of Chinese society, for the Chinese do seem compelled to make all of their leaders into imperial figures. Yet, the fact remains that many non-Chinese, who have no affinity for his rural origins but represent a host of varied social and personal backgrounds, seem to find inspiration for their political lives in his words and his example.

What is the character of the man that lies behind all this greatness? Merely to raise the question is an act of sacrilege for many. For the Chinese and other worshipers of Mao and his thoughts, it is enough to dwell on his public virtues, read only hagiographies, and reject all else as being in bad taste. For his detractors, the whole spectacle is revolting, and Mao the man must be the devil behind the Chinese version of socialist totalitarianism. Yet between these extremes there are those who are honestly curious. These are the people to whom this article is addressed.

The public record reveals a man at home in rural China, a man of the peasantry, who knows the myths and folklore of traditional China. Yet, although he received a Confucian education, Mao was also part of the first full generation of Chinese to explore Western knowledge. From his rural isolation, he moved effectively into the chaotic, competitive world of Chinese student politics and revolutionary scheming. As soldier, ideologist, and planner, he became the symbolic leader of the Chinese Communist guerilla struggle. As victorious ruler he was a visionary who looked beyond immediate problems of administration to the goals of a new society and to the molding of a new form of man. Chinese to the core, he also has been a principal shaper of our two contemporary international systems: His judgment helped to create the postwar world of two sharply divided blocs, and his decisions contributed to the 1970s concept of a more fluid and complex balance of states. His genius has thus extended from the era of China's first awakening, through the drama of World War II, the intense bitter struggles of the cold war, to a new era of the future, whose outlines we can barely perceive today.

In recent years, numerous attempts have been made to understand what lies behind the renown of Mao Tse-tung. Students of intellectual history, for example, have tried to suggest ways in which he has enriched Marxism; but while they have shown Mao to have been an astute, indeed shrewd, thinker, they have all had to concede that his ultimate claim to greatness does not lie in his work as a philosopher. Others have suspected that his reputation springs from his successes as a military strategist; but in spite of all their sympathetic effort, it is clear that Mao's genius lies elsewhere. Still other champions of Mao's fame have argued that he envisaged entirely novel goals for the economic order which would render obsolete all conventional ambitions for greater industrial and material well-being; but a careful review of Mao's policies makes it clear that he appreciates the near universal craving for higher standards of living and greater personal security.

The paradox of Mao Tse-tung is that while his claim to greatness is unassailable, in every specific sphere whether as philosopher, strategist, economic planner, ideologue or even world statesman, his qualities are not the match of his right to greatness.

The secret of his greatness lies elsewhere—in his extraordinary ability to understand, evoke, and direct human emotions and the innumerable ways in which he has used his own persona to command the sentiments and passions of others.

Since Mao's greatness lies so clearly in the realm of emotions, the problem of Mao Tse-tung is a problem in political psychology. To treat Mao merely as an intellectual or as a calculating strategist is to miss the essential dimensions of his historic role. Furthermore, if we are to understand how Mao came to be so successful in mobilizing the feelings of the Chinese, and of others, we must explore his own emotional world and discover the dynamics of his psychic relations with others.

When the story of modern China is systematically related to the activities of Mao, a key element of Mao's genius is immediately highlighted: his remarkable capacity to perform different, and even quite contradictory, roles at different times. As Mao took on the roles of peasant organizer, military commander, ideological spokesman, political strategist, and ruling statesman, he also vacillated between such contradictory public persona as fiery revolutionary and wise philosopher; dynamic activist and isolated recluse; preacher of the sovereign powers of the human will and patient planner who knows that history cannot be rushed.

The idea that Mao's greatness lies in the relationship between his own psychological needs and the psychological needs of masses of people is a part of Mao Tse-tung's political consciousness. When Mao saw Edgar Snow after the Cultural Revolution he confessed that the Chinese people had probably gone too far in attributing magical power to his thoughts, but then he added that there are times when there is a need for a personality cult, and that in human affairs one thing that will always exist is "the desire to be worshiped and the desire to worship."

With these words Mao identified the essential relationship between leader and follower: The politician serves a psychic function for the crowd just as the crowd performs a function for the politician. Leaders and followers are each dependent upon the other and they need to extract from the other something which fulfils their needs, and yet there is a peculiar singularity but vital difference in what each seeks. The desire "to worship" and the "desire to be worshiped" are symmetrical, but not similar sentiments.

Mao's insight into the needs of leaders and followers takes us directly to the essence of charismatic leadership. The need to worship taps the basic human need for dependency; the need to be worshiped goes to the core sentiment of narcissism; and, of course, dependency and narcissism have their common roots in infancy. The comforts of dependency and the exhilirations of narcissism are linked in the earliest of human experiences when the self has not been differentiated from others or from the environment, and when there is a confusion of omnipotence and helplessness. At that stage the distance is infinitesimal between the cries of weakness and vulnerability, and the joys of every wish becoming an instant command for attention. Out of this universal experience most people, in varying degrees, can sense that their hero's joy in being worshiped barely masks his anxieties over being ignored; and most leaders, in even more subtle degrees, can sense that lurking in the dependency of their followers is a mighty craving for potency, and that a people's sense of justice rests upon the infantile longing that their own inherent goodness will be rewarded by the blessing of their own total command of their situation. The followers can see their leader's psychic vulnerability, but they do not want to see through him for fear of destroying the memories of the only magic that ever worked in their lives. The capacity for the leader to tap his own narcissism reminds his followers that they too have their potential for greater goodness and strength.

The theory of narcissism, in grossly oversimplified form, holds that in earliest infancy when separation of ego and non-ego has not taken place, the ego is extremely weak, and anything pleasant is considered ego. The baby, if his environment is appropriately supportive, senses no differentiation between himself and the world, and thus he and his world are one, his every wish becomes a command, and his sense of his own goodness is the center of his magical universe. When he cannot relieve every pain by crying and hence commanding his world, he experiences deep frustrations, anxieties over his own goodness, and possibly the beginnings of guilt. Thus omnipotence and self-esteem are intimately linked to a longing for the "oceanic feeling of primary narcissism." Later after the child has developed a sense of his separate ego and differentiation between ego and non-ego has taken place, it is possible to revive the fantasy of being incorporated as one in the world, of recapturing the sense of omnipotence and inherent goodness that went with primary narcissism. It is this form of "secondary narcissism" which is the basis of the narcissistic personality, who is constantly in search of self-esteem (as in Lasswell's theory of the political man) that is the basis of our theory of the charismatic leader. Narcissism makes possible the focusing of tremendous psychic energies on the ego.[1]

Out of the interplay of narcissism and dependency those who need to be worshiped and those who need to worship are linked together as each depends upon the other's vulnerabilities.[2] The charm of the great man is that we can see his capacity for both self-deception and for having fun with the public; the great man in turn is charmed and exhilarated that his actions can bring such exaggerated responses from the public. A Franklin D. Roosevelt could never completely hide his pleasure at being able to manipulate public passions, and the American public never completely hid their pleasure at being able to see through the self-satisfaction of their popular president. The great appeal of John F. Kennedy was based on a very human relationship in which his admirers appreciated his refusal to take himself too seriously, and he understood their readiness to be teased and humored. The key to why the sly element of the imposture inspires heroism in the viewer rather than disenchantment seems to be the universal human appreciation of narcissism. People can instinctively understand that the great man enjoys his sense of greatness, and they may respond in kind by relaxing their inhibitions about their own narcissistic urges and in their turn aspire to act in ways which rise above their humdrum roles.

Notes

[1] For technical details about narcissism see: Sigmund Freud, "On Narcissism: An Introduction," in Ernest Jones (Ed.), Joan Rivere (Trans.), *Collected Papers (Vol. IV)* (New York, 1959), pp. 30-59; and Otto Fenichel, *The Psychoanalytical Theory of Neurosis* (New York, 1945).

[2] I am indebted to discussion with Dr. Steve Pieczenik, M.D., for help in arriving at this concept of the *mutual exploitation of vulnerabilities* as the basis of the charismatic relationship between leader and followers.

The American Presidency: Leadership in the Balance

Alexander M. Haig, Jr.

Americans have always cherished a hardy insistence that American institutions were equal to any task, no matter the challenge. Over the past decade, however, serious questions have been raised about the adequacy of our institutions to deal with the problems besetting us. These problems are not new in themselves; we have confronted conflict abroad, and inflation and unemployment at home in the past. But the most recent ills, like a mysterious virus, seem impervious to our remedies. Our troubles exhibit a malignant interdependence. Thus, domestic inflation is fueled by our imports of foreign oil, most of which comes from the world's most politically volatile areas; unemployment at home is affected by our declining competitive position in foreign markets; and the dollar's low international standing symbolizes the extent to which foreigners currently discount America's ability to manage its affairs both at home and abroad.

As we struggle with an apparently seamless web of foreign and domestic entanglements, American confidence in major institutions has shown an alarming decline. This is particularly devastating in the case of the presidency. Some observers are suggesting that the institution itself needs major reform. Others are persuaded that a different personality is

Published by permission of Transaction, Inc., from *The Washington Quarterly*, Vol. 3.S.S. Copyright © 1980 by The Center for Strategic and International Studies, Georgetown University.

required for the job; a more muscular president could trans-
form the situation. Still others find the flaw to be in the recent
incumbents, who are derided for lacking confidence or suffer-
ing from a weak will.

It is my thesis that the presidency, properly understood, is
still a vital and effective institution. The muscular personality
would not be the source of its strength; any man capable of
winning an American presidential election cannot be described as weak-willed or unsure of himself. However, what
has been missing is the notion of a balanced presidency.

The Constitution of the United States is an open invitation to struggle, with an intricate system of checks and
balances designed to keep our government from ever becoming monolithic. But the eighteenth century concept of balance
is as essential to our Constitution as is its emphasis on checks.
The machinery of government becomes harmonious not in
paralysis but in balanced action.

The presidency is our system's essential balance wheel.
The president is the hub of this wheel, and the spokes connect
him to an extraordinary range of relationships. But the lack of
proper balance in several of the president's most important
relationships is the root of the institution's recent troubles.
Again, like the problems facing the country, these distortions
were tolerable so long as they were few in number and
distinct from each other. But the imbalances that have developed in the president's role as educator, in his relations with
Congress, and in his function as executive are together a
paralyzing force. The proper balance in these areas must be
restored if public confidence in the presidency is to be
renewed.

Intrinsic to our system is the right of the citizen to
demand redress of his grievances—to demand answers to the
problems besetting him. But the presidential response is
unique, for the president's task is not simply to broker such
demands but also to articulate the interests of the entire
nation. Both aspects of the dialogue have fallen badly out of
sync in recent years.

The vocation of political lobbyist (foreseen by the
Founding Fathers) has become ever more popular.[1] Over
2,200 entities are now registered for such activities as the
traditional organizations advocating business, labor, agricultural, or other interests [and] have been joined by a steadily
increasing number of single issue groups. Furthermore, the

technological revolution in radio, television, and travel and the steady expansion of media outlets give each of these groups exposure and ready access to audiences undreamed of in the days when our Constitution was first drafted—an era of handbills, broadsheets, stump speeches, and communications limited by the speed of a horse or sailing ship.

Our president must be cognizant of our nation's often conflicting currents of interests, desires, and opinions; but it likewise is the president's task to lead public opinion, to mold it, and to shape a national consensus on issues of major importance. Often this will require him to take positions or actions that are temporarily unpopular, even stridently opposed by many, but as Winston Churchill observed, a politician with his ear always to the ground assumes a very vulnerable position. Franklin Roosevelt put the concept very well:

> The presidency is...preeminently a place of moral leadership. All our great presidents were leaders of thought at times when certain historic ideas in the life of a nation had to be clarified...that is what the office is—a superb opportunity for reapplying, applying new conditions, the simple rules of human conduct to which we always go back. Without leadership alert and sensitive to change, we are all boggled up or lose our way.

Franklin's cousin Theodore, our first President Roosevelt, expressed the same thought more succinctly in terming the presidency "a bully pulpit."

Given the idealistic, even utopian, strains that permeate American thought and our instinctively optimistic national approach to problems, telling the truth to the American people is no easy task. But no president can provide the leadership America and its allies desperately need unless he understands the stark, often unpalatable, realities that shape our domestic and international life. He must be willing and able to explain them and their consequences convincingly to the American people and to the world.

Unfortunately, the concepts of presidential leadership fostered by the Constitution have been sidetracked by those of Madison Avenue. Both presidents and presidential aspirants have become mesmerized by polls. Rather than showing the lonely courage of an Abraham Lincoln or taking full advantage of the bully pulpit, presidents now hire public relations specialists and advertising executives in the apparent belief that marketing techniques and gimmicks are adequate substitutes for sound, coherent policies. To the detriment of America and the world, some of our elected would-be leaders have cultivated the image rather than the substance of leadership.

Our forefathers created a republic. They believed—with Edmund Burke—that an elected political leader owed those who put them in office his wisdom and judgment, not just deference to their often changing and less than totally informed opinions of the moment. The Constitution's basic concept was that America's voters would review periodically the stewardship of those entrusted with elective office. Officials whose performance was deemed wanting would be replaced with others who might do better. This is another key area in which the concept of balance is central to the effectiveness of our constitutional system.

THE PRESIDENT AND THE CONGRESS

The indispensable partner of any American president is the Congress. The success or failure of any president is usually shaped by the success or failure of that partnership. This alliance is seldom totally harmonious, often uneasy, and sometimes marked by open or thinly-veiled hostility. Readily, often gleefully, our government's various branches have accepted the Constitution's open invitation to struggle. The swinging pendulum of primacy between the White House and Capitol Hill (which includes the Supreme Court) is the dialectic of American constitutional history.

The parties most directly involved have seldom agreed on the rightness of the balance struck at any given moment. Senator Harry Truman felt differently from President Truman, who once remarked, "I've always said that a president who didn't have a fight with Congress wasn't any good anyhow"—a view also held, if differently expressed, by all presidents who came to the Oval Office from Capitol Hill, including John Kennedy, Lyndon Johnson, Richard Nixon, and Gerald Ford.

In the wake of Vietnam, Watergate, and what were widely perceived as the dangers of an "Imperial Presidency," this pendulum has now taken a long swing toward Capitol Hill. Congress has become far more assertive, particularly in the area of foreign policy, than it was even a few years ago. Through a variety of legislative mechanisms, it has sought and secured a much greater measure of detailed control over executive branch agencies. This process was furthered by an historical coincidence: the movement of many former members of the executive branch into congressional staffs, giving the Congress unprecedented expertise in executive branch activity. The result was what David Abshire has termed "neo-congressional government."

Neo-congressional government would not be harmful if we had a parliamentary system. But our Congress is neither temperamentally nor structurally adapted to discharge executive branch responsibilities, nor is it constitutionally mandated to do so.

In the days of Franklin Roosevelt, Truman, Eisenhower, John Kennedy, and Lyndon Johnson, a president could enlist the aid of key congressional leaders and committee chairmen. Together, they could hammer out a consensus on the issue in question, a consensus likely to be endorsed by the Congress as a whole. This technique has become a casualty of the 1970s.

There are now over 250 autonomous (or virtually autonomous) congressional subcommittees, each with independent legislative mandates and staffs. On the critical issue of energy, for instance, 83 committees and subcommittees in the House of Representatives pass on energy related issues. Four hundred twenty-one of the four hundred thirty-five members of the House belong to a committee or subcommittee with jurisdiction over some facet of energy legislation. Capitol Hill's coherence and consistency are the casualties of such arrangements.

The waning power of congressional consensus-makers and the proliferation of congressional committees are not the only phenomena making Congress a difficult partner for the president. The Congress is supported by large and growing staffs. The Senate is served by 7,148 staff members, double the number of a decade ago. House aides total 11,738; House Committees employed 2,014 in 1977, up from 634 a decade earlier.[2] Some staff members have acquired considerable influence and authority; none were elected.

The ability of Congress to discharge its responsibilities efficiently and authoritatively while acquiring a growing influence over the executive branch has been damaged by such developments. In foreign affairs, where such attributes as coherence, consistency, and dispatch are of great value, the consequences have been dismaying, to say the least. America's cherished and hard-won consensus on our basic interests abroad, a casualty of the Vietnam period, has not been recovered. Executive authority in dealing with other countries is diminished inevitably by the knowledge that our main lines of policy, our alliances, and our reputation for fidelity may be at the mercy of a constant struggle to establish a fleeting consensus.

One overlooked aspect of the difficulties of reestablishing consensus is to be found in the congressional staff system itself. The demoralization of the executive bureaucracy has contributed to a new phenomenon. Aggrieved or disappointed professionals move from the executive departments (State, the Pentagon, the NSC, and the White House) into congressional staff positions. Deprived of meaningful participation in policymaking in their former posts, they seek it through Congress itself. Hence, when administrations change, the new president will find himself with a bureaucracy at war with itself, the establishment, and its opponents in the new-boy network. What is worse, the new boys will have entered at a much higher level than would have been the case had they stayed in the executive branch. They will lack the knowledge and experience they might have gained, but they will not lack a taste for promoting discontinuity in an adversarial fashion.

No president can reorganize the Congress, and it would be suicidal for any president to attempt it. Congress is as jealous of its prerogatives as any other component of our government and because it controls the others' appropriations, most effective in protecting its jurisdiction. Congress alone is master of the Capitol and bears full responsibility for putting and keeping its own house in order.

If he is to succeed, a president must learn how to deal effectively with the Congress. No hard and fast rules exist to determine the techniques. Experience suggests, however, a number of avoidable mistakes. These concern the executive's basic stance toward Congress, relationships with individual members, and consultation.

Despite the example of Harry Truman, a president who campaigns against Congress as an institution is unlikely to forge a constructive partnership with its members. This does not mean that a president who is forceful in dealing with Congress is not more likely to have good relations with the Congress than one who projects an image of weakness or diffidence. An essential attribute of effective leadership, in any field, is a willingness to take heat for allies, colleagues, and subordinates. A president who takes the lead in forging a national consensus on complex, controversial issues and forcefully takes a firm stand on them will not only be respected in the Congress; his position is likely to be privately applauded and greeted with considerable private relief—and appreciation—by many individual congressmen. If the issue in question is highly controversial in a congressman's home state or district—particularly if the member in question has a tight election coming up—it is extremely useful for the member to be able to make electorally anodyne statements for the record, to vote with the president, then be able to cite White House pressure and a need to support the president as the rationale for his or her vote on the House or Senate floor.

Particularly on issues that are important and contentious, dealings between the White House and the Capitol are most likely to be effective if conducted in an amicable atmosphere. Such an atmosphere does not exist naturally. It is rather the product of a special political hot house, the persistent and meticulous cultivation of common courtesy and small details. Even in a crisis, as I know from personal experience, substantive discussion is greatly facilitated when, for example, the White House has a consistent record of promptly answering all mail and returning all telephone calls from Capitol Hill. As a White House staff member, I never went home until I had returned all my congressional calls. This may have startled some honorable members who heard from me at one or two in the morning but it certainly strengthened my own legislative relations.

Contrary to some impressions, congressmen and senators are not averse to public association with the president, and the Congress—particularly its leaders—appreciate being consulted by the president, especially before presidential action is taken or announced on major, contentious issues. Those consulted will not necessarily agree with the president, or support him publicly, but such consultations will greatly improve the climate for discussion. They will improve it even more if serious consultation is a regular White House practice, not something that occurs only in times of crisis. Congress, as has often been said, likes and wants to be in on the take-offs as well as the landings—particularly the crash landings.

This process must of course be a two-way street, entailing reciprocal responsibilities: candor by the president, discretion by the congressmen. Mutual confidence is impossible if the chief executive is not candid or if his confidants rush their information to the camera or press. Effective consultation between the president and Congress requires a continuing balance on both sides.

THE PRESIDENT AS EXECUTIVE

The president's essential instrument for the translation of his vision into concrete goals and policies is the executive branch. This instrument has four key components: the cabinet, policy-level political appointees below the cabinet level, the government's corps of civilian and military professionals, and the White House staff.

America does not have a parliamentary system of government and the American cabinet is not a functioning body with independent power of decision. In successful presidencies, Lincoln's rule is operative: how the president votes at the cabinet table determines whether the ayes or nays have it. No president can delegate his ultimate responsibility, but if a government as large and complex as ours is to function, he must delegate a measure of authority. How well, consistently, and effectively the executive branch functions under any given administration will depend to a great extent on how wisely its president chooses, and uses, his cabinet.

The basic criteria of selection should be excellence and competence, preferably demonstrated by successful experience in fields at least related to those for which any particular cabinet officer is to be made responsible. One hallmark of a true leader is a willingness to pick, and effectively use, outstandingly able subordinates. A fear of being overshadowed is an almost certain indicator of inner weakness and insecurity. Harry Truman's formal education was limited, and he never expected to have the presidency thrust upon him, but he rose impressively to its challenges. Two things that enabled him to do so were his willingness to have people like George Marshall, Dean Acheson, and James Forrestal in his cabinet, and his ability to harness their talents effectively without any of them—or the country—ever forgetting who was president. A president willing and able to relieve General MacArthur for insubordination would not have allowed his administration, or the country, to be embarrassed by an ambassador to the United Nations.

The president's best use of his cabinet is something that cannot be determined by immutable rules. Nonetheless, experience teaches a few things about the necessary balance in this sphere of presidential activity. A president cannot squander time on minutiae; cabinet members must be responsible for managing their respective departments, for which they need a delegation of requisite authority or the right kind of presidential support and backing.

On policy matters affecting the responsibilities or interests of more than one cabinet department the president should compel every cabinet officer to make policy recommendations to the president in front of, and open to challenge by, other cabinet officers—especially those whose responsibilities or interests are affected by the issue in question. Here, however, the consideration of balance again comes into play; every cabinet officer must have periodic private access to the president; otherwise that officer's morale, prestige, and hence effectiveness will be gravely undermined.

When presidential decisions are taken, cabinet members must know and understand those decisions. This may sound so self-evident as to be trivial, but I know from experience and first-hand observation that it is not. There have been many Oval Office, Cabinet Room, or other meetings such as Lyndon Johnson's "Tuesday lunches"—often not held on Tuesdays, or over lunch—convened by a president from which cabinet officers attending have returned to their respective departments and given radically different, sometimes diametrically opposed, accounts to their subordinates of presidential decisions and instructions. The methods used by the president to accomplish this vital task may vary, but the task is essential to the functioning of the presidency and is frequently overlooked.

If well chosen, cabinet officers will be strong personalities with independent minds and views—and often, independent constituencies. To be effective, however, our government must speak with a coherent, reasonably consistent voice. The balance to be struck here is difficult and tenuous, subject to continual adjustments dictated by circumstances. Each cabinet officer must have enough free rein to run his or her department effectively and to exhibit the independence of spirit and judgment that is of such great value to the president. Nonetheless, the cabinet as a whole must pull together as a team toward the administration and party goals that, in the final analysis, the president must define and over which he must be the final arbiter. In short, if the executive branch is to be effective, essential cabinet independence has to be balanced with equally essential cabinet discipline.

The same holds true for responsibility. In our government's executive branch, as in any large organizational structure, decisions cannot be discussed and debated forever. At some point they have to be made and, once made, executed. No cabinet officer has the authority of the president; an unpalatable fact every cabinet officer must accept. No administration can function effectively if cabinet officers refuse to accept presidential decisions or if they feel free to try to undercut or reverse decisions they may not like by personal lobbying with Congress, the media, or anyone else.

Cabinet members can be invaluable in expounding, defending and lobbying for the president's own programs in Congress, with the media, and through each cabinet officer's personal range of contacts. Cabinet officers will want to be as responsive as possible to congressional needs and desires—in fact, they have to be, since Congress controls their departments' budgets. Still, no cabinet officer can spend all or even much of the time testifying before a plethora of congressional committees and subcommittees and still properly discharge the many other responsibilities of cabinet office. A recent secretary of the treasury, for example, made more than 400 public appearances on Capitol Hill. No one can do that and also devote proper attention to the functioning of the Treasury Department.

The particular techniques and procedures used to follow the precepts outlined above will vary in each administration. Wherever possible, however, already existing procedures or organizational instruments—especially ones of proven utility—should be employed, with any necessary adaptation, rather than devising entirely new ones to be layered on top of the old. It is essential, for example, that policies that have an impact on more than one cabinet department's responsibilities be framed in consultation with all departments affected— even when only one department will have primary responsibility for implementation. The National Security Council exists, and was established by statute in 1947, for precisely this purpose in the field of foreign and defense-related affairs. It should be used; this wheel may need improvement, but it does not need to be reinvented. A similar device could well be useful in matters of primarily domestic concern, but in developing any kind of domestic council, an administration should draw on the history and experience of the NSC. No president, cabinet, or effectively functioning executive branch has time to do work already done by its predecessors.

The considerations applicable to the selection, management, and effective use of the cabinet itself also apply with some modification and adaptation to the immediate, policy-level subordinates of cabinet officers. These include the deputy, under and assistant secretaries, special assistants, and other second and third echelon figures. They are political appointees in the sense that they are placed in their positions to help develop and carry out a particular administration's policies and goals. They must expect to be replaced if an administration changes.

In selecting and using this essential group of key officials, however, many balance questions come into play. A cabinet officer—especially a strong one—will insist on having a considerable voice in the selection of his immediate subordinates. However, a president (or his immediate staff) will need to ensure that all those chosen for sub-cabinet positions are essentially in accord with the president's basic goals and philosophies—and so not unduly reflect the personal hobby horses of any individual cabinet member or other senior administration official.

The touchstones for selecting such officials should be talent, competence, and experience. After threshold standards in these fields are met, many other factors come into play. More than the cabinet itself, this is the place to ensure the representation of those groups or constituencies the president deems necessary to his administration's policy formulation. These positions are especially vulnerable to change, and the president's expectations of loyalty from his political appointees at the subcabinet level must be reciprocated. A president who neglects his troops, especially those who have followed and supported him in adversity, will soon face adversity alone.

LEADERSHIP IN THE BALANCE

Over the past decade, the American presidency has lost some of the essential balance necessary for effective leadership, particularly in foreign policy. Some of this was due to circumstances, the rest to misunderstanding and error. Some of it will be corrected by the turn of events, the rest will depend on the competence of the chief executives to come.

The shift of power towards Congress in the ever present constitutional struggle between the executive branch and the legislative branch is neither unnatural nor deplorable in itself. Unhappily, this shift occurred as Congress itself suffered a crippling loss of discipline through internal reforms, leaving the Senate and House woefully disorganized. As the memories of Vietnam and Watergate recede, the executive will regain power; simultaneously, the Congress will restore its own discipline in response to voter antipathy. The signs are therefore hopeful that the ragged performance of the federal government will improve as a different external and internal balance emerges between president and Congress.

It is not necessary to be hindered by adversary government any more than was ordained by the Constitution. The debilitating disloyalty that has disfigured relations between the president and his professional servants, the emergence of centers of power in the White House staff, are signs of poor management. The restoration of professionalism to the bureaucracy is an urgent task that can be accomplished only if the president realizes what the professionals have to offer— expertise—and what the professionals can never offer—strategic decision.

The president's resumption of this role as teacher and educator is more problematic. He can succeed only if he has a message to give, if he understands that policymaking means setting priorities, if he sees communication as a process for enlisting the electorate in a common course rather than just shaping his image. A muscular president cannot succeed in this task. If all he has to offer is strength of personality, he will be frustrated by equally willful men. The power of persuasion and the art of consensus, both deriving from forceful convictions, are the presidential tools, not sheer virility or infinite flexibility.

These attributes are especially important in the realm of foreign policy. In a crisis, the president does not always have the chance to pursue lengthy consultations with Congress and intricate lobbying with interest groups. The chief executive requires a fund of good will and confidence in his competence so that he can deal with emergencies as an executive rather than as a committee chairman. If his performance has been an accomplished one, he will enter the crisis with a good balance of confidence and trust. If he must develop such a fund in the course of the emergency itself, he will find himself seriously weakened in the pursuit of American interest abroad.

Perhaps as a legacy of the 1960s, a period of unusual presidential initiative, we have grown accustomed to demanding action from the president as if he were all powerful. At the same time, we have sought to limit what we conceived to be an excess of presidential power, especially in the conduct of foreign affairs. The awesome range and complexity of public business has found chief executives less able to execute even as greater demands have been made upon them. Here, too, there is every prospect that the situation will improve. Over-promise and underperformance usually culminate in electoral defeat. Sooner or later the two will be brought back into balance.

Given this tumultuous background, it seems clear that a strong-willed president will not be enough to conduct an effective presidency in the 1980s. Indeed, the first and essential characteristic of such a leader must be a realization of his own limitations and the limitations of his office. He will understand that he is a chief magistrate, not secretary of defense, state, or health and welfare. He cannot reconcile all interest group demands at his level, nor can he administer great departments of governments. He certainly cannot dictate to the Congress.

In the end, the president can act only in the constitutional sense of a leader whose action springs from a balanced sense of limitation and opportunity. More than ever, today's president must aspire to his role as educator and teacher to set the agenda and tone of public debate. To succeed, perhaps he should begin by expounding his own concept of where the balance of presidential action lies for the new decade.

Our presidential form of government can work. No passing crisis should panic us into amending or discarding an institution that has stood the test of time, becoming a symbol of American stability and leadership. Issues that appear to be increasingly complex and the special interests promoting them can still be managed by an attentive president. The task before our would-be leaders is to reestablish the balance required by an effective presidency.

Experience suggests that an American president who is at once cognizant of his own limitations, yet fully committed to maximizing the effectiveness of the institutions with which he must work, can assert the leadership that is crucial to sustaining the requisite confidence at home and abroad.

The potential for effective leadership is written into the institution of the Presidency. How well the elements of that leadership are realized depends upon the experience and the capacity for leadership of the individual in office and how well he uses the resources of the office. As a time-tested institution, it is the man and not the institution that invites our attention.

Notes

[1]See in particular, *Federalist Paper #10* by James Madison.

[2]*U.S. News and World Report,* December 17, 1979.

[3]At the moment, furthermore, this is the only type of incentive a president can utilize. In the upper military and civilian ranks, there are now no financial incentives because of "compression" and the growing disparity between the emoluments such levels of responsibility carry in the government and those with which they are rewarded in private life. Furthermore, another balance question: "ethics" legislation requires those who advance to senior military or civilian career positions within the government to surrender their personal privacy in a manner not required of those successful in private life.

Endnote

As we reflect on the content of the preceding sections, it becomes clear that our knowledge has been considerably enhanced during the preparation of this volume. We approached the task with extensive leadership development experience, direct involvement in research on the topic, and a strong interest in further developing our knowledge of the field. The senior editor has focused on community leadership analysis, and the junior editor has been primarily concerned with organizational leadership. The joint editing endeavor has exposed us to a most interesting variety of new viewpoints, which eventually led to the five-part organization of the book. The section on social and political leadership was added to the four parts from the Second Edition; the materials on educational and community leadership were refocused; new "basic" concepts were added; and the section on organizational leadership was greatly expanded.

Two sets of basic themes pervade all five parts: (a) a micro level, or a focus on individual leader behavior, and (b) a macro level, emphasizing the large-scale and cross-social-unit issues. It is clear that there is a considerable body of knowledge about the micro level. The dimensions of "task" and "relationship" behavior (identified as "rational and emotional" needs in the Introduction) have been repeatedly emphasized in one form or another. However, as originally conceived, these categories are too broad and have been refined to much more discrete leadership behaviors.

Individuals who engage in both types of leadership behavior are likely to be at least somewhat successful (Bass, 1960; Hall & Donnell, 1979). We cannot be certain, on the basis of present evidence, whether they are effectively and simultaneously achieving personal, subordinate, organizational, community, and national goals. The definition of "effective" leadership is much debated at the theoretical level but has not been empirically tested with sufficient thoroughness (Blake & Mouton, 1982; Hersey & Blanchard, 1982). It is not clear whether a strong combination of task and relationship behaviors is always desirable, or whether the balance should be altered depending on the leadership context.

At the macro level, several consistent but complex themes are evident. The basic rational-emotional dimensions of leader behavior are evident across all levels of social systems (i.e., communities, social movements, nations). The most common component of effective leadership is participation. There is, moreover, substantial support for the efficacy of participative leadership (Sashkin, 1982). We can explain *why* participation is important for effective leadership.

One basic factor seems to be important at any level— business organization, educational institution, community, social movement, or nation: the "connectedness" of the system or the "looseness" or "closeness" of connections among system elements. That is, the various divisions of a manufacturing firm are to some degree independent and to some degree interdependent. Likewise, the schools and colleges of a university are to some extent autonomous and to some extent dependent on one another. We refer to the "loose coupling" noted in Parts III and IV (on educational institutions and community organizations). Connectedness is associated with the time it takes for actions of one part of a system to have some effect on other parts. Actions in the more loosely coupled system will have slower effects. For example, when system elements are "tightly coupled" or very connected, such as the functional departments of a manufacturing organization, interunit interdependence is great, and considerable interunit coordination will be needed if vital interdependencies are to be accounted for. The role of the leader as coordinator is critical. If such coordination is not carried out, the consequences will be negative, immediate, and obvious.

When systems are less tightly coupled, as is the case in large, state educational institutions, the effects of interdependencies are less immediate. For example, a new engineering-management program developed by the College of Engineering may have strong effects on the School of Business, but such impacts may not be immediate; it may take considerable time before the School of Business faculty realizes that students are being diverted into the engineering program. Although the consequences may be less immediate and obvious, interdependencies do exist.

Finally, some community or national systems are so loosely coupled that we do not normally view them as single organizations. The elements in each—organizations, programs, interest groups, social movements, political units, etc.—are, in the very long run, definitely interdependent, but viewed in the short run, such interdependencies are not evident. Thus, it may be many years before the actions of the Co-op members and the councilmen in Wildavsky's town have impacts on other community organizations and institutions. Nonetheless, some form of impact is highly probable. The coordinating role of "community" or "political" leaders is much less visible but no less important.

Complex, "intensive" interdependencies can be coordinated *only* through open channels for feedback and mechanisms for mutual adjustment (Thompson, 1967). This is essentially a process of mutual involvement and, perhaps, explains why participation has been found to be so generally useful. Intensive interdependencies apparently exist in most social systems. Thus, the quality of participative leadership may actually be critical even though it is not obviously needed.

The role of the leader as a "participation coordinator" is nontraditional; taking on this role is a sophisticated leadership act. The traditional conception of leadership emphasizes the leader as an authority figure. However, the role of coordinator seems to be crucial, on the micro level, if social units are to prosper.

There is, then, a sufficient basis for applying available knowledge to the enhancement of leadership in each major realm of social organization: small-group settings such as the administrative group of a hospital; organizational settings such as United Way or the Chamber of Commerce; community settings of every size and complexity; educational units such as the extended learning units of colleges and universities; or local, state, and national social-political movements such as Common Cause.

We hope that this book is useful in each of the areas where leadership is exercised. Despite our efforts to be thorough and comprehensive, however, it is clear that much is *not* known about either leadership *or* social change. The research literature is sparse and incomplete. We are not yet prepared to construct a complete theory that will fit all of the situations alluded to in the various parts of this book. It is our view, however, that despite the shortcomings of knowledge, we should not hesitate to diligently use those elements of theory and wisdom for which there is a reasonably sound base. The best test of knowledge is how it works in practice.

References

Bass, B.M. *Leadership, psychology, and organizational behavior.* New York: Harper & Row, 1960.

Hall, J., & Donnell, S.M. Managerial achievement: The personal side of behavioral theory. *Human Relations,* 1979, *32,* 77-101.

Blake, R.R., & Mouton, J.S. Grid principles versus situationalism: A final note. *Group & Organization Studies,* 1982, *7,* 211-215.

Hersey, P., & Blanchard, K.H. Grid principles and situationalism: Both! *Group & Organization Studies,* 1982, *7,* 207-210.

Sashkin, M. *A manager's guide to participative management.* New York: American Management Associations, 1982.